MAY 1 8 2005

The
Anatomy of
Impact

The Anatomy of Impact

WHAT MAKES
THE GREAT WORKS
OF PSYCHOLOGY
GREAT

EDITED BY

Robert J. Sternberg

American Psychological Association, Washington, DC

Published by
American Psychological Association
750 First Street, NE
Washington, DC 20002
www.apa.org

To order
APA Order Department
P.O. Box 92984
Washington, DC 20090-2984
Tel: (800) 374-2721; Direct: (202) 336-5510
Fax: (202) 336-5502; TDD/TTY: (202) 336-6123
Online: www.apa.org/books/
E-mail: order@apa.org

In the U.K., Europe, Africa, and the Middle East, copies may be ordered from
American Psychological Association
3 Henrietta Street
Covent Garden, London
WC2E 8LU England

Typeset in Goudy by AlphaWebTech, Mechanicsville, MD

Printer: Port City Press, Baltimore, MD
Cover Designer: Michael Hentges Design, Alexandria, VA
Technical/Production Editor: Jennifer L. Zale

The opinions and statements published are the responsibility of the authors, and such opinions and statements do not necessarily represent the policies of the American Psychological Association.

Library of Congress Cataloging-in-Publication Data
The anatomy of impact : what makes the great works of psychology great /
edited by Robert J. Sternberg.— 1st ed.
    p. cm.
Includes bibliographical references and indexes.
    ISBN 1-55798-980-X (alk. paper)
    1. Psychology—History—20th century. 2. Psychology—History—19th century. I.
Sternberg, Robert J.
    BF105 .A46 2003
    150'.9—dc21
                                                                    2002151478

British Library Cataloguing-in-Publication Data
A CIP record is available from the British Library.

Printed in the United States of America
First Edition

CONTENTS

CONTRIBUTORS

Michael Alcee, Fordham University, New York
Ellen Berscheid, University of Minnesota, Minneapolis
M. H. Clark, University of Memphis, Memphis, TN
Linda Jarvin, Yale University, New Haven, CT
David E. Leary, University of Richmond, Richmond, VA
Nancy McWilliams, Rutgers University, Piscataway, NJ
Stanley B. Messer, Rutgers University, Piscataway, NJ
Glenn Phillips, University of Memphis, Memphis, TN
Donald E. Polkinghorne, University of Southern California, Los Angeles
Frank C. Richardson, University of Texas at Austin
Daniel N. Robinson, Oxford University, Oxford, England
Theodore R. Sarbin, Carmel, CA
William R. Shadish, University of Memphis, Memphis, TN
Dean Keith Simonton, University of California, Davis
Brent D. Slife, Brigham Young University, Provo, UT
Robert J. Sternberg, Yale University, New Haven, CT
Frederick J. Wertz, Fordham University, New York
Matthew Whoolery, Brigham Young University, Provo, UT

PREFACE

The ultimate goal of any publication in psychology (or anything else) is to have an impact—to make a difference to a field. Yet most published research is never or only scarcely cited, and many works are read by only small numbers of people. Although students of psychology learn a great deal in their professional education regarding how to design, conduct, analyze, and write up research, they learn much less, if anything, about what they can do to propose theory, review literature, or conduct research that will make a major difference to the field of psychology. What is it that separates the most successful psychological works—in terms of impact—from the less successful ones?

The goal of this book was for experts in the philosophy and history of psychology as well as other distinguished psychologists each to choose a work of monumental impact and to analyze why, in their opinion, the work was so successful in terms of influencing the field. They were asked to analyze the factors that underlay the impact of the work and how this work differs from others that have had less impact on the field. In this way, students of psychology as well as professionals are provided with diverse points of view on the kinds of aspirations one can have to make a difference in the field of psychology.

Ultimately, what distinguishes greater from lesser psychologists is the impact of their work. Many research psychologists wish to make a substantial long-term difference to the development of the field but, arguably, do not succeed in doing so. What can a psychologist do to maximize the impact of his or her work? One is not taught how to maximize impact in graduate school, and it is unclear that one *ever* is taught it. Thus, arguably, the most important aspect of a research career typically is never taught and may never be learned.

Each chapter author was asked to accomplish five goals in his or her chapter:

1. to identify a great work or collection of works that the author wished intensively to analyze for its impact;
2. to describe the origins of the work and its place in the field of psychology;
3. to analyze why the work has had such great impact, emphasizing general as well as specific attributes that lead to impact;
4. to compare the work with works of lesser impact and state why the analyzed work has been so successful;
5. to give advice to students and professionals alike as to how they can strive to achieve substantial impact in the work they do.

This book was sponsored by Division 24, Theoretical and Philosophical Psychology, of the American Psychological Association in conjunction with my presidency of the division during the 2000–2001 year. All royalties for the project are to be donated to the division.

I am grateful to Cynthia Blankenship for her assistance in preparation of the manuscript.

Preparation of this book was supported under the Javits Act Program (Grant R206R000001) as administered by the Office of Educational Research and Improvement (OERI), U.S. Department of Education and Grant REC-9979843 from the U.S. National Science Foundation (NSF). Grantees undertaking such projects are encouraged to express freely their professional judgment. This book, therefore, does not necessarily represent the position or policies of NSF, OERI, or the U.S. Department of Education, and no official endorsement should be inferred.

Robert J. Sternberg

The
Anatomy of
Impact

1

FRANCIS GALTON'S *HEREDITARY GENIUS*: ITS PLACE IN THE HISTORY AND PSYCHOLOGY OF SCIENCE

DEAN KEITH SIMONTON

Psychology's history is replete with great psychologists. Yet certainly even a short list of the greatest of the great would have to include the name of Francis Galton. For instance, one survey of an international collection of experts put Galton in the highest possible category, along with Sigmund Freud, Wilhelm Wundt, William James, Ivan Pavlov, and John B. Watson (Annin, Boring, & Watson, 1968). In another investigation, a psychologist's impact was assessed according to the amount of space assigned to him or her in history of psychology textbooks (Zusne & Dailey, 1982). Galton was ranked 18th. Actually, if you delete those figures who cannot be considered psychologists in the modern sense—such as Aristotle, Plato, René Descartes, Immanuel Kant, and John Locke—Galton's ordinal position rises to 11th or 10th (depending on whether or not Hermann von Helmholtz is considered a psychologist). As additional demonstration of his distinction, Galton's publications continue to receive abundant citation in scientific articles published decades after his death. For example, according to one inquiry, Galton continued to receive more citations in the 1970s and 1980s than did most of his contemporaries, which included such big names as Helmholtz, Jean-Martin

Charcot, G. Stanley Hall, and Hermann Ebbinghaus (Simonton, 2000). One last indicator of Galton's enduring fame is his eponymic status (Boring, 1963). In particular, he has given his name to the Galton bar, the Galton whistle, Galton's Laws, and Galton's questionnary (Zusne, 1987).

So what is the basis of all this acclaim? In one respect, this is an impossible question to answer. Galton was a scientist of many accomplishments. Indeed, he would have been eminent today even if he had not made a single contribution to psychology. This reputation would be based on his notable contributions to geography (African exploration), meteorology (isobars and weather stations), and criminology (finger print identification). In fact, Galton's early career showed no signs of directing itself toward psychology at all. Having received enough inheritance to lead the life of a gentleman farmer and dilettante scientist, he kept his mind active by conducting electrical experiments, engaging in various inventions, and being involved in other assorted inquiries. What sent him on the path toward behavioral science was reading a book written by his cousin Charles Darwin. That book, *Origin of Species*, was published in 1859, when Galton was already 37 years old. For Galton, it became what can be called a "crystallizing experience" (Walters & Gardner, 1986). That is, by reading *Origin*, Galton discovered that his interests and capacities were best aimed at the scientific study of human beings.

Although Galton was profoundly influenced by Darwin's masterpiece, it was not by any means the sole definitive influence. To Darwin's evolutionary theory Galton added an inveterate enthusiasm for quantification and mathematics—for statistics. Unlike his cousin, who attended Cambridge University in the quest of a liberal arts degree, Galton's Cambridge education began with the serious study of mathematics. His devotion to the subject was reflected in the fact that his room contained the bust of Sir Isaac Newton, one of the greatest mathematicians of all time. Galton competed in the notoriously difficult "Mathematical Tipos," with the aspiration of graduating with the highest honors. The competition was so intense that Galton suffered a nervous breakdown under the pressure and eventually had to settle for an ordinary degree. Even so, his appreciation for numbers, calculations, and formulas was to permeate the manifestations of his Darwin-inspired curiosity about human psychology.

The first concrete realization of these influences was an article that he published in 1865. Titled "Hereditary Talent and Character," this study constitutes his first contribution to psychology (Watson, 1974). Indeed, the entire text of this investigation has been reprinted in a Web site that is specifically devoted to classic works in the history of psychology (Classics in the History of Psychology: http://psychclassics.yorku.ca/Galton/talent.htm, retrieved January 1, 2001). Nevertheless, Galton soon realized that the issues treated in this 20-page article deserved more extensive, book-length treatment. Just 4 years later, he published the monograph that is the subject of the present chapter: *Hereditary Genius: An Inquiry Into Its Laws and Consequences* (Galton, 1869).

To appreciate fully the significance of this work requires that it be scrutinized from two highly distinctive perspectives. In this chapter, *Hereditary Genius* is first examined from the standpoint of the history of science, with special stress on the history of psychological science. Then the book is considered from the viewpoint of the psychology of science, with the emphasis placed on the psychology of scientists who have earned a place in history.

THE HISTORY OF PSYCHOLOGICAL SCIENCE

Galton's (1869) *Hereditary Genius* is rich in ideas. For instance, Galton was the first behavioral scientist to discuss multiple discovery and invention. This is the phenomenon in which two or more scientists independently come up with the same idea (Merton, 1961; Simonton, 1988b). In addition, Galton conjectured that immigration might have positive consequences for the level of talent enjoyed by a given nation, a notion that has been confirmed empirically (Simonton, 1997b). Nonetheless, these observations and hypotheses are somewhat peripheral to the main thrust of Galton's book. In particular, the bulk of *Hereditary Genius* centered on the concept of *natural ability*, which he discussed in terms of four core issues: (a) its cross-sectional distribution, (b) its adaptive consequences, (c) its familial inheritance, and (d) its deliberate enhancement, or what he termed *eugenics*. All four of these ideas have deep roots in Darwin's evolutionary theory, and all four exerted a profound influence on subsequent research.

The Cross-Sectional Distribution: The Bell-Shaped Curve

An absolutely essential feature of Darwin's theory is the assumption that organisms vary on various characteristics. It is this variation that provides the raw material on which natural selection operates—no variation, no selection. Not surprisingly, Galton argued that human beings were no different. But in line with his mathematical predilections, Galton went a step further by attempting to describe precisely the probability distribution of individual differences. His point of departure was Adolphe Quételet's work establishing that individual differences in physical characteristics, such as height, could be accurately described by the Laplace–Gauss distribution. Galton then proceeded to argue that exactly the same "normal" or "bell-shaped" curve could be applied to human psychological attributes. In particular, he claimed that this distribution was descriptive of individual differences in what Galton called *natural ability*. To establish this claim, he analyzed the distribution of test performance—on the Cambridge Mathematical Tipos and the Royal Military College entrance exams—and found a conspicuous concordance with statistical expectation.

The importance of this extension cannot be overstated. The normal distribution has since become the bedrock on which much of psychology has been built. Most standard inferential statistics begin with the assumption of normality, whether in the variables or in the residual (error) terms. The bell-shaped curve is featured in virtually every introductory psychology text, in which the curve is most frequently applied to the distribution of intelligence, as gauged by "IQ tests." Indeed, a person's IQ is most often defined in terms of his or her placement on the normal curve. If anything, Galton's influence in this regard has been too great. Although the normal curve does a pretty good job predicting the distribution of performance on intelligence tests (Burt, 1963), it provides an extremely poor description of how people vary on other critical psychological and behavioral attributes (Burt, 1943; Walberg, Strykowski, Rovai, & Hung, 1984). Ironically, the bell curve is especially inept at describing the distribution on traits that provided the main focus of *Hereditary Genius*, namely, creativity, leadership, and talent (Simonton, 1999b). Nevertheless, the broad applicability of the normal curve can still be considered one of the book's major contributions to psychology.

The Adaptive Consequences: Genius Born, Not Made

According to Darwin's theory, variations feed natural selection because the variants differ in adaptive fitness. That is, some variations better facilitate survival and reproduction. By the same token, Galton believed that each individual's natural ability underwrote his or her ultimate success in life. Those people whose natural ability placed them on the upper tail of the normal distribution would display this inherently superior adaptive advantage as overt achievements so exceptional that the originators would necessarily attain a wide and enduring reputation (Simonton, 1991b). For Galton, supreme natural ability, eminence, and genius were essentially synonymous terms. In contrast, those on the lower trail of the normal distribution would be ill equipped for an adaptive life and would most likely have to be institutionalized.

At the time Galton promoted this linkage, he had no instruments by which to measure directly natural ability. Only later did he devise "anthropometric" measures that purported to assess individual differences on this key construct (Galton, 1883). Unfortunately, it was eventually discovered that these instruments failed to predict adaptive superiority in the sense Galton anticipated. Even so, Galton's followers could argue that the fault rested with the measures, not with Galton's theory. Especially crucial was Lewis Terman's (1925) decision to define natural ability and genius in terms of scores on the Stanford–Binet intelligence test that he had just recently developed. Galton's belief in the adaptive value of natural ability became thereby translated into widespread conviction that general intelligence provides the single most critical psychological factor underlying success in life (see, e.g., Herrnstein & Murray, 1994).

Although Galton might have been pleased with this outcome, he might also have entertained one serious reservation about these recent developments. Galton's (1869) concept of natural ability was far more complex than encompassed by general intelligence. According to him, it consisted of a mix of at least three ingredients, namely, intellect, energy, and persistence. Only the first of these is cognitive, whereas the last two are clearly motivational in nature. It is significant, therefore, that subsequent research has demonstrated that motivation plays a much stronger role in the attainment of distinction than does general intelligence (e.g., Cox, 1926; Eysenck, 1995; Roe, 1953). The old saying that "where there's a will, there's a way" has a grain of truth.

The Familial Inheritance: The Nature–Nurture Issue

Where does this natural ability come from? How does one become "born" with "genius"? Until more modern times, such events were often attributed to divine intervention. In Giorgio Vasari's (circa 1550/1968) *Lives of the Painters, Sculptors, and Architects*, for example, Michelangelo's appearance occurred because "the great Ruler of Heaven looked down" and decided "to send to earth a genius universal in each art" (p. 347). However, Galton had no more need for such miraculous occasions than did Darwin for the emergence of new life forms. Indeed, just as Darwin believed that adaptive fitness was passed down from parents to offspring, so did Galton argue that natural ability was the upshot of familial inheritance—like parent, like child.

In partial support of this assertion, Galton pointed to the bell-shaped curve. Because physical traits like height were both genetically inherited and normally distributed, the normal distribution of natural ability may indicate that this trait originates by a similar process. This argument, we now know, is plain wrong, for environmental factors can also generate normally distributed psychological attributes.

Fortunately, most of *Hereditary Genius* is devoted to providing empirical evidence of an utterly different kind. If exceptional natural ability leads to achieved eminence, and if natural ability arises from familial inheritance, then genius should cluster into family lines. To make his case, Galton compiled extensive family records for a wide range of achievement domains, including politicians, commanders, religious figures, scientists, poets, musicians, painters, and athletes. By performing a systematic statistical analysis, he was able to show that notable achievers were disproportionately represented among lineages that featured other outstanding figures. Furthermore, the closer the degree of biological relationship, the higher were the statistical odds. This demonstration constitutes the first significant application of the family pedigree method in psychology—and thus constitutes the beginning of modern behavioral genetics. In addition, because Galton subjected historical and biographical data to statistical analysis, this inquiry can also be considered the most important use of historiometric methods since Quételet's (1835/1968) pioneering application a few decades earlier (Simonton, 1999a).

Not everyone in Galton's day was willing to accept his argument, many affirming that the environment plays a much bigger role than does genetic inheritance. Such criticisms inspired Galton to conduct what can be considered a follow-up study to *Hereditary Genius*, namely, *English Men of Science: Their Nature and Nurture* (Galton, 1874). Rather than study historic geniuses, Galton here decided to investigate famous contemporaries. In particular, he distributed questionnaires to Fellows of the Royal Society of London, the greatest British scientists of his day. This constitutes the first major use of the survey–questionnaire method in the behavioral sciences. The questionnaire asked the respondents to provide information about both genetic and environmental influences. In the latter category were such family background factors as birth order—the first scientific inquiry on the developmental relevance of that variable. Even more critical is the subtitle. Although the alliterative terms *nature* and *nurture* had been linked before in William Shakespeare's *The Tempest* and in Richard Mulcaster's even earlier *Elementary* (Teigen, 1984), Galton still deserves credit for establishing the nature–nurture issue as one of the major substantive problems in developmental psychology.

The Active Encouragement: Eugenics

Darwin chose the term *natural selection* to contrast that hypothesized process against its better-known alternative, namely *artificial selection*. Darwin's thinking was strongly influenced by the breeding of domestic animals. If human breeders could generate such an immense variety of dogs, cats, and pigeons in such a relatively brief span of time, then certainly Nature could produce an even more impressive diversity of life forms over an even longer span of time. Curiously, Galton (1869) reversed this argument in *Hereditary Genius*. If human beings were the product of natural selection, so could they become subjected to artificial selection. Specifically, those individuals who display higher levels of natural ability should be encouraged to reproduce their kind. Galton thereby introduced what became known as the eugenics movement, a movement that he played a major role in promulgating.

Galton's discussion of this topic includes many passages that cause his admirers considerable embarrassment today. Believing that not all human races were equally evolved, Galton (1869) tried to rank the races according to the general level of natural ability in their respective populations. This racial hierarchy was an integral part of his treatment of dysgenic practices that caused decline in certain historic populations. In particular, he had to explain why the ancient Greeks, whom he considered the supreme race, ceased to occupy the center of civilization after the Athenian Golden Age. This deterioration could be then explicated in terms of miscegenation, in which the superior Greeks bred with inferior races, especially after the conquests of Alexander the Great (Kroeber, 1944). As abhorrent as these ideas appear to most modern psychologists, Galton's views must be placed in the context of the Victorian times in which he lived. His racial hierarchies were not too out of step in a zeitgeist that featured Social Darwinism, imperialism, and colonialism as active public policies and widespread personal beliefs. Certainly his assertion that the African Blacks were inferior to "English stock" dovetailed nicely with British colonial conquests throughout the African continent.

THE PSYCHOLOGY OF HISTORIC SCIENTISTS

I have just outlined the central aspects of Galton's (1869) treatment of natural ability. Besides indicating their antecedents in Darwin's evolutionary theory, I also sketched the significance of those ideas in the history of psychological science. I now scrutinize *Hereditary Genius* from an entirely different perspective—the psychology of science. The latter discipline entails the application of psychological methods and theory to the scientific enterprise (Feist & Gorman, 1998). A special subfield within this domain entails the psychological study of distinguished scientists (Simonton, 1988b). Significantly, none other than Galton himself first introduced this latter research tradition. In the first place, his *Hereditary Genius* contains a whole chapter devoted to establishing the pedigrees of great scientists (including Darwin, who was related not just to Galton but also to Erasmus Darwin, their shared grandfather, and to his eminent sons, Francis, George, Leonard, and Horace). Better yet, the follow-up study, *English Men of Science*, concentrated exclusively on the contributions of nature and nurture to the emergence of notable British scientists. In any case, the cumulative literature on the psychology of great scientists has now grown to encompass psychologists as well (Simonton, 2002). As a consequence, we now have a fairly secure set of nomothetic findings that should help us comprehend why *Hereditary Genius* can be counted as a noteworthy contribution. Let us specifically consider the results regarding professional influence, career output, and conceptual content.

Professional Influence

The best single predictor of a scientist's eminence is the impact his or her work has on the field, and the best predictor of that influence is the number of citations that work receives in the professional literature (Simonton, 1988b). In particular, citation rates are strongly associated with such professional honors as election to the National Academy of Sciences and reception of the Nobel Prize. The same association holds for great psychologists as well (Simonton, 2002). Moreover, citation rates can also be used to distinguish the relative merit of singular contributions, such as journal articles, chapters, or books.

By this criterion, *Hereditary Genius* does very well. According to the *Social Sciences Citation Index Five-Year Cumulation* (1992), this work was still garnering about a dozen citations per year. Only one of Galton's publications, *Inquiries Into Human Faculty and Its Development* (Galton, 1883), exhibited a higher citation rate. Yet unlike *Hereditary Genius*, *Inquiries* is actually a compilation of previously published work dealing with a great variety of topics—an anthology of reprints. Of all his books and articles devoted to a single subject, *Hereditary Genius* is by far the most frequently cited.

What makes this citation success all the more impressive are the following two considerations. First, most scientific publications are not cited at all. To provide specifics, of the 783,339 papers that appeared in scientific journals in the year 1981, 81% were cited 10 times or less, and 47% were not cited at all between 1981 and June 1997 (Redner, 1998). Second, even among those publications that do earn citations, the rate of citation decays rapidly, until the work recedes into oblivion (MacRae, 1969). Only those publications that become "citation classics" manage to survive this obsolescence process. And for a book published back in 1869 to average about a dozen citations a year well over a century later certainly bestows on this work classic status.

Sadly, citation indexes do not extend back to years that followed shortly after the publication of *Hereditary Genius*. Even so, there exists ample documentary evidence that the book's impact was immediate, profound, and widespread. Just 2 years later, Charles Darwin published his next masterwork, *The Descent of Man and Selection in Relation to Sex*, in which he devoted several pages to discussing Galton's (1869) ideas (Darwin, 1871/1952). So impressed was Darwin with *Hereditary Genius* that he wrote Galton on December 3, 1869, "I do not think I ever in all my life read anything more interesting and original" (Galton, 1892/1972, p. 3). Moreover, within a short time, the book's influence went beyond the borders of Great Britain. Most notably, Alphonse de Candolle (1873), the great French scientist, published his *Histoire des Sciences et des Savants depuis Deux Siècles* with the specific aim of contradicting Galton's (1869) conclusion that genius was born, not made. Instead, Candolle presented data showing that the appearance of genius (at least in the sciences) could be explained in terms of the political, cultural, economic, and religious milieu. In fact, it was de Candolle's 1873 counterargument that provided the primary impetus for Galton's (1874) *English Men of Science* (Hilts, 1975). In this latter work, Galton compromised a little by admitting that environmental factors may play some role, even if that role is secondary to biological inheritance.

The foregoing events illustrate another feature of a great work's impact on the discipline. Although Darwin's treatment of Galton's ideas in *Descent* were very favorable, de Candolle's were more critical. Research on scientists' citation practices show that this is typical (e.g., Moravcsik & Murugesan, 1975). Frequently, work is cited to make manifest where the author is taking issue with some predecessor. In the case of *Hereditary Genius*, it is probably safe to say that many references to this work by subsequent investigators fell into the critical category. For instance, Alfred Kroeber (1944), the great cultural anthropologist, wrote his classic *Configurations of Culture Growth* as an explicit repudiation of Galton's genetic determinism (Simonton, 1988a).

Hence, a great work is not one that inspires universal consent. If that were true, then Darwin's *Origin of Species* would not count as a masterpiece. Rather, a great work contains ideas so powerful that they cannot be ignored. *Hereditary Genius* clearly falls in that category by this criterion as well.

Career Output

According to Darwinian theory, those who display superior adaptive fitness should exhibit more reproductive success. Likewise, according to Galton's (1869) theory, those who exhibit greater natural ability should make themselves known by their numerous accomplishments. In the case of scientists, the magnitude of achievement is most commonly gauged by the number of publications that appeared during the course of their career (Simonton, 1988b). In Galton's case, *Hereditary Genius* was just one out of 227 items that he published during his lifetime. To place this figure in context, Sigmund Freud could claim 330; William James, 307; Johannes Müller, 285; Gustav Fechner, 267; Hermann von Helmholtz, 229; Alfred Binet, 227; Abraham Maslow, 165; and Charles Darwin, 119 (Bringmann & Balk, 1983). Certainly Galton rubs elbows with some good company! Yet to comprehend fully the specific status of *Hereditary Genius*, we must discuss how this productivity is distributed across the career course.

The first behavioral scientist to study the relation between age and creative output was none other than Quételet (1835/1968). In general, he found that productivity first increases very rapidly, reaches a peak, and thereafter gradually declines. Although Quételet's focus was on career trajectory for the production of plays by notable French and English dramatists, this basic age curve has been replicated many times for various scientific disciplines, including psychology (e.g., Lehman, 1960; Simonton, 1985). What is especially fascinating about this curve is the specific location of what have been termed *career landmarks* (Simonton, 1991a). These are the first major contribution, the last major contribution, and the best (most influential) contribution. Typically, eminent scientists produce the first high-impact work in their late 20s or early 30s, their last high-impact work in their mid-50s, and their single most influential work in their early 40s. However, this generalization must be qualified by three complicating factors (Simonton, 1997a). First, the trajectory is actually a function of career age rather than chronological age. Late bloomers have their age curves shifted over to the extent their career onsets were delayed. Second, holding career onset constant, the most prolific scientists tend to have their first high-impact work appear earlier in their career and their last high-impact work appear later but without any change in the career placement of their single best work. Third, the career trajectory is contingent on the specific discipline. For instance, mathematicians tend to produce their career landmarks at younger ages than do earth scientists. In the particular case of psychology, one study of 69 eminent American psychologists found that the first highly cited work appeared at age 30, the last highly cited work at age 63, and the most cited work at age 47 (Simonton, 1992). The obvious question is how Galton's own career fits these empirical findings.

At age 31 Galton published his first major work, the book *Narrative of an Explorer in Tropical South Africa*, which recounted his experiences leading a geographical exploration. As said before, Galton got a late start as a psychologist, and this cannot be considered a contribution to the field. Around age 63, Galton had published two major books, the already-mentioned *Inquiries Into Human Faculty*, which came out when he was 61, and *Natural Inheritance*, which appeared when he was 67. Actually, given Galton's overall output and impact, we should expect his last influential work to emerge yet later. In line with this expectation, Galton's has several publications in his 70s and 80s that still receive citations today, most having to do with eugenics and statistics.

Last but not least, what was Galton doing at age 47, the age at which the 69 eminent American psychologists tended to publish their most influential work? Well, that is the age at which he published *Hereditary Genius*, to the year! Admittedly, this may seem a glib point given his delayed career onset in the field. Perhaps his *Inquiries* better matches the developmental pattern, particularly in light of its slightly higher citation rate. If so, then *Hereditary Genius* might be best considered his first high-impact contribution rather than his most influential work. In either case, the book must be seriously considered for the privileged status of a career landmark.

One final consideration must be brought to bear on this issue. The study of 69 eminent American psychologists found that high-impact publications are more likely to be books than articles (Simonton, 1992). Corroborative results were found in another study that had eminent psychologists list the publications that most significantly influenced their own work (Heyduk & Fenigstein, 1984, p. 556). Extremely few articles were mentioned. And in every case but one, when a scientific paper was deemed influential, a book or monograph by the same author proved even more so. Hence, Galton's most influential work is most likely to be a book, a position that *Hereditary Genius* can fill nicely.

Conceptual Content

Thus far I have cited nomothetic findings that have absolutely nothing to do with the content of *Hereditary Genius*. Instead, I have focused on its objective impact and its career placement. Not surprisingly, however, empirical research has indicated that the content of a work does indeed have relevance to its disciplinary influence. In particular, consider two research findings, one having to do with consistency, the other with audacity.

Conceptual Consistency

The inquiry into the careers of 69 eminent American psychologists mentioned earlier included a computerized content analysis of the titles of the major publications (Simonton, 1992). The analysis divulged what kinds of topics are most likely to yield research programs with high impact, again as gauged by continued citation in the literature. Among the several findings was one especially pertinent to this evaluation: Exceptional psychologists do not jump around from topic to topic but rather display considerable consistency and coherence in their research programs. In other words, the careers of high-impact psychologists exhibit impressive determination, doggedly pursuing a self-selected set of themes or issues throughout their career. Just think of the big names in psychology, such as Sigmund Freud, Ivan Pavlov, Jean Piaget, or B. F. Skinner to realize the importance of this intellectual persistence. Furthermore, this asset is not unique to psychology. Another study applied the same content analysis to the publications of natural scientists and obtained the same results (Feist, 1993).

The implication of these findings to Galton's own work should be obvious. Once he decided to become a psychologist, certain themes cropped up repeatedly throughout his career: the wide dispersion of individual differences, the behavioral consequences of such variation, the role of biological inheritance in producing those differences, the potential use of eugenic interventions to elevate highly desirable traits, and the use of innovative statistical analyses to study individual differences, their inheritance, and their consequences. One or more of these themes underlie every major contribution Galton made, such as correlation and regression, twin studies, and facial composites. Although not everything Galton published dealt with all of these issues at once, *Hereditary Genius* is certainly among the few publications that did so. Hence, this book can be considered a seminal work that established the conceptual framework for virtually all of his subsequent research.

Conceptual Audacity

Another empirical study examined the long-term impact of 54 eminent psychologists born between 1801 (Gustav Theodor Fechner) and 1919 (William K. Estes), including Galton himself (Simonton, 2000). Each of the 54 had been previously assessed according to the positions they took on several theoretical and methodological issues that have proved divisive in the history of psychology. For instance, should concepts be quantitative or qualitative, atomistic or holistic, objective or subjective, impersonal or personal, static or dynamic? Those psychologists with the most long-term impact on the field were found to be those who took the most extreme positions on these controversies. Interestingly, the same effect was observed in a study of the 2,012 thinkers who define the Western intellectual tradition from the ancient Greeks to the 20th century (Simonton, 1976). Those philosophers who attained the greatest long-term distinction were those who tended to take strong positions on such issues as empiricism versus rationalism, materialism versus idealism, determinism versus free will, and individualism versus collectivism.

Here, too, the relevance of these findings to Galton's work should be manifest. His stance on the nature–nurture issue was clearly extremist. Although he sometimes yielded a little, as is most apparent in his *English Men of Science* (Galton, 1874), this compromise was rather minimal, as is obvious from his lifelong commitment to research on biological inheritance and to the eugenics movement. In fact, the nature–nurture issue was among those on which the 54 psychologists were assessed, and Galton's score was the farthest out in the direction of nature: 2.5 standard deviations above the mean. Although Galton's placement at the extreme end of this nature–nurture dimension is based on the entire body of his research contributions, it is also evident that some publications express this genetic determinism with the least qualification. And of Galton's most frequently cited works, *Hereditary Genius* takes the most extremist stance on the nature–nurture issue. As a consequence, this book helped ensure that Galton might be criticized, attacked, and belittled by psychologists advocating a more environmentalist viewpoint.

IMPLICATIONS

One benefit from adopting a nomothetic approach is that it makes it easier to generalize beyond this particular case. By comparing *Hereditary Genius* with what psychologists have learned about the nature of great scientists and their works, it has been shown to possess several attributes that can be considered fairly representative of influential contributions in general. As a consequence, the foregoing discussion has potential implications for anyone who aspires to make a substantial impression on psychological science. To be specific, the discussion leads to the following three recommendations:

1. *Build on the best ideas of the past, for great contributions do not emerge de novo.* Newton once admitted that he saw farther than his colleagues because he "stood on the shoulders of giants." Galton, too, built on the work of illustrious predecessors, most notably Darwin. It is especially helpful to adopt an integrative strategy that puts together ideas for two or more sources. Newton integrated the new heliocentric astronomy of Copernicus and Johannes Kepler with the new mechanics of Galileo. Likewise, to Darwin's evolutionary theory Galton added mathematical analysis, including Quételet's work on the normal curve. When a scientific publication extends and integrates the contributions of past luminaries, it becomes part of a "great conversation" in the advancement of scientific ideas.

2. *After putting forward your ideas, don't ever rest on your laurels.* For any innovative idea to make a significant impact on the field, it must receive the development and elaboration it deserves. Great scientists do not attain their elevated status by publishing a single classic journal article and then waiting for the awards to fall on their heads. Almost invariably, the initial idea must be expanded, the implications worked out, and the predictions tested—in publication after publication after publication. Einstein did not cease his endeavors with the appearance of his relativity theory at age 26 but rather spent most of the remainder of his life pursuing the idea, extending first the special theory, and then proposing and expounding his general theory. By the same token, Galton devoted his whole career to working out his core ideas. In sciences like psychology, moreover, full-fledged conceptual development usually requires a book-length treatment. A single journal article can seldom do justice to all the theoretical complications and methodological niceties that a truly powerful idea requires. Hence, Galton's 1865 article on "Hereditary Talent and Character" was enlarged into his 1869 book *Hereditary Genius*. His impact on psychology's history gained as a consequence.

3. *Don't be wishy-washy, but rather take forthright positions.* Too often ideas of great potential importance fail to see the light of day because their originators want to avoid controversy or are too timid to face possible criticism. Where would Copernicus, Galileo, Darwin, or Freud be now had they been unwilling to defy the crowd? Galton was repeatedly willing to challenge received notions or conventional ideas. He once even conducted a study to test the efficacy of prayer—in the heyday of Victorian religious sentimentalism! To be sure, controversial stances are not necessarily true, but great scientists are not afraid of making mistakes. They are risk takers who are willing to tolerate failures for the sake of the successes. Those who set out to disprove Galton's (1869) extreme genetic determinism have tremendously enhanced our understanding of the origins of genius and talent.

Perhaps from Galton's *Hereditary Genius*, I can derive yet a fourth recommendation: *It's never too late to start applying the first three.* After all, Galton did not even launch his career as a psychologist until he was 43 years old. If the trajectory is a function of career age rather than chronological age, then late bloomers always have hope. Perhaps you are still waiting for that influential book that will stimulate you with the needed "crystallizing experience." If so, when that epiphany finally arrives, be sure to enact at once the three other implications of Galton's life work.

REFERENCES

Annin, E. L., Boring, E. G., & Watson, R. I. (1968). Important psychologists, 1600–1967. *Journal of the History of the Behavioral Sciences, 4,* 303–315.

Boring, E. G. (1963). History, psychology, and science (R. I. Watson & D. T. Campbell, Eds.). New York: Wiley.

Bringmann, W. G., & Balk, M. M. (1983). Wilhelm Wundt's publication record: A re-examination. *Storia e Critica della Psicologia, 4*, 61–86.

Burt, C. (1943). Ability and income. *British Journal of Educational Psychology, 12*, 83–98.

Burt, C. (1963). Is intelligence distributed normally? *British Journal of Statistical Psychology, 16*, 175–190.

Cox, C. (1926). *The early mental traits of three hundred geniuses*. Stanford, CA: Stanford University Press.

de Candolle, A. (1873). *Histoire des sciences et des savants depuis deux siècles* [History of the sciences and scientists in the last two centuries]. Geneva, Switzerland: Georg.

Darwin, C. (1952). The descent of man and selection in relation to sex. In R. M. Hutchins (Ed.), *Great books of the Western world* (Vols. 49, pp. 253–600). Chicago: Encyclopaedia Britannica. (Original work published 1871)

Eysenck, H. J. (1995). *Genius: The natural history of creativity*. Cambridge, England: Cambridge University Press.

Feist, G. J. (1993). A structural model of scientific eminence. *Psychological Science, 4*, 366–371.

Feist, G. J., & Gorman, M. E. (1998). The psychology of science: Review and integration of a nascent discipline. *Review of General Psychology, 2*, 3–47.

Galton, F. (1869). *Hereditary genius: An inquiry into its laws and consequences*. London: Macmillan.

Galton, F. (1874). *English men of science: Their nature and nurture*. London: Macmillan.

Galton, F. (1883). *Inquiries into human faculty and its development*. London: Macmillan.

Galton, F. (1972). *Hereditary genius: An inquiry into its laws and consequences* (2nd ed.). Gloucester, MA: Smith. (Original work published 1892)

Herrnstein, R. J., & Murray, C. A. (1994). *The bell curve: Intelligence and class structure in American life*. New York: Free Press.

Heyduk, R. G., & Fenigstein, A. (1984). Influential works and authors in psychology: A survey of eminent psychologists. *American Psychologist, 39*, 556–559.

Hilts, V. L. (1975). *A guide to Francis Galton's English Men of Science*. Philadelphia: American Philosophical Society.

Kroeber, A. L. (1944). *Configurations of culture growth*. Berkeley: University of California Press.

Lehman, H. C. (1960). The age decrement in outstanding scientific creativity. *American Psychologist, 15*, 128–134.

MacRae, D., Jr. (1969). Growth and decay curves in scientific citations. *American Sociological Review, 34*, 631–635.

Merton, R. K. (1961). Singletons and multiples in scientific discovery: A chapter in the sociology of science. *Proceedings of the American Philosophical Society, 105*, 470–486.

Moravcsik, M. J., & Murugesan, P. (1975). Some results on the function and quality of citations. *Social Studies of Science, 5*, 86–92.

Quételet, A. (1968). *A treatise on man and the development of his faculties*. New York: Franklin. (Reprint of 1842 Edinburgh translation of 1835 French original)

Redner, S. (1998). How popular is your paper? An empirical study of the citation distribution. *European Physical Journal B, 4*, 131–134.

Roe, A. (1953). *The making of a scientist*. New York: Dodd, Mead.

Simonton, D. K. (1976). Philosophical eminence, beliefs, and zeitgeist: An individual–generational analysis. *Journal of Personality and Social Psychology, 34*, 630–640.

Simonton, D. K. (1985). Quality, quantity, and age: The careers of 10 distinguished psychologists. *International Journal of Aging and Human Development, 21*, 241–254.

Simonton, D. K. (1988a). Galtonian genius, Kroeberian configurations, and emulation: A generational time-series analysis of Chinese civilization. *Journal of Personality and Social Psychology, 55*, 230–238.

Simonton, D. K. (1988b). *Scientific genius: A psychology of science*. Cambridge, England: Cambridge University Press.

Simonton, D. K. (1991a). Career landmarks in science: Individual differences and interdisciplinary contrasts. *Developmental Psychology, 27*, 119–130.

Simonton, D. K. (1991b). Latent-variable models of posthumous reputation: A quest for Galton's G. *Journal of Personality and Social Psychology, 60*, 607–619.

Simonton, D. K. (1992). Leaders of American psychology, 1879–1967: Career development, creative output, and professional achievement. *Journal of Personality and Social Psychology, 62*, 5–17.

Simonton, D. K. (1997a). Creative productivity: A predictive and explanatory model of career trajectories and landmarks. *Psychological Review, 104*, 66–89.

Simonton, D. K. (1997b). Foreign influence and national achievement: The impact of open milieus on Japanese civilization. *Journal of Personality and Social Psychology, 72*, 86–94.

Simonton, D. K. (1999a). Significant samples: The psychological study of eminent individuals. *Psychological Methods, 4*, 425–451.

Simonton, D. K. (1999b). Talent and its development: An emergenic and epigenetic model. *Psychological Review, 106*, 435–457.

Simonton, D. K. (2000). Methodological and theoretical orientation and the long-term disciplinary impact of 54 eminent psychologists. *Review of General Psychology, 4*, 1–13.

Simonton, D. K. (2002). *Great psychologists and their times: Scientific insights into psychology's history*. Washington, DC: American Psychological Association.

Social sciences citation index five-year cumulation 1986–1990. (1992). Philadelphia: Institute for Scientific Information.

Teigen, K. H. (1984). A note on the origin of the term "nature and nurture": Not Shakespeare and Galton, but Mulcaster. *Journal of the History of the Behavioral Sciences, 20*, 363–364.

Terman, L. M. (1925). *Mental and physical traits of a thousand gifted children*. Stanford, CA: Stanford University Press.

Vasari, G. (1968). *Lives of the painters, sculptors, and architects* (A. B. Hinds, Trans.). New York: Dell. (Original work published ca. 1550)

Walberg, H. J., Strykowski, B. F., Rovai, E., & Hung, S. S. (1984). Exceptional performance. *Review of Educational Research, 54,* 87–112.

Walters, J., & Gardner, H. (1986). The crystallizing experience: Discovering an intellectual gift. In R. J. Sternberg & J. E. Davidson (Eds.), *Conceptions of giftedness* (pp. 306–331). New York: Cambridge University Press.

Watson, R. I., Sr. (1974). *Eminent contributors to psychology* (Vol. 1). New York: Springer.

Zusne, L. (1987). *Eponyms in psychology: A dictionary and biographical sourcebook.* New York: Greenwood Press.

Zusne, L., & Dailey, D. P. (1982). History of psychology texts as measuring instruments of eminence in psychology. *Revista de Historia de la Psicología, 3,* 7–42.

2

A PROFOUND AND RADICAL CHANGE: HOW WILLIAM JAMES INSPIRED THE RESHAPING OF AMERICAN PSYCHOLOGY

DAVID E. LEARY

Who before or since William James has had as great an impact on the way that American psychologists—and many others—describe and explain psychological experiences and activities?[1] The noted historian of psychology, E. G. Boring (1950), could think of only three others—Charles Darwin, Hermann von Helmholtz, and Sigmund Freud—none of whom was an American or psychologist per se (p. 743). John Dewey (1910) expressed the view of his generation when he noted that "by common consent" James was "far and away the greatest of American psychologists" (p. 506). Indeed, Dewey felt

---

[1]This chapter discusses James's influence on American psychology, but it should be noted that his influence was also felt by psychologists in many other countries and that a wide array of thinkers, writers, scientists, and artists have acknowledged a debt to James—individuals as varied as Bernard Berenson, Niels Bohr, Jorge Luis Borges, John Dewey, W. E. B. DuBois, Nelson Goodman, Helen Keller, Walter Lippmann, Stephen Pepper, Hilary Putnam, Richard Rorty, Oliver Sacks, Gertrude Stein, Wallace Stevens, and Cornel West. The great philosopher and historian of ideas Alfred North Whitehead considered James to be one of the four major thinkers in the entire Western tradition, along with Plato, Aristotle, and Gottfried Wilhelm von Leibniz (Whitehead, 1938, pp. 3–4).

that James was the greatest psychologist "in any country—perhaps of any time" (p. 506). Speaking for a later generation, John B. Watson (1924/1963) showed less reserve, asserting that James was "the most brilliant psychologist the world has ever known" (p. 141).

Since Watson proffered this opinion, it has been repeated over and over, right up to the present time. And even though recent commentators often express regret that contemporary psychologists cite James more often than they actually read his work (e.g., Miller, 1983, p. xviii) and that too few have absorbed the full wisdom of his insights (e.g., Mandler, 1979, p. 744), it is nonetheless clear that James's influence has been both fundamental and pervasive.

Why was James so successful in stimulating the growth of the "new psychology" that was still struggling for life and for its own disciplinary identity in the late 19th century? How did he help this not-fully-formed offspring of philosophy and physiology develop into a major scientific and academic field? I address these questions in this chapter, making particular reference to the development and impact of his masterwork, *The Principles of Psychology* (1890/1981).[2]

In trying to understand James's influence on psychologists and psychology, we need first to grasp what it was like to encounter James's *Principles* on "the other side" of the discipline's history, when his treatise first appeared. Comments by James R. Angell, a major psychologist in the early 20th century who was a graduate student when *Principles* was published, express the experience with particular immediacy and clarity:

> With the publication of this great work . . . a profound and radical change
> came over the scene. Who does not remember the sense of glowing de-
> light with which we first read the pages of the big, cumbrous, ill-bound
> and rather ill-printed volumes? It was like inhaling a rare, pungent moun-
> tain air, vital, bracing and almost intoxicating. To many of us of the
> younger generation the book was assigned as a text. We read it as one
> reads the most fascinating tale of a master—spell-bound and transported

---

[2]Focusing on James's *Principles* makes sense, not only because it has been the most influential of his many works but also because his subsequent presentations and publications—including his psychological articles, his *Talks to Teachers on Psychology and to Students on Some of Life's Ideals* (1899/1983b), and his *Varieties of Religious Experience* (1902/1985), as well as his important writings on pragmatism, pluralism, and radical empiricism—were outgrowths, in various ways, of the perspective, conceptual framework, suppositions, and insights expressed in *Principles*. Of course, when I speak about the influence of James's *Principles of Psychology*, I am referring also to the influence of its much abbreviated version, James's *Psychology: Briefer Course* (1892/1984). For decades, because of its smaller size and cheaper price, the latter served more commonly than *Principles* as a textbook for undergraduates and even graduates. (As a result of its continuing use, *Briefer Course* was reprinted by its original publisher at least 17 times between 1892 and 1945; after that, it has been reissued periodically by other publishers. Like *Principles*, it continues to be cited frequently up to the current day. See Sokal, 1984a, pp. xl–xli.) Both treatises—*Principles* and *Briefer Course*—were so well known in the decades after they were published that they were often referred to, simply, as "James" and "Jimmy." Although there are some differences (other than longer and shorter treatments) between these two texts, these differences do not matter for the arguments presented in this chapter.

and yet withal feeling ourselves acquiring new powers, and gaining command of pregnant thoughts. Scores of other readers fared as did we and so it came to pass that almost over night James became the recognized fountain head of the most original and most vigorous psychological thinking in our country. . . It is difficult to appreciate how much that is now familiar and commonplace in psychological writing was introduced by James. (Angell, 1911, pp. 78–79)

How did this come about? How did James inspire a reshaping of what was "familiar and commonplace" in psychology? Certainly, one could say that the time was right for someone to think and write what James thought and wrote. But this begs essential questions: What was it about his thinking and writing that facilitated such a "profound and radical change"? What made James's *Principles* so "spell-binding" that it "transported" so many who read it? What has helped his work remain fertile to this very day? I believe we can come to some useful answers—after tracing some general lines of development that proceeded from James's work—by reflecting on the constitutive factors and distinctive characteristics of his psychology and by considering the special role played by his innovative central vision. In the end, I argue that the connections between James's life experiences, his time and place, and his psychology, as well as the new and coherent story that he told about humans (and animals in general), help explain the powerful effects of his *Principles of Psychology*.

THE VARIETIES OF JAMES'S INFLUENCE

Although the main objective of this chapter is to elucidate *why* and *how* James has had such a great impact on psychology, it is reasonable to begin with a broad, if necessarily selective survey of *what* influence he has had.

Elucidating Issues, Questions, and Problems; Offering Ideas; Clearing the Way

First of all, James played an important role in introducing, clarifying, and recasting some of the important issues, questions, and problems that have preoccupied psychologists since his time. As a special committee of the American Psychological Association (APA) asserted in 1969:

James' *Principles* is without question the most literate, the most provocative, and at the same time the most intelligible book on psychology that has ever appeared in English or in any other language. Part of James' genius was his ability to recognize a fundamental problem, to formulate it clearly, to marshall [sic] the available facts and theories, and then to throw it back to the reader, cleaned and polished, as a challenge to his curiosity. In 1890 the "new psychology" was in the making. James found some aspects of it exciting, others boring, but in every chapter of his great book we find him burrowing through masses of observation and opinion, patiently sorting and discarding, and then coming through with an invitation to further inquiry. If there ever was a man who knew how to ask searching questions, it was William James. (Bray, Boring, MacLeod, & Solomon, 1969, p. iii)

But James did more than ask questions; he posited many answers and did so in a way that invited further thought, observations, experimentation, and even rebuttals. It was the "unfinished business" of psychology, as the APA committee put it, that excited James and was communicated to his audience. Although his powers of expression were considerable, it was his "gift of suggestion," as one friend pointed out (Chapman, 1915/1996, p. 53), that energized his contemporaries and later psychologists. Three decades later, Edna Heidbreder (1933) noted that James's treatment of psychological topics was more often than not "far more suggestive than conclusive" and "raised many more questions than it answered," but it usually contained "the unformed stuff of which science is made" and persistently turned the reader "directly toward experience" for answers (p. 200).

Besides insisting on fidelity to experience—to experienced *facts*—James continually emphasized the need for *psychological* facts. As Heidbreder (1933) said, other psychologists at the time were intent on "making the new psychology a science," whereas James was more concerned "that the new science be psychology" (p. 152). After pushing persistently in this direction as he worked for 12 long years on his text, James produced a psychological treatise—the *Principles of Psychology*—that many have found to be "the most stimulating and provocative ever written," a treatise that "today, as in 1890," is "a seemingly inexhaustible source of ideas" (Myers, 1981, p. xl) and "still offers fresh insights (and delights) to the psychologist who takes the trouble to read it" (Johnson & Henley, 1990, p. xix).

James's fertility of mind and thought is clearly an important aspect of his contribution to psychology. It is not simply that his discussions in *Principles* are provocative; as the APA committee suggested, they are *intelligibly* provocative. Almost as important as what he offered by way of fresh hypotheses and speculations was the "sorting and discarding" that the APA committee mentioned. In this regard, as I have argued elsewhere, James can be seen as "a sort of John Locke of the 19th and 20th centuries" (Leary, 1990b, p. 124). By this I mean that James, like Locke, was devoted to "clearing the ground . . . and removing some of the rubbish that lies in the way of knowledge" (Locke, 1690/1959, Vol. 1, p. 14). James did this preparatory work very well: In exposition after exposition in *Principles*, "he did more than simply regurgitate what others thought. James organized the material in such a way as to reveal the underlying issues" (Park & Kosslyn, 1990, p. 195). That was an enormous contribution to a fledgling discipline, and it is one of the reasons that people still return to James's work: not simply out of historical interest or curiosity but for clarification of issues as well as inspiration and stimulation.[3]

James cleared the way for closer observations and offered better thinking in virtually all areas of what is now recognized as the domain of psychology. However, in this relatively short chapter, it makes sense to focus on just a few areas in which his impact has been apparent: his analysis of habit, his phenomenology of consciousness, and his theory of the self. It would be easy to select additional areas.[4] But discussions of these three should serve as adequate stepping stones to the discussion that follows.

Habit

At the end of his chapter on brain activity—Chapter III of *Principles of Psychology* (1890/1981, Vol. 1)—James concluded that the most important

[3]In all of these regards—in his ability to sort and discard previous conjectures, in his ability to highlight key issues, and in his ability to offer stimulating observations, ideas, and theories of his own—James was different from the other major figures of his day and generation, most notably George Trumbull Ladd, G. Stanley Hall, and James McKeen Cattell. For all their historical significance, none of these other "founders of modern American psychology" has had a similar continuing impact on the discipline, although Hall and Cattell were both instrumental in establishing psychological organizations and journals, and Hall played an important role in the growth of modern scientific pedagogy and in the development of "genetic psychology" (especially the psychology of childhood, adolescence, and senescence). Regarding Ladd, see Mills (1969); regarding Hall, see Ross (1972); regarding Cattell, see Sokal (1984b). It bears noting that Ladd's *Elements of Physiological Psychology* (1887) appeared 3 years before James's *Principles of Psychology* (1890/1981) and was important in its time. However, Ladd's insistence on spiritualistic dualism and his subsequent attack on the natural scientific approach to psychology (Ladd, 1892) forfeited him the preeminence and continuing influence that he craved. James's (1892/1983a) reply to Ladd's attack, although appropriately modest about the actual achievements of psychology to date, became a rallying point for those who followed his lead. In addition, as Seashore (1921) noted, Ladd was more "an organizer . . . than an inspirer, or an original contributor" (p. 242), and even Ladd's devoted biographer confessed, reluctantly, that Ladd's "endless stream of dry prose made me impatient" so that "when weary of the solemn style I would turn to William James for relief" (Mills, 1969, p. viii). Let no contemporary undergraduate or graduate student think that the impact of one's work can be separated from the vitality of one's writing! I say all of this, and could say more about Hall and Cattell, to underscore that James's impact was *not* simply a function of being in the right place at the right time, while the discipline was in formation. Others—now more or less forgotten—were there too.

[4]For instance, a great deal of interesting empirical observation, experimental work, and theoretical speculation have been stimulated by James's novel explanation of the emotions, which has come to be known as the James–Lange theory. But this hardly exhausts the other possibilities. As the APA committee assigned to plan a series of lectures and discussions to clarify James's ongoing legacy in the late 1960s reported: "We found it difficult to agree on which of James' questions we should select, because there were so many of them" (Bray, Boring, MacLeod, & Solomon, 1969, p. iii). It should be noted that some aspects of James's impact—for instance, his influence on the development of broader, open-ended conceptions of consciousness and on the establishment of abnormal and clinical psychology—were foreshadowed in *Principles* but were more clearly generated through his teaching and lectures in the years following the publication of *Principles* (see Taylor, 1982, 1996, pp. 40–81). Recent overviews and assessments of various aspects of James's legacy were prompted by the centennial anniversary of *Principles*. See Donnelly (1992) and Johnson and Henley (1990), and confer Taylor (1996, pp. 194–204) for useful summaries and comments on these works as well as on many of the articles that appeared in special "James issues" of the *American Journal of Psychology*, *History of the Human Sciences*, *Personality and Social Psychology Bulletin*, and *Psychological Science*. Taylor saw, as I do, that James's influence has been pervasive, even though much of 20th-century American psychology has evolved in ways that James would have criticized. Taylor also saw,

feature of general brain physiology "for psychological purposes" is "the aptitude of the brain for acquiring *habits*" (p. 108). As a result, he devoted all of his next chapter to habit. He began that chapter by noting that "when we look at living creatures from an outward point of view, one of the first things that strike us is that they are bundles of habits" (p. 109). Those habits for which there is an innate tendency he called "instincts"; those that are due to "education" he saw as resulting from "acts of reason." Although the efficacy of reason (and will) are attenuated as habits become more and more engrained, it seemed clear to James that habits, being variable across individuals, illustrate the "plasticity" of organic matter and the tendency for "channels" or "paths" to be worn into this matter, and especially into its nervous tissue, as a result of repeated "exercise" (pp. 111, 117).

With this basic scenario in place, James went on to list some "practical applications of the principle [of habit formation] to human life": (a) "habit simplifies the movements required to achieve a given result, makes them more accurate and diminishes fatigue," and (b) "habit diminishes the conscious attention with which our acts are performed" (pp. 117, 119). Then, in typical Jamesian fashion, he gave some vivid and effective illustrations from life, including his own life, intermixing these accounts with theoretical elaborations. Finally, with his "law of habit" graphically and firmly lodged in the reader's mind, James made the "very natural transition" to the ethical implications of this law. In some of his most famous sentences, he wrote that habit is

> the enormous fly-wheel of society, its most precious conservative agent.
> . . . It dooms us all to fight out the battle of life upon the lines of our
> nurture or our early choice. . . . The great thing, then, in all education, is
> to *make our nervous system our ally instead of our enemy.* (pp. 125–126)

James then proffered a series of maxims that, if observed, would help individuals develop the kind of habits that would increase the probability of success in life, while making "automatic and habitual, as early as possible, as many useful actions" as possible (p. 126). Doing the latter, he pointed out, frees "our higher powers of mind" from the mere "details of our daily life" so that they can address "their own proper work" (p. 126).

The thing to emphasize, after this all-too-succinct summary, is that James was unique in his particular emphasis on habit, which was in fact an emphasis on learning and reflected, in the tradition of the "old psychology" of mental and moral philosophy, a distinctly American concern for the practical application of psychological theory.[5] This emphasis and concern were both

---

as I do, that there is much in James's overall corpus of work (e.g., his treatment of the "further reaches of consciousness") that remains unknown, overlooked, or ignored by psychologists and could be of considerable benefit to psychology.

[5]The distinctive character of James's emphasis on habit is illustrated by the fact that 4 years after *Principles* appeared, George Trumbull Ladd was still writing in traditional ways about "ideo-motor movements," without any of the ethical fervor or practical applications (much less the stylistic flair) that James brought to the topic (Ladd, 1894, pp. 227–228).

underscored in James's subsequent *Talks to Teachers on Psychology and to Students on Some of Life's Ideals* (1899/1983b), with its influential claim that education could best be described as "the organization of acquired habits of conduct and tendencies to behavior" (p. 27). By the time James wrote this later work, one of his graduate students, Edward L. Thorndike, had already performed his groundbreaking animal learning experiments in James's basement, thus preparing the way for his subsequent study of human learning and his important contributions to educational psychology (Thorndike, 1898, 1913, 1913–1914).

As is well known, Thorndike's classic research on cats, chickens, and dogs trying to escape from "puzzle boxes" in order to be fed, which led to the articulation of his famous "law of effect," was a clear forerunner of B. F. Skinner's studies of operant conditioning. Although he never formally called himself a "behaviorist," Thorndike was one of several links between James and the later functionalist–behaviorist tradition in American psychology (another link being James R. Angell, who taught John B. Watson at the University of Chicago). Without Thorndike, who was attracted to psychology through his reading of *Principles*, a book that he found "more stimulating than any books that I had read before, and possibly more so than any book read since" (Thorndike, 1936, p. 263), the study of learning in the United States may have followed a slightly different course, but learning would still have moved, as it did, to the center of American psychological concerns for the coming century. This was a key part of James's legacy: an emphasis on the role of habit formation in the "nurture" or "education" of individual character, leading to an elevation of the importance of learning as a topic of psychological study. It was not a major subject of empirical study before William James, but it has been ever since. Similarly, a concern for the practical, for what really matters regarding human welfare, was firmly entrenched by those who took their cue from James.

Consciousness

Virtually everyone who knows about James's psychology is aware of his description of mental life as a "stream of consciousness." The concept has become so commonplace that we may not realize how revolutionary it was. No longer was consciousness depicted as some kind of encompassing mental container more or less full of such "contents" as sensations, images, ideas, thoughts, feelings, and the like; rather, it was now portrayed as a continually ongoing, wholistic experience or process from which one can carve out "objects" (like sensations or images) *after the fact* by abstracting them from all the "connections" and "relations" in which they are embedded. In place of a relatively static and mechanistic conception of mind, James substituted a dynamic process-oriented view and called on everyone to attend to his or her own experience for verification.

Isn't it true, James asked, that consciousness—*your* consciousness—flows from moment to moment, that it undergoes continual change, that its experienced continuity is better described with metaphors like "river" and "stream" than with images like "chain" and "train"? Surely, if you take the trouble, you will notice that there are parts of the stream that stand out, because consciousness, like a bird's life, "seems to be made of an alternation of flights and perchings." But even though some parts of conscious experience are more "substantive" and others more "transitive," none is experienced, in the first place, as separate from the stream (see James, 1890/1981, Vol. 1, pp. 233–236).

As James proceeded with his description of consciousness, he mapped out territory that had never been surveyed in quite the same way. In particular, he noted that

> it is very difficult, introspectively, to see the transitive parts [of consciousness] for what they really are. If they are but flights to a conclusion [i.e., to the next more substantive resting place], stopping them to look at them before the conclusion is reached is really annihilating them. (p. 236)

In this context, he shared some of his deservedly well-known insights. For example, "we ought to say [that we have] a feeling of *and*, a feeling of *but*, and a feeling of *by*, quite as readily as we say [that we have] a feeling of *blue* or a feeling of *cold*" (p. 238). If we were to attend closely enough to our conscious experience, we would see that these feelings of relation, just like feelings of tendency (or expectation), are just as *real* within the ongoing stream of thought as the more easily noted and named "substantive parts."

James also discussed the cognitive function of human consciousness—how thinking puts us in touch with objects independent of the mind—and he insisted that careful reflection on mental experience makes it clear that thoughts enter consciousness as a whole, not as parts to be assembled, as the association theorists claimed. He pointed out, too, that consciousness "is always interested more in one part of its object than in another, and welcomes and rejects, or chooses, all the while it thinks" (p. 273). Saying that "the phenomena of selective attention and of deliberative will" are obvious examples of this "choosing activity," James underscored that "few of us are aware how incessantly it [the mind's selecting or choosing activity] is at work in operations not ordinarily called by these names" (p. 273). Beyond that, "we do far more than emphasize things, and unite some, and keep others apart. We actually *ignore* most of the things before us" (p. 273). From this insight, he proceeded to ask, "what are our very senses themselves but organs of selection?" (p. 273), and then argued that the same selective function operates in perception, reasoning, aesthetics, and ethics. At each level of consciousness, he claimed, the mind is selective. That is, the mind

> works on the data it receives [from the previous level of the cognitive process] very much as a sculptor works on his block of stone. In a sense

the statue stood there from eternity. But there were a thousand different ones besides it, and the sculptor alone is to thank for having extricated this one from the rest. Just so the world of each of us, however different our several views of it may be, all lay embedded in the primordial chaos of sensations. . . . Other sculptors, other statues from the same stone! Other minds, other worlds from the same monotonous and inexpressive chaos! My world is but one in a million alike embedded, alike real to those who may abstract them. How different must be the worlds in the consciousness of ant, cuttle-fish, or crab! (p. 277)

Here we have William James at his best and most insightful. This compelling sculptor-and-stone example conveys an accurate sense of the cognitive psychology (and philosophical epistemology) that was emerging from James's own personal introspection and reflection. While serving as one of the starting points of philosophical as well as psychological phenomenology (see Edie, 1987; Herzog, 1995), this incipient cognitive psychology anticipated several other psychological movements, including Gestalt psychology, and it continues to be a "time bomb" waiting to explode some of our fondest prejudices. In short, while some of the things James was getting at have been addressed by others more or less independently, other aspects of his treatment of consciousness await their full effect. Even with the reemergence of cognitive psychology in the 1960s, after decades of behaviorist domination of the field, psychologists have not fully exploited James's treatment of *consciousness*. They have chosen, instead, to focus on a narrower conception of *thinking*, and they have tended to treat thinking in some of the same associationistic and mechanistic ways that James opposed with compelling reasons and examples. As a result, James's treatment of consciousness continues to beckon those who are uncomfortable with computer-generated and computer-dependent models of thought processes. How should we account for those "feelings of relation" and "feelings of tendency"? And how are we to understand the "vague" intimations we often have? Isn't the sense of vagueness as real, as factual, as *sui generis* as crystal-clear perceptions?

Asking these questions and admitting the unfulfilled potential in James's thought does not mean that James's treatment of consciousness had no contemporary impact. Indeed, together with his treatment of habit, it spurred a tradition of "motor theories of consciousness," of ideational stimuli leading to action. Acknowledging his debt to James, John Dewey advanced this tradition with his important paper on "The Reflex Arc Concept in Psychology" (1896). In this paper, Dewey argued for what is essentially a feedback-loop approach that makes consciousness one of three stages in a continually revolving cycle of sensory input, ideation, and behavior, with each stage in the cycle leading to the next. Ideas can lead to behaviors, which lead to sensations that confirm whether or not the ideas were correct, or at least whether they led to a desirable result. Alternatively, the environment can stimulate awareness of a situation, leading to a response. Or a random act can lead to a result of which the mind may take notice. In any and all of these ways, the reflex circuit accounts for the coordination of action as the behaving organism changes and adjusts to its environment.

From Dewey, thus building on concepts in James's *Principles*, the functionalist tradition grew within American psychology. James R. Angell gave it more formal status with his APA presidential address, "The Province of Functional Psychology" (1907). In many ways, functionalism has defined the spirit, if not the daily activity of psychologists in the United States. In a very real sense, Watsonian behaviorism can be seen as a retrograde child of this tradition, though it must be admitted that once consciousness was seen as leading to action, it was natural for poor introspectionists, like Watson, to simplify matters by focusing on just two of the three parts of Dewey's reflex circuit. More recent forms of cognitive behaviorism are more in line with the tradition, and more reflective of their Jamesian origins.[6]

Self

James's example of different sculptors deriving different statues from the same stone illustrates an additional feature of consciousness: Consciousness is deeply and essentially personal. As experienced, it is always *mine*, not *yours* or *his* (James, 1890/1981, Vol. 1, pp. 220–224). Not surprisingly, then, James's chapter on the stream of consciousness leads to his chapter on the consciousness of self. Here, too, James broke new ground, some of which proved to be fertile in the shorter term and some of which remains promising, or at least challenging, in the longer term.[7]

James started his chapter on the self with an admission that it is difficult to draw a line between "what a man calls *me* and what he simply calls *mine*." This led him to argue that

> in the widest possible sense . . . a man's Self is the sum total of all that he can call his, not only his body and his psychic powers, but his clothes and his house, his wife and children, his ancestors and friends, his reputation and works, his lands and his horses, and yacht and bank-account. (James, 1890/1981, Vol. 1, p. 279)

---

[6]Psychologists in this tradition often acknowledge an affinity to, if not direct descent from, Edward C. Tolman (1932) as well as James. Tolman was a student of E. B. Holt (1914), who drew his inspiration from James. William K. Estes (1990) pointed out how often "James' ideas have been rediscovered at points of important shifts in theoretical orientation" (p. 159) in the area of cognition. He cited Miller, Galanter, and Pribram (1960), Broadbent (1963), and Waugh and Norman (1965) as examples.
[7]Those who wish to know more about James's views on the self should consult Leary (1990b). Markus (1990) argued, relevantly, that "we have yet to give serious consideration to his ideas about the truly pervasive and fundamental role of the self in individual behavior," that is, in "the fundamental psychological processes—attention, perception, emotion, conception, reasoning, will, consciousness" (p. 181). In addition, she felt that "we have only just begun to realize the significance" of some of the questions James has raised regarding the nature and functioning of the self (p. 184). Smith (1992) provided some additional reflections from the vantage point of a sympathetic critic of James.

Encompassed in this opening statement are the four "constituents" of the self that he went on to discuss: the material self, the social self, the spiritual self, and the pure ego. These are different aspects, not separate parts, of the self—either of the self as experienced and known (which James called the *empirical ego* or *me*) or of the self as inherent in the sense of personal identity associated with one's ownership of cognitive experiences (which James called the *pure ego* or *I*). James felt that the material and social dimensions of the self, and much of its spiritual dimension, belong to the empirical *me*, whereas some aspects of the spiritual self and all of the pure ego are aligned with the *I*, traditionally expressed as "the soul."

What is most relevant for our purpose is the way in which James's discussion of the material and social dimensions of the self set an agenda, whether explicit or implicit, for later psychologists. For instance, one of the founders of modern personality psychology, Gordon Allport (1937), made explicit use of James's treatment of the material dimensions of the self, arguing that "clothing, ornamentation, and special grooming contribute their share to self-consciousness" (p. 164) and that "possessions, friends, one's own children, other children, cultural interests, abstract ideas, politics, hobbies, recreation, and most conspicuously of all, one's *work*, all lead to the incorporation of interests once remote from the self into selfhood proper" (p. 217). In elaborating his views on "the bodily self" in later works, Allport gave direct credit to James (e.g., Allport, 1961, p. 127). In more recent times, Mihaly Csikszentmihalyi and Eugene Rochberg-Halton's *The Meaning of Things: Domestic Symbols and the Self* (1981) has extended James's insights regarding the material aspects of self, although its authors seem unaware of the relation between their work and his. Clearly, this is an area of research that is far from exhausted, especially given current social and ethical concerns regarding our consumerist culture and the theoretical issues involved in understanding materialism and its effects on the human spirit.

Even more prominent over the past century, however, have been the elaborations of James's *social self*. In this regard, James's (1890/1981) central insight about the social nature of the self bears quotation:

> Properly speaking, *a man has as many social selves as there are individuals who recognize him* and carry an image of him in their mind. To wound any one of these his images is to wound him. But as the individuals who carry the images fall naturally into classes, we may practically say that he has as many different selves as there are distinct *groups* of persons about whose opinion he cares. He generally shows a different side of himself to each of these different groups. . . . From this there results what practically is a division of the man into several selves; and this may be a discordant splitting, as where one is afraid to let one set of his acquaintances know him as he is elsewhere; or it may be a perfectly harmonious division of labor, as where one tender to his children is stern to the soldiers or prisoners under his command. (Vol. 1, pp. 281–282)

What is remarkable in this quote is the way in which James, in contrast to the authors of the old mental and moral philosophy, treated the individual person neither as an indivisible, autonomous unit nor as a simple accretion of discrete, associated ideas, but rather as an emergent reality created over time in relation to its social as well as material connections with the surrounding world. As is well known, a whole host of "relational theories of the self" have been proposed and developed over the past century, from Charles Cooley (1902/1964) and George Herbert Mead (1934) through Harry Stack Sullivan (1953) and more recent social constructionists. While degrees of dependence on James vary from theorist to theorist, James's influence and his continuing relevance to this tradition are widely acknowledged (e.g., see Schellenberg, 1990).

If the social aspect of the self is rooted in the self's embeddedness in a physical world of other selves, so too is the spiritual (or subjective) aspect of the *me* rooted, for James, in the physical experiences of the embodied self. Based on introspective analysis, James concluded that his own sense of subjectivity—of being the subject of his own experience—was related to a collection of "peculiar motions in the head or between the head and throat," including such physiological experiences as "the opening and closing of the glottis" (p. 288). Although he did not claim that everyone's sense of "the Self of selves" had to be grounded in the same experiences, he assumed that introspection by others would always reveal physical correlates of the subjective sense of self. This assumption seems not to have been pursued in any systematic manner by subsequent psychologists.

As regards the ultimate nature of "the Thinker" or "pure ego," James refused to conjecture. Still, he devoted 27 pages to a review of the relevant philosophical theories of the spiritualists, associationists, and transcendentalists, with an eye toward reaching an "empirical consensus" on which all of these thinkers could agree. That consensus, James concluded, is that "personality implies the incessant presence of two elements, an objective person, known by a passing subjective Thought" (p. 350). On the basis of this simple formulation, which at first seemed to confirm his distinction between the *me* and the *I*, James proceeded to complicate matters: His review of the phenomena of delusion, altered and multiple selves, mediumship, possession, and the like—in effect, the phenomena of "exceptional mental states" of which he would write more fully in subsequent years—led him to express doubts about the assumed unity of the self or personality. (It is important to note that he was now questioning the unity of the pure ego or *I*, not simply referring to the pressures toward disunity emanating from the coexistence of multiple social selves in the same empirical self or *me*.) Beyond this, his reflections on the fact that one never has a sense of being a "thinker" outside the context of having "thoughts" made him wonder if "thought is itself the thinker" (p. 379). Why, in short, should we posit an entity when it is only a function (thinking) that we actually experience?

The ramifications of these radical questions and reflections have yet to be worked out in full. It took John Dewey (1940/1988) 50 years to draw attention to this fact, but the critical story, as James suspected it might unfold, was not "the vanishing subject in the psychology of William James," as Dewey put it, but the possible immersion of individual consciousnesses, in ways that somehow preserve their pluralistic identities, into "some sort of an *anima mundi*" or world-soul that is "thinking in all of us" (p. 328). Although James himself found this "a more promising hypothesis" than other philosophical conclusions about the nature and functioning of personal self-consciousness—partly because it would help explain various altered states of consciousness, multiple personalities, possessions, automatisms, and the like—he let the matter stand there, at least as far as his *Principles of Psychology* was concerned. However, he returned to the notion of individual selves as aspects of a larger field of consciousness in his later works (see Leary, 1990b, pp. 112–119). Although conventional psychology has not assimilated, and may never assimilate, this kind of thinking, it resonates with issues raised in various realms of religious and postmodernist thought.

SOME CONSTITUENTS AND CHARACTERISTICS OF JAMES'S PSYCHOLOGY

We have seen that James had a way of providing enlightening descriptions of psychological phenomena, useful surveys of thinking and research in a given area, relevant and probing questions, and stimulating (sometimes persuasive) theories. Clearly, these facts account for much of his historical influence. But James's impact on psychology is rooted in deeper and less obvious causes. If his distinctive approach to psychological issues has guided later psychologists, what guided *him* to create his distinctive approach?

First and foremost, it was his own unique life experiences, to which he gave a great deal of attention. In essence, his intellectual life was devoted to "saving the appearances" of his life, to acknowledging, describing, explaining, understanding, and drawing lessons from the experiential realities afforded to him. Perhaps most notably, some of James's core psychological insights proceeded from his famous free will-versus-determinism crisis in the late 1860s and early 1870s, which occasioned personal depression and thoughts of suicide as he confronted with horror the thought that "not a wiggle of our will" might happen "save as the result of physical laws" and, consequently, that he as an individual might not be able to make the slightest "nick" in the inevitable unfolding of history (as he wrote to his friend Thomas W. Ward in March and January, 1868, respectively, as reproduced in H. James, 1920, Vol. 1, pp. 152–153, and p. 132). The insight that he gained through this crisis—that materialistic determinism need not be the final word, although it necessarily has much to say—was built into his psychology, with its strong insistence that only through attention and will—before overpowering habits are formed—can we direct our lives in the ways we want them to go. Similarly, as we have seen, James argued that our own individual interests can lead to particular cognitive experiences being highlighted and selected, even though we may have little choice regarding the array of potential sensations, perceptions, thoughts, and feelings with which we are confronted. And consistent with his view of self, James noted that of the many potential selves we *could* become, we need to select one for emphasis while relinquishing the rest (see H. James, 1920, Vol. 1, pp. 295–296). This doctrine was clearly based on the resolution of his own existential crisis (see Anderson, 1982; Feinstein, 1984; Fullinwider, 1975).

Another salient part of James's life experience pertained to religion, stemming both from the unique religious concerns and expressions of his father (a noted advocate of Swedenborgian thought) and from his own concern to find an honest and satisfying—inclusive rather than exclusive—accommodation between religion and science. Although most apparent in his *Varieties of Religious Experience* (1902/1985), this concern underlay many aspects of his psychology, including his treatment of consciousness and the self.

Even these few paragraphs suggest an important fact: James's own life reflected, in heightened form, many of the key facts and issues of his time and place: the rise of science and the impact of materialism on American culture, the crisis of religion in relation to the rise of science as well as to its own internal developments (as many nontraditional viewpoints, like the secular–religious views of Emerson and the scientific–religious views of Swedenborg, became a larger part of the general cultural mix in the United States), and the associated frequency of individual crises of subjectivity, spirituality, and will. In short, James's own particular life circumstances fostered an unusual sensitivity to issues that were, and have remained, relevant and even crucial in American culture. (Some of these issues are treated in Leary, 1987.)

As part of these life circumstances and experiences, James received an unorthodox education. He was essentially "home schooled," not in one home, but in homes on several continents (in Europe as well as the United States) where he learned multiple languages, was exposed to different cultures and perspectives, established far-flung networks of friends and acquaintances, and read widely and according to his own interests in several different national literatures. He also absorbed all the insights he could from a wide range of arts, from poetry and literature to architecture and painting. Because he focused on understanding and dealing with his own personal concerns, his exposure to the arts and his education in general were tailored to the issues that would become pertinent as he developed his psychology. And James's broad connections were not hindered when he became a faculty member at Harvard in the early 1870s. While adding numerous contacts with leaders in academic life at Harvard and in the United States, his frequent European trips allowed him to maintain and expand his acquaintances abroad.

The essential point is that James brought a wealth of relevant personal experience, an unusually broad range of reading, thinking, discussion, and communication, and a long list of personal, quasi-professional, and professional contacts to his work in psychology. He might have been influential in any case, but the fact that he was *uniquely* and *exceptionally* influential is certainly related to the fact that he drew honestly and passionately from every aspect of his exceptionally broad and in many ways emblematic existence.[8] This is what I mean by referring to the formative constituents or constitutive elements of his psychology: The insights and concerns that he derived from his own life history formed the basis of his distinctive perspective and shaped the psychology that proceeded from it.

Beyond this, James's psychology has obviously been more effective, historically speaking, because of certain characteristics that are reflective of his own distinctive style. Besides being a remarkably astute observer and articulator of his own experience (including his own reading), James's graphic descriptions demonstrate an extraordinary capacity to express even vague, previously undescribed experiences. To be able to combine sharply delineated and compelling descriptions with novel analyses that highlight key issues and offer rich and suggestive vistas was enormously consequential with regard to the impact of his psychology. And the vistas that he offered, more frequently than not, added to rather than subtracted from the possibilities that he saw (and that his readers were shown) in nature and science. James's openness to new facts and to new ways of thinking, combined with his ability to be critical (but not preemptively so), made his work stimulating as well as challenging and potentially enlightening.

In summary, unlike many psychologists, James drew his psychology from his very being and invested it with the distinctive qualities of his personality: His psychology addressed real, current, *felt* issues, and it did so in ways that opened more doors than it closed. In addition, it offered a distinctive vision that provided a consistent framework for a timely and compelling set of psychological descriptions and explanations. For all the talk of James's psychology being "unsystematic" (Kimble, 1990, is only one of many instances of such talk), the underlying coherence of his psychology has too often gone unnoted. It too has contributed, in essential ways, to the power and historical significance of his psychological work.

JAMES'S CENTRAL VISION

For many years, analyses of the various "schools of psychology" focused on the methods of empirical data gathering and the modes of theoretical

---

[8]It may seem odd to call James's experience "emblematic," but although it was unusual, it highlighted many of the specific issues confronting Americans in the late 19th century.

explanation that distinguished each of these schools. Rarely did these analyses clarify the central vision underlying these different approaches to empirical and theoretical work. Although any adequate treatment of James's influence must take into account his devotion to gathering facts from immediate, direct experience (which we have already noted), as well as his exceptionally effective use of metaphors in describing and explaining these facts (which this chapter has illustrated, albeit without specific commentary up to this point), such treatments would miss a crucial point if they failed to reveal the special vision that provided the basic framework, or perspective, that gave James's psychology its innovative conceptual structure and its distinctive rhetorical force.

James's use of metaphor is an important and salient topic that I have addressed elsewhere (e.g., Leary, 1990a, pp. 19–21, 45–49; Leary, 1992). It has been illustrated in this chapter's summaries of his discussion of living organisms as "bundles of habits," of consciousness as a "stream," of awareness as a series of "flights" and "perchings," of the mind as a "sculptor," and of reality as a "stone" to be carved. Some of these metaphors are primarily descriptive rather than explanatory; even so, they contribute to the conceptual context within which James explained psychological phenomena. Others, however, are essential parts of the explanatory framework of his psychology. One set of such metaphors expresses James's central vision; or, if you prefer, it conveys the underlying story that gives James's psychology a coherence greater than the sum of its parts.

I am referring to James's Darwinian metaphors and to the fact that he was one of the first scientists or intellectuals in any field to see and accept the larger significance of Charles Darwin's way of thinking. Although Darwin's *On the Origin of Species* (1859) convinced many of the *fact* of evolution, it was much less successful in convincing them of his *theory* of evolution (see Hull, 1973). Long before Darwin's theory of natural selection was accepted by the majority of biological scientists, James had accepted it and was drawing out its implications for psychology in a way that allowed him to address the phenomena and issues with which he was confronted (see Richards, 1987). At the center of his vision were a set of Darwinian metaphors, most particularly those clustering around Darwin's three crucial notions of variation, selection, and utility.[9] With these metaphors, James created a new way of imag-

---

[9]One of the reasons that Whitehead saw James as so far ahead of his contemporaries and as one of the crucial intellects in Western history (see footnote 1 in this chapter) was that James recognized so clearly that the old world that celebrated "being," permanence, and certitude as hallmarks and standards (whether in the form of essential species, eternal ideas, or definitive explanations) was giving way, in the wake of Darwin and other "intellectual shocks," to a new world in which "becoming," change, process, transformation, even chaos, and at best probabilities were primary characteristics (see Whitehead, 1956, p. 272). Besides creating a psychology that reflected this radical change of perspective and experience, James developed a philosophy featuring pragmatism, pluralism, and radical empiricism to serve as a platform for dealing with this profoundly new worldview, which others sensed but more often than not tried to ignore. In turning to Darwin for inspiration, James was deeply aware that he was using Darwin's basic concepts metaphorically, as means to insight and

ining human functioning, which left the door open for what James called the "dramatic possibilities" of nature and experience, including phenomena that were outside the pale of conventional consideration. While the new scientific psychology, as advanced by others, was moving toward allowing experimental methodology to determine which phenomena were worthy of study—or even belief—James was moving in a different direction, one that helps account for the fruitfulness of his psychology.

To James, following Darwin, the world is characterized by overabundance, by the unexpected, by variations even in the things we know best and rely on most. Whether speaking of the "chaos of experience," the "stream of consciousness," or any number of similar metaphors for ever-changing experience, James made it clear that the world *and the way we experience, think, feel, and act within it* are characterized by flux and variation. From this ever-changing flow of occurrences, sensations, perceptions, ideas, feelings, and so on, we typically select for attention those that conform to our interests.[10] In selecting from the range of possibilities thus presented to us, we entertain sensations, perceptions, actions, and so on that sooner or later will be shown to have more or less utility for us, whether in helping us navigate the physical world, recognize pertinent features of our social environment, solve a cognitive problem, address a moral dilemma, or experience an object in a way that gives us pleasure. What we learn from our ongoing experience, whether it is successful or not, generally helps us make better selections in the future. In ways that others have studied in subsequent years, our senses become attuned, our minds become focused, our emotions are channeled, and our ac-

---

probabilistic understanding. Yet, in doing so, he was truer to Darwin's intentions than others who used Darwinian concepts, ironically as well as unfortunately, as essential categories of analysis, as if they captured the full, literal, once-and-for-all truth. On Darwin's own reliance on metaphor and on the abuse (overextension) of Darwinian metaphors by later psychologists, such as B. F. Skinner, see Leary (1990a, pp. 10–11, 21, 48–49).

[10]I have touched on James's view of the selectivity of the mind in my discussion of consciousness. From early on, the *variation* and *selection* of random thoughts, feelings, and impulses were crucial concepts in James's psychology and philosophy: Beyond asking in *Principles* (1890/1981), "what are our very senses themselves but organs of selection?" (p. 273), he stated, "Reasoning is but another form of the selective activity of the mind" (p. 276). "If we now pass to [the mind's] aesthetic department, our law is still more obvious" (p. 276). "Ascending higher still, we reach the plane of Ethics, where choice reigns notoriously supreme" (p. 276). In sum, "the mind is at every stage a theatre of simultaneous possibilities. Consciousness consists in the comparison of these with each other, the selection of some, and the suppression of the rest" (p. 277). Indeed, "without selective interest, experience is an utter chaos. Interest alone gives accent and emphasis, light and shade, background and foreground—intelligible perspective, in a word. It varies in every creature, but without it the consciousness of every creature would be a gray chaotic indiscriminateness, impossible for us even to conceive. Such an empirical writer as Mr. Spencer, for example, regards the creature as absolutely passive clay, upon which 'experience' rains down. . . . If such an account were true, a race of dogs bred for generations, say in the Vatican, . . . ought to become . . . accomplished *connoisseurs* of sculpture" (p. 381).

As is well known, James spent a good deal of time and effort, especially in the decades after *Principles*, articulating the importance of *utility*. The practical consequences of our thoughts, feelings, and behaviors—and of our religious beliefs as much as our scientific theories—are what define their meaning and worth for James (see, e.g., James, 1907/1975).

tions are adjusted, not once and for all but in an ever-ongoing process of choosing and learning from the variety of options available to us.

To the extent that our lives are shaped by processes in which variation, selection, and utility play significant roles, Jamesian insights are likely to retain their relevance, even as newer versions of this kind of thinking come to the fore. One thing that has sustained this relevance is the fact that James, like Darwin, but unlike many subsequent thinkers in their tradition, espoused an important role for consciousness in the overall scheme of things (see Darwin, 1871). To be sure, James concluded that the relative efficacy of consciousness is circumscribed, but the tipping-of-balance between free will and determinism that an individual consciousness, with its own particularized interests, can bring into the natural world remained for James a beacon of hope and a call to personal responsibility. And by insisting that nature has unknown parameters and that human experience is open-ended, James offered reasons for wonder and for trusting in the possibility of realities beyond any we have yet encountered.

Thus, rather than prescribing and narrowing the world within which psychologists work, James widened its horizons and invited exploration. His psychology may not have the "finished" quality that some critics would have preferred, but that is because he felt that no psychology can be complete, just as no system of thought can have the final word, as long as there are more experiences to be had. Who knows what might be possible—what startling revelation may occur—tomorrow?

SOME USEFUL LESSONS, OR, CAN WILLIAM JAMES INSPIRE US TOO?

We began by asking why and how William James has had such an impact on the development of American psychology. We have come, in the end, to appreciate the relevance of his life experiences and of his ability to draw on them in ways that helped him create a psychology that addressed timely and meaningful issues. We have also seen that he cleared away much of the conceptual confusion and many of the theoretical constraints that stood in the way of a truly *new* psychology, freed of the assumptions and practices of old ways of psychologizing. We noted, too, that the results of James's efforts in these regards have not yet been fully exploited, so that his work remains a source of useful ideas and criticisms. And we have recognized that beyond his flair for graphic expression, he had a remarkable ability to identify metaphors that have fruitful implications for theoretical as well as descriptive purposes. All of these factors contributed to his historical impact and suggest things you should keep in mind as you do your own psychological work:

1. Broaden your experience through reading, travel, exposure to the arts, and communication with a wide range of acquain-

tances as well as through attending to your daily life and to the empirical, experimental, or applied work in which you are engaged. *Then trust your own experience.*[11]

2. Be aware of the critical issues, problems, and questions of your times—not just of your discipline, or your neighborhood within that discipline, or even your nexus between disciplines—and address those issues, problems, and questions, either directly or indirectly.

3. Think clearly and act intelligently, actively seeking to avoid letting old perspectives and procedures blind you to new possibilities and opportunities.

4. Do not hide your light under a basket. Take risks. Present and publish your radical ideas, together with evidence and reasons for them. Obviously, your evidence and reasons should be as compelling as possible, but neither your evidence nor your reasons need necessarily conform to the canons of description and explanation that presently govern your field. Any major advance in any field, as James liked to point out, comes at the expense of previous authority.

5. Share fertile conjectures along the way, even if they are only afterthoughts—thoughts that might stimulate further consideration and action long after your current work is a distant memory.

6. Attend carefully to the metaphors you use, to the broader vision or story that they convey, and to the attractiveness of your writing. If they inspire as well as persuade, you may have an impact beyond your hopes and expectations.

Of course, these things will be easier to accomplish if you happen to be a genius, with novel data and brilliant ideas that impress your colleagues as

---

[11]This is perhaps the main lesson that an analysis of James's impact can give us. It is a harder lesson to follow than it may seem. It has been articulated more recently, without specific reference to James, by Sigmund Koch (1999), whose criticism of "rule-governed" behavior on the part of psychologists and his call for more "sensibility-based" thinking suggest, correctly, that many psychologists have not heeded this lesson, resulting in a great deal of what Koch called "ameaningful" theory and research. The ending of a recent article on Koch's hope for psychology is relevant here: "It would be well for us to attend to meaningful topics in meaningful ways. Relying on our own inherent sensibilities, trusting our own instincts regarding what is really important, and applying careful analysis of whatever kind that promises to elucidate and persuade us about what is truly problematic to us as humans, we can still opt to make psychology a human science as well as a science of humans. Of course, a truly human science—a science oriented by human agency rather than dictated by abstract rules—would be no science at all to some people, but the results of its studies would matter. Drawn from and relevant to actual human experiences, these studies would generate better, if still fallible, understanding—and more salutary, if not miraculous, effects" (Leary, 2001, p. 431).

Even though Koch did not think of himself as a "Jamesian," there was good reason for Taylor (1992) to conclude his discussion of "a uniquely American Jamesian tradition" with a section on Koch.

worthy of attention; but there is not much you can do to arrange for that, as James himself noted in a discussion on our very topic: the historical impact of "great men" and their "great thoughts."[12] The fact that there are great men (and women) who have ideas capable of influence, James said, is simply a given that we have to accept, "just as Darwin accepts his spontaneous variations," without trying to give any final explanation or prescription for them. But having accepted that there are such individuals, the crucial question for James was, "How does the environment affect them, and how do they affect the environment?" Following Darwin's lead, although focusing on the social rather than physical environment, James concluded that

> the relation of the visible environment to the great man is in the main exactly what it is to the "variation" in the darwinian philosophy. It chiefly adopts or rejects, preserves or destroys, in short *selects* him. And whenever it adopts or preserves the great man, it becomes modified by his influence in an entirely original and peculiar way. He acts as a ferment, and changes its constitution, just as the advent of a new zoological species changes the faunal and floral equilibrium of the region in which it appears. (James, 1880/1897/1979, p. 170)

In short, "the mutations of societies," and (I note) changes in the psychological theories and practices of those societies, are "in the main due directly and indirectly to the acts or the example of individuals" (p. 170). James gave some instances:

> Rembrandt must teach us to enjoy the struggle of light with darkness, Wagner to enjoy certain musical effects; Dickens gives a twist to our sentimentality, Artemus Ward to our humor; Emerson kindles a new moral light within us. If shown a certain way, a community may take it; if not, it will never find it. (p. 172)

Certainly we can add James to the list of individuals whose unique genius has made a difference in how we conceive and do our work. He constructed a distinctive path to understanding human nature and the processes by which humans think, feel, and behave. Without James opening the way, it is entirely conceivable that we would not have discovered all of the interesting possibilities that he pointed out to us. But if James's ideas have inspired the psychological community, the psychological community has in turn done much—although perhaps not yet enough—to preserve and extend the profound and radical change that he initiated.[13]

---

[12]This discussion appeared originally in an 1880 article with the title "Great Men, Great Thoughts, and the Environment," which was retitled "Great Men and Their Environment" when it was republished in 1897 as part of *The Will to Believe and Other Essays in Popular Philosophy* (James, 1880/1897/1979). For more detail about the historiographic implications of this and other related pieces of James's work, see Leary (1995).

[13]As James himself (1880/1897/1979) wrote, "the community stagnates without the impulse of the individual. The impulse dies away without the sympathy of the community" (p. 174).

REFERENCES

Allport, G. W. (1937). *Personality: A psychological interpretation*. New York. Holt.

Allport, G. W. (1961). *Pattern and growth in personality*. New York: Holt, Rinehart & Winston.

Anderson, J. W. (1982). "The worst kind of melancholy": William James in 1869. *Harvard Library Bulletin, 30*, 369–386.

Angell, J. R. (1907). The province of functional psychology. *Psychological Review, 14*, 61–91.

Angell, J. R. (1911). William James. *Psychological Review, 18*, 78–82.

Boring, E. G. (1950). *A history of experimental psychology* (2nd ed). New York: Appleton-Century-Crofts.

Bray, C. W., Boring, E. G., MacLeod, R. B., & Solomon, R. L. (1969). Preface. In R. B. MacLeod (Ed.), *William James: Unfinished business* (pp. iii–iv). Washington, DC: American Psychological Association.

Broadbent, D. E. (1963). Flow of information within the organism. *Journal of Verbal Learning and Verbal Behavior, 2*, 34–39.

Chapman, J. J. (1996). William James. In L. Simon (Ed.), *William James remembered* (pp. 53–57). Lincoln: University of Nebraska Press. (Original work published 1915)

Cooley, C. H. (1964). *Human nature and the social order*. New York: Schocken Books. (Original work published 1902)

Csikszentmihalyi, M., & Rochberg-Halton, E. (1981). *The meaning of things: Domestic symbols and the self*. New York: Cambridge University Press.

Darwin, C. (1859). *On the origin of species*. London: Murray.

Darwin, C. (1871). *The descent of man, and selection in relation to sex* (2 vols.). London: Murray.

Dewey, J. (1896). The reflex arc concept in psychology. *Psychological Review, 3*, 357–370.

Dewey, J. (1910). William James. *Journal of Philosophy, Psychology, and Scientific Methods, 7*, 505–508.

Dewey, J. (1988). The vanishing subject in the psychology of William James. In J. A. Boydston (Ed.), *The later works of John Dewey, 1925–1953* (Vol. 14, pp. 155–167). Carbondale: Southern Illinois University Press. (Original work published 1940)

Donnelly, M. E. (Ed.). (1992). *Reinterpreting the legacy of William James*. Washington, DC: American Psychological Association.

Edie, J. M. (1987). *William James and phenomenology*. Bloomington: Indiana University Press.

Estes, W. K. (1990). Introduction: *Principles of Psychology*: 1890–1990. *Psychological Science, 1*, 149–150.

Feinstein, H. M. (1984). *Becoming William James*. Ithaca, NY: Cornell University Press.

Fullinwider, S. P. (1975). William James's "spiritual crisis." *The Historian, 38*, 39–57.

Heidbreder, E. (1933). *Seven psychologies.* New York: Appleton-Century-Crofts.

Herzog, M. (1995). William James and the development of phenomenological psychology in Europe. *History of the Human Sciences, 8*, 29–46.

Holt, E. B. (1914). *The concept of consciousness.* London: Allen.

Hull, D. (1973). *Darwin and his critics.* Cambridge, MA: Harvard University Press.

James, H., III. (Ed.). (1920). *The letters of William James* (2 vols.). Boston: Atlantic Monthly Press.

James, W. (1975). *Pragmatism: A new name for some old ways of thinking.* Cambridge, MA: Harvard University Press. (Original work published 1907)

James, W. (1979). Great men and their environment. In *The will to believe and other essays in popular philosophy* (pp. 163–189). Cambridge, MA: Harvard University Press. (Original work published as an article in 1880 and as a book chapter in 1897)

James, W. (1981). *The principles of psychology* (2 vols.). Cambridge, MA: Harvard University Press. (Original work published 1890)

James, W. (1983a). A plea for psychology as "natural science." In *Essays in psychology* (pp. 270–277). Cambridge, MA: Harvard University Press. (Original work published 1892)

James, W. (1983b). *Talks to teachers on psychology and to students on some of life's ideals.* Cambridge, MA: Harvard University Press. (Original work published 1899)

James, W. (1984). *Psychology: Briefer course.* Cambridge, MA: Harvard University Press. (Original work published 1892)

James, W. (1985). *The varieties of religious experience.* Cambridge, MA: Harvard University Press. (Original work published 1902)

Johnson, M. G., & Henley, T. B. (1990). Preface. In M. G. Johnson & T. B. Henley (Eds.), *Reflections on The principles of psychology: William James after a century* (pp. xix–xx). Hillsdale, NJ: Erlbaum.

Kimble, G. A. (1990). A search for principles in *Principles of Psychology. Psychological Science, 1*, 151–155.

Koch, S. (1999). *Psychology in human context: Essays in dissidence and reconstruction.* Chicago: University of Chicago Press.

Ladd, G. T. (1887). *Elements of physiological psychology.* New York: Scribner's.

Ladd, G. T. (1892). Psychology as so-called "natural science." *Philosophical Review, 1*, 24–53.

Ladd, G. T. (1894). *Psychology: Descriptive and explanatory.* New York: Scribner's.

Leary, D. E. (1987). Telling likely stories: The rhetoric of the new psychology, 1880–1920. *Journal of the History of the Behavioral Sciences, 23*, 315–331.

Leary, D. E. (1990a). Psyche's muse: The role of metaphor in the history of psychology. In D. E. Leary (Ed.), *Metaphors in the history of psychology* (pp. 1–78). New York: Cambridge University Press.

Leary, D. E. (1990b). William James on the self and personality: Clearing the ground for subsequent theorists, researchers, and practitioners. In M. G. Johnson & T. B. Henley (Eds.), *Reflections on* The Principles of Psychology: *William James after a century* (pp. 101–137). Hillsdale, NJ: Erlbaum.

Leary, D. E. (1992). William James and the art of human understanding. *American Psychologist, 47*, 152–160.

Leary, D. E. (1995). William James, the psychologist's dilemma and the historiography of psychology: Cautionary tales. *History of the Human Sciences, 8*, 91–105.

Leary, D. E. (2001). One big idea, one ultimate concern: Sigmund Koch's critique of psychology and hope for the future. *American Psychologist, 56*, 425–432.

Locke, J. (1959). *An essay concerning human understanding.* New York: Dover. (Original work published 1690)

Mandler, G. (1979). A man for all seasons? *Contemporary Psychology, 24*, 742–744.

Markus, H. (1990). On splitting the universe. *Psychological Science, 1*, 181–185.

Mead, G. H. (1934). *Mind, self, and society.* Chicago: University of Chicago Press.

Miller, G. A. (1983). Introduction. In W. James, *The principles of psychology* (pp. ix–xxi). Cambridge, MA: Harvard University Press.

Miller, G. A., Galanter, E., & Pribram, K. H. (1960). *Plans and the structure of behavior.* New York: Holt.

Mills, E. S. (1969). *George Trumbull Ladd: Pioneer American psychologist.* Cleveland, OH: The Press of Case Western Reserve University.

Myers, G. E. (1981). Introduction: The intellectual context. In W. James, *The principles of psychology* (Vol. 1, pp. xi–xl). Cambridge, MA: Harvard University Press.

Park, S., & Kosslyn, S. M. (1990). Imagination. In M. G. Johnson & T. B. Henley (Eds.), *Reflections on* The Principles of Psychology: *William James after a century* (pp. 183–196). Hillsdale, NJ: Erlbaum.

Richards, R. J. (1987). *Darwin and the emergence of evolutionary theories of mind and behavior.* Chicago: University of Chicago Press.

Ross, D. (1972). *G. Stanley Hall: The psychologist as prophet.* Chicago: University of Chicago Press.

Schellenberg, J. A. (1990). William James and symbolic interactionism. *Personality and Social Psychology Bulletin, 16*, 769–773.

Seashore, C. E. (1921). George Trumbull Ladd. *Science, 54*, 242.

Smith, M. B. (1992). William James and the psychology of self. In M. E. Donnelly (Ed.), *Reinterpreting the legacy of William James* (pp. 173–187). Washington, DC: American Psychological Association.

Sokal, M. M. (1984a). Introduction. In W. James, *Psychology: Briefer course* (pp. xi–xli). Cambridge, MA: Harvard University Press.

Sokal, M. M. (1984b). James McKeen Cattell and American psychology in the 1920s. In J. Brozek (Ed.), *Explorations in the history of psychology in the United States* (pp. 273–323). Lewisburg, PA: Bucknell University Press.

Sullivan, H. S. (1953). *The interpersonal theory of psychiatry.* New York: Norton.

Taylor, E. (1982). *William James on exceptional mental states: The 1896 Lowell Lectures.* New York: Scribner's.

Taylor, E. (1992). The case for a uniquely American Jamesian tradition in psychology. In M. E. Donnelly (Ed.), *Reinterpreting the legacy of William James* (pp. 3–28). Washington, DC: American Psychological Association.

Taylor, E. (1996). *William James on consciousness beyond the margin.* Princeton, NJ: Princeton University Press.

Thorndike, E. L. (1898). Animal intelligence: An experimental study of the associative processes in animals. *Psychological Review, Monograph Supplements, 2*(Serial No. 8).

Thorndike, E. L. (1913). *The psychology of learning.* New York: Columbia University Press.

Thorndike, E. L. (1913–1914). *Education psychology* (3 vols.). New York: Columbia University Press.

Thorndike, E. L. (1936). Edward Lee Thorndike. In C. Murchison (Ed.), *A history of psychology in autobiography* (Vol. 3, pp. 263–270). Worcester, MA: Clark University Press.

Tolman, E. C. (1932). *Purposive behavior in animals and men.* New York: Century.

Watson, J. B. (1963). *Behaviorism* (rev. ed.). Chicago: University of Chicago Press. (Original work published 1924)

Waugh, N. C., & Norman, D. A. (1965). Primary memory. *Psychological Review, 72,* 89–104.

Whitehead, A. N. (1938). *Modes of thought.* New York: Macmillan.

Whitehead, A. N. (1956). *Dialogues of Alfred North Whitehead* (L. Price, Ed.). New York: New American Library.

3

FRANZ BRENTANO'S *PSYCHOLOGY FROM AN EMPIRICAL STANDPOINT*

DONALD E. POLKINGHORNE

The aim of producing a publication is to make an impact on the field. One of the texts that has made a great impact on the field of psychology is Franz Brentano's *Psychology From an Empirical Standpoint* (PES). The purpose of this chapter is to understand why *PES* made an impact and to see if contemporary writers can learn from it how they might create a book that has a similar impact. *PES* was written in 1874 and is one of the two founding texts of the scientific study of consciousness, and it helped establish psychology as a scientific discipline. The views expressed in *PES* exerted a powerful impact in Austria, Germany, Poland, and Italy, influencing such varied developments as Husserl's phenomenology, Meinong's theory of objects, Gestalt psychology, and early analytic philosophy in Poland and England.

The impact of *PES* derives from its depiction that two different phenomena appear in consciousness: physical phenomena, which make up the contents of consciousness, and mental phenomena, which make up the acts of consciousness. Mental phenomena consist of acts such as perceiving, remembering, and feeling, which always are directed at or intend mental content. *PES* is most known for this idea of intentionality, which is a property unique to the acts of consciousness. *PES* may seem like an unlikely choice as a great work in psychology, having been neglected or given a minor mention by American historians of psychology. However, in the return to the study of consciousness in recent decades by American psychology and philosophy, *PES* and its idea of intentionality are being looked to for a corrective to contemporary reductive models of mentality.

Thinès (1987) called Brentano "one of the most original figures in the history of philosophy and psychology" (p. 117). And Chisholm, Baumgartner, and Müller (1995) stated,

> It would be difficult to exaggerate the influence, direct or indirect, of Franz Brentano's thought upon both philosophy and psychology. . . . Brentano's teachings are by no means merely of historical interest. His doctrines of *intentionality* and *evidence* . . . remain highly relevant to present-day philosophy of mind, psychology and ethics. (p. x)

Writing in *The Concept of Intentionality*, Mohanty (1972) said,

> Whatever might have been the history of the concept of intentionality before Brentano, there is no doubt that modern philosophy owes it to him to have both drawn attention to the centrality of this concept for philosophy of mind and given it a formulation which is essentially original. (p. 3)

Brentano's impact occurred primarily through those he taught. He was an extraordinary teacher but not a natural producer of books. Papers and the occasional monograph appeared, but *PES* was his one attempt at a comprehensive treatise, and he only completed its first two of a planned six books. An English translation has recently been published of a collection of his lectures under the title *Descriptive Psychology* (Brentano, 1982/1995b); nevertheless, he is primarily known for *PES*, and it is this text that is the primary focus of the chapter. The first section describes the historical context in which *PES* was produced, including the competing texts and positions. The next section presents a summary outline of the two books contained in *PES* followed by a section on why it has and has not had an impact on American psychology. The chapter closes with lessons that can be learned from *PES* for contemporary scholars about how their work might make a similar impact on psychology.

THE HISTORICAL CONTEXT OF *PSYCHOLOGY FROM AN EMPIRICAL STANDPOINT*

Beginning with the Enlightenment, the authority of theologians and metaphysicians had diminished for explaining the operations of the physical world (including the human body). Their place was taken over by the new scientists of the Enlightenment and their methods of discovery. Scientific inquiry was progressively uncovering the order of the physical realm and thereby providing humans with knowledge they could use to control nature for their benefit. However, the use of scientific inquiry had been limited to investigations of the physical realm; the human soul or mind was thought to have divine properties and, thus, could not be investigated using scientific methods. Knowledge of the mind remained the purview of the theologians and metaphysicians.

However, the success of experimental science in studying the natural realm was taken as evidence that the scientific method of investigation was the one method that produced reliable knowledge. There was a move to apply scientific methods to the study of human consciousness. By the mid 1800s, scientifically guided studies in physiology began to show mathematical relationships between changes in environmental stimuli and changes in mental phenomena. In parallel with these experiments, Darwin proposed that human beings were an evolved part of nature, not special beings divinely created outside of nature (Peters, 1962). Brentano believed these events provided the circumstances for the emancipatory possibility of a science of the mind unconstrained by religious doctrine and traditional, theologically informed philosophy.

Resistance to the scientific study of the mind came from those who held that the human realm contained special properties, such as meaning and values, that were not susceptible to scientific investigation. Giambattista Vico, writing in 1725, was a forerunner of this resistance (Vico, 1725/2000); he was followed by Johann Droysen, who in 1858 proposed that, although the methods of science could produce explanations of physical events, the human realm required a method that would produce understanding (Droysen, 1858/1893). A center for the debate over the proper method for the study of the human realm was the so-called Southwest German (or Baden) school, which later in the 1800s produced Wilhelm Windelband's distinction between the nomothetic or natural sciences and the ideographic or historical sciences and also Heinrich Rickert's distinction between the cultural and natural sciences (Polkinghorne, 1983). The notion that the methods of natural science are inappropriate for the study of the human realm has remained as a subtheme throughout the history of psychology and, more recently, has manifested itself in the "paradigm wars" of the 1980s between advocates of traditional quantitative methods and champions of qualitative methods.

Prior to the publication of *PES*, there were two basic methods used for the study of the mind: introspective or philosophical psychology and physiological or experimental psychology. These were the competing methods against which *PES* was written. Much of the text of *PES* consists of critiques of authors who used physiological experiments or traditional philosophical introspection as methods to study the mind. *PES* proposed to correct the errors and limitations of these two methods. Wilhelm Wundt, as the most advanced proponent of the use of physiologically based experimentation, was the most competitive contemporary author to Brentano.

The Introspective Method

The method of introspection for the investigation of consciousness as a systematic and ethically neutral practice of self-observation was not in general use until the 1850s (Danziger, 1990). Reflection on everyday self-awareness, called *introspection,* had been appealed to by John Locke and the other empiricist philosophers. They used the model that treated introspection or inner sense as analogous to the outer senses, through which representations of the external world are provided. Immanuel Kant asked whether the experiences conveyed by the inner sense can serve as the basis of a mental science (psychology) in the way that the experiences conveyed by the outer sense serve as the basis of physical science. Kant's answer to his question was no. He thought that, although the experiences of the outer sense could be mathematically ordered, the experiences of the inner sense were resistant to mathematization—there could be no science of mentation, that is, no psychology. But Kant did identify the mental realm as a separate sphere of specialized investigation, although it would have to be more like botany of his day—a classification enterprise, which he did not consider a science because it lacked mathematized relations.

Another issue regarding introspection was that, like the evidence of the external sense, what was given was knowledge of phenomena; that is, what appeared in consciousness, not a direct awareness of the reality. Brentano in *PES,* along with Wundt, drew a distinction between actual introspection (simply perceiving mental events) and internal perception (observing mental events in a methodical way). *PES* is concerned with these problems and attends to the issues raised by Locke and Kant in developing its own use of internal perception to study the mind.

The Experimental Method

Experimentation in psychology is related to a specific historically developed form of experiment developed in physiology rather than experiments developed in physics. The idea that there was a universal form of experimentation and scientific method ignores the history of science with its various kinds of experimentation (Danziger, 1990). It was not until 1860 that physiology became a primarily experimental science.

The physiological studies that were most relevant for the development of psychology were stimulation studies. These studies sought to establish connections between changes in the physical stimulation of the body's sense organs and changes in a person's consciousness. Physical stimulations, such as sounds, were varied and compared with the variations in what was reported to have occurred in what was heard in consciousness. The kinds of questions the experimental studies in physiology could address were those about the dependence of aspects of conscious experience on conditions of stimulation, such as intensity, spatial location, and temporal duration. This was the model of experimentation that was proposed by Wundt for use in the new science of psychology.

Among the physiologists addressed in *PES* are Ernst Heinrich Weber, Gustav Theodor Fechner, Rudolph Lotze, and Hermann von Helmholtz. Weber discovered the first quantitative psychological law based on experimental results. In his *Sense of Touch and the Common Sensibility* (1846/1978), Weber presented experiments in which he varied the distance between points of contact on the skin. He found that at close distances, the two points were experienced as one. By continuously lengthening the distance between points, at a certain distance they were experienced as two separate contacts. The smallest detectable distance he termed *the just noticeable distance*. Weber expanded his research to cover experienced differences related to other sense modalities and found that there was a constant fraction corresponding for each sense modality. Weber provided an experimental method whereby psychological phenomena could be studied and quantified, something declared by Kant to be impossibility.

Fechner (*Elements of Psychophysics*, 1860/1966) advanced Weber's research and further contributed to the use of experimentation to measure mental experiences. Lotze's *Outlines of Psychology* (1881/1886) was the first book that attempted to be a physiological psychology. The focus of his experimental research was on space perception. Helmholtz (*Handbook of Physiological Optics*, first published in 1867) measured the rate of nerve conduction by stimulating a nerve at different distances from its responsive muscle. Helmholtz's studies challenged the notion that the mind and body were independent and that actions in the mental realm (not being physical) were instantaneous.

Although these authors' positions are much more complex than this brief outline conveys, they represent the growing conviction that the mental realm could be studied using the experimental methods developed in physiology. The critique of the experimental method offered in *PES* is not that experimentation itself was wrong (Brentano himself hoped to develop a psychological laboratory in Vienna) but that the subject matter it could study, mental sense experiences, was too limited; it was not able to investigate the higher mental processes, such as willing, feeling, and acting.

Wilhelm Wundt

Wundt was the founder of the German school of psychology while Brentano was the founder of the Austrian school of psychology. The ideas of both men changed over time; however, I limit my discussion to the positions presented in their early books, both published in 1874: Wundt's *Principles of Physiological Psychology* and Brentano's *Psychology From an Empirical Standpoint*. (Wundt published the first half of his *Physiological Psychology* in 1873, and *PES* includes comments on this portion of the book.) Wundt's use of the term *physiological* in the title of his book is equivalent to the term *experimental* as it was practiced in the physiological studies (described earlier). Edward B. Titchener, a prominent voice in early American psychology, commented on the two books:

> The year 1874 saw the publication of two books which, as the event has shown, were of first-rate importance for the development of modern psychology. Their authors, already in the full maturity of life, were men of settled reputation, fired as investigators with the zeal of research, endowed as teachers with a quite exceptional power to influence younger minds, ready as polemists to cross swords with a Zeller or a Helmholtz. (Titchener, 1921, p. 108)

Physiological Psychology is a continuation of the approach to the study of the mind developed by physiology. Wundt's approach also emphasized stimulation experiments that studied how "internal" experiences in the mind varied when differing stimuli were presented. His experiments replicated much of the work on audition and vision and on absolute and differential thresholds that the physiologists had done. Kurt Danziger (1980a) examined 189 studies performed in Wundt's laboratory between 1883 and 1903. He found that all but 4 used experimental internal perception. Wundt's specific contribution was to advance the methods used in stimulation studies and to set up the first laboratory devoted exclusively to these kinds of studies.

The problem Wundt addressed was how to set up conditions under which internal perception could resemble the precision of external perception. Because ordinary reflective or introspective views of one's own mental contents were distorted by feelings, memories, and higher order conscious processes, a procedure was needed that would allow the reporting of unaltered mental contents as they appeared immediately upon application of the stimuli and thereby make reports of internal perceptions as reliable as external perceptions.

Wundt held that this could be accomplished by establishing laboratory conditions in which variation of the stimulus could be tightly controlled and through extensive training of the reporters of the various contents of conscious processes that occurred with the presentation of a stimulus. Edwin G. Boring (1953) wrote that reporters in Wundt's reaction-time experiments had to perform approximately 10,000 internal perception observations before they were considered skilled enough to provide valid data. By having the reports follow immediately on the original perception, the data would approximate the conditions of external perception. Wundt held that these conditions would allow replication of specific experiments because identical stimuli would produce the same or very similar subjective experiences.

The purpose of psychology as outlined in *Physiological Psychology* was to analyze or break down the basic contents of consciousness into its most elemental components that would emulate the work being done in the natural sciences. The work took place within the context of the excitement over Dmitriy Mendeleev's publication of the chemical periodic table (1869/in press). Wundt thought that consciousness, like chemical compounds, was composed of elements that combined to produce compound experiential contents.

For Wundt, experimental psychology was limited to the study of only simple perceptual appearances. More robust and complex mental phenomena, such as thoughts, volitions, and feelings, were not sufficiently amenable to experimental control to be included within a scientific study of the psyche (Lyons, 1986). The deeper processes that make up conscious experience are beyond the reach of internal perception or any other experimental technique. However, in the full scope of Wundt's work, beyond *Physiological Psychology* shows interest in the full range of human experience, including its higher, synthetic operations, human will, and feelings (Viney, 1993). While experimentation and, thus, the experimental science of the mind needed to be limited to stimulus experiments, he also proposed that other kinds of nonexperimental studies were needed, such as the development of mind as it occurs in individuals and in communities across the historical contexts. Thus, in the last 20 years of his life (1900–1920), Wundt turned his attention to the development of his *Völkerpsychologie*, or "cultural psychology," and produced a 10-volume work on higher mental operations (Wundt, 1900–1920). He believed that the form and content of people's mental life was fashioned by the culture in which they lived. His later studies of the development of mind focused on the languages, myths, and customs that composed the collective life of various communities. Wundt's most substantial contribution in his *Völkerpsychologie* was his theory of psycholinguistics, which closely resembles modern psycholinguistic notions (Leahey, 1980).

Wundt's *Physiological Psychology* was the primary competitor to Brentano's *PES* in Europe during the beginning decades of scientific psychology; in the United States, however, the initial impact of the ideas was far greater than those of *PES*. It is only in recent years with the turn to studies of cognition that the ideas of *PES* have had their direct impact in the United States.

THE ORIGINS OF *PSYCHOLOGY FROM AN EMPIRICAL STANDPOINT*

Psychology From an Empirical Standpoint was written in a context in which study of the mind was approached from two directions: the traditional metaphysical–theological approach and the new physiological–experimental approach. *PES* presents a third approach that, although it replaces the metaphysical and theological views with rigorous scientific study, proposes a nonexperimental study of the mind. Although *PES* does not oppose experimentation as a method of investigation, it views it as limited in that it can only study specific contents of the mind, not the activity of the mind. The term *empirical* in the title of *PES* calls attention to its position that psychology should not be limited to experimental or *physiological* methods of study; nevertheless, Brentano held that "the true method of philosophy [psychology] is none other than that of the natural sciences" (quoted in B. Smith, 1994, p. 31).

Explanations about why a book is produced at the time it is with the contents it has are varied. They range from holding that its source is the underlying social or intellectual factors to holding that its source is the individual genius of the author. An account of the origin of *PES* requires a mixed explanation. The time was filled with admiration for science and its accomplishments, and this is reflected in *PES*'s view that study of the mind must be scientific. *PES* is a work that reflects the differences between the German-speaking countries of Germany and Austria. *PES* was produced in Vienna and reflects the antimetaphysical spirit of Viennese philosophy (a spirit that would later inform principles of the logical positivism of the Vienna Circle). In addition to this intellectual milieu, *PES* grew out of the personal genius and creative powers of Brentano. He was an Aristotelian scholar before turning to the development of a new psychology. He had studied and taught philosophy and the new experimental physiology. He acted on the basis of his own beliefs, even as his actions impaired his career. On top of the influences of the social milieu, individual history, and personal characteristic, he was a creative thinker who produced new ideas. "The source of [Brentano's] philosophy is complex, especially because it is a mixture of both modernization of old doctrines and a highly creative mind which produced new ideas difficult to trace in the history of philosophy" (Velarde-Mayol, 2000, p. 8). It is *PES*'s new idea of a classificatory science for psychology (which became known as phenomenology) and the new idea that mental phenomena have the property of action that have served to produce the impact *PES* had in the decades after its publication and is having in contemporary cognitive psychology.

Brentano was born into a family of German Catholic intellectuals. He was educated at several universities in Bavaria and Berlin in preparation for his ordination as a priest, which occurred in 1862, when he was 26. He wrote two books on Aristotle and came to be recognized as an authority on Aristotle's philosophy. From 1866 to 1874 he was a faculty member at the University of Würzburg, where he lectured on the history of philosophy, logic, and psychology. During this period Brentano's relationship with the Catholic Church became contentious. He opposed the proposed doctrine of papal infallibility and produced a paper that argued that such a doctrine contradicts the Gospels, the Church Fathers, and the historical positions of the Church. In 1873, when he was 35 years old, he broke completely with the Church and left the priesthood.

In 1874, a year after his rupture with the Church, he published *Psychology From an Empirical Standpoint* and was appointed to the University of Vienna as a professor. He spent his next 22 years (from his 36th to 57th years) in Vienna. However, after his 6th year at the University of Vienna, he married, which for ex-priests was not permitted in Austria. He had to resign his professorship and, although the faculty of the university frequently appealed to the government to reappoint him to a professorship, it never did. It also rejected his proposal to create a laboratory for experimental psychology. Thus, for his remaining 18 years at Vienna, he was only able to hold an unsalaried lecturer position. Nevertheless, a large and strong following was influenced by his ideas and teaching.

Brentano published the two books that make up PES when he was 36 years old. During the remaining 43 years of his life, he revisited some of the ideas developed in PES, changing his positions on some of them and refining others. (The appendix and supplemental writings that are part of the English translations of PES include some of these later writings.) As did Wundt, Brentano became interested in other areas of philosophy, including logic, ethics, and ontology; nevertheless, his influence on psychology came primarily from PES. Brentano left Vienna in 1895 without regaining his professorship. He moved to Italy, where he lived until he was 77. When Italy entered into World War I in 1915, Brentano, who by then had become nearly blind, moved to Switzerland, where he died 2 years later.

Brentano committed himself to bring about a transformation to a philosophical psychology based on scientific principles. He considered it "his task to bring about a 'universal revolution, or better, a fundamental reformation of philosophy' in the service of mankind" (see Spiegelberg, 1976, p. 29). His students said that he had a messianic sense of a mission to renew philosophy. In his early writings, Brentano proposed that historically philosophy passes through four phases. The first phase is the most fruitful phase and is characterized by concern for theoretical questions without concern for the possibility of application. The approach used is based on the adoption of the best methods and results of the science of the day. The second phase is the beginning of the decline. Concern with practical application, such as ethics, overtakes the interest in theoretical questions. Philosophical growth is slow, and its questions are more superficial because of the attempt to popularize philosophy. The third phase, which is the natural outcome of the second phase's abandonment of the profound theoretical questions, is a skeptical phase. The skeptical phase is replaced by a fourth, mystical phase. This phase is the most extreme decay of philosophy. Argumentation is replaced by dogma, and mystical intuitions replace natural methods of inquiry (Velarde-Mayol, 2000).

Brentano considered that in his day philosophy of the mind was in the final mystical phase as represented by Kant, post-Kantian idealism, and, especially, Georg Hegel. Brentano believed that it was his vocation to move philosophy to a new first phase that would deal with basic theoretical concerns and would be based on the methods of natural science. As sources to assist him in creating this new first phase, Brentano looked to the philosophers who produced other first phases, for example, Aristotle, John Locke, and Gottfried Leibniz, for guidance. Although these philosophers, who produced the most creative and scientific periods of philosophy, were Brentano's heroes, he sought to use what was worthwhile from their accounts yet move beyond them. The approach to a new scientific psychology developed in *PES* shows a strong influence from Aristotle, about whom Brentano had previously written two books. *PES* advocates an Aristotelian-type of science, which does not use experimentation but instead reaches conclusions by abstracting from careful descriptions of experience. *PES*'s idea of intentionality is an adaptation of Aristotle's theory of perception in which the form but not the material substance of a perceived object is in the mind. Aristotle's notion that the mind is active shows up in Brentano's emphasis on the mind as actively engaging the world. Even the plan for *PES* parallels Aristotle's *De anima* (Simons, 1992). Nevertheless, *PES* is not simply a modification of Aristotle's thought but an original and unique contribution to psychology as a science.

Brentano hoped his own approach would make psychology truly scientific and intended that *PES* would start psychology on a unified path. He held that *PES* was "no more than a mere preparation for future, more perfect accomplishments" (Brentano, 1874/1995c, p. xxix) and intended the book to be a large work that would "embrace all the different and essential fields of psychology" (p. xxvii).

PSYCHOLOGY FROM AN EMPIRICAL STANDPOINT

The original plan for *PES* called for a work consisting of six books. The first five were to be about psychology as a science, mental phenomena in general, and the three classes of mental phenomena. The sixth book was to deal with the mind–body problem. However, after publishing the first two books—on the method of psychology and on its subject matter—Brentano became ill with smallpox and never returned to the final envisioned four books. The two books of *PES* were republished in 1911 under a new title, *The Classification of Mental Phenomena*, and with an added appendix "intended to explain and defend, as well as to correct and expand upon the theory" (Brentano, 1874/1995c, p. 271). In 1924 a new edition was published by Oskar Kraus, who added previously unpublished materials from Brentano. The current English translations of *PES* contain the first two books, the appendix, and the additional Brentano publications (Brentano, 1924/1995a).

Book One: Psychology as a Science

Psychology is the study of consciousness, that is, the mental realm. The mental realm has different characteristics than the physical objects in the world; nevertheless, it is a real realm, and as such, it is susceptible to scientific study. In *PES*, Brentano argued against the traditional metaphysical and theological approaches that based their understandings of the mind on revelation or assumed axioms. He argued that gaining true knowledge of the mental realm needs to follow the approach developed by the natural sciences. The approach of the natural sciences means having evidence to support one's knowledge claims. It does not necessarily mean imitating the particular methods of inquiry used for the study of physical objects. Rather, the methods for collecting evidence and analyzing that evidence should be designed according to characteristics of the realm under study. Thus, the scientific study of the mental realm, because of its unique characteristics, will require its own method of study. In Brentano's view in *PES*, "natural science basically 'teaches and disciplines us to change our method in conformance with the specific nature of the objects' of research" (Rancurello, 1968, p. 24).

PES points out that the previous psychologies have not clarified the fundamental categories of the mental realm and, thus, their attempts at developing causal relations among psychological phenomena lacked the necessary precision. It holds that what is needed is a science of classification (descriptive psychology or psychognosy) that will lay out the various kinds of things that make up the mental realm. Only after this work has been accomplished should psychology undertake to uncover regularities or causes in the appearance and disappearance of mental events (genetic psychology).

Thus, the new science of psychology should follow Aristotle's example and become a science of classification to complete the task of categorizing the kinds of mental phenomena that exist. This is the type of science that is used in the disciplines of anatomy, botany, and geology. These sciences develop careful descriptions of the objects in their field of inquiry that are methodical, painstaking, and detailed. Through careful inductive analysis of these descriptions, one can note the different classes or kinds of things referred to in the descriptions. The findings of a science of classification are a taxonomy or categorization system of the things that make up the object of study. When applied to the mental realm, a science of classification will yield a detailed description of the kinds of contents and actions that make up the complex experiences of mental realm or consciousness.

Sciences of classification must be empirical; that is, they must be grounded in experience. The term *empirical* in the title of *Psychology From an Empirical Standpoint* emphasizes this position in opposition to the nonempirical-based claims of the theologians and traditional philosophers. An empirical science is one whose knowledge is based entirely on what is experienced, not on dogma or philosophical reasoning. A science of the mental realm should not borrow assumptions about the mind from theology or philosophy, rather it should learn about the nature and characteristics of consciousness from a close examination of conscious experiences. Thus, a scientist of the mental realm needs to place his or her own beliefs out of the way when engaged in inquiry about the mind. (Brentano believed that the psyche or soul continued on after the death of the body, but he remarked that he had no scientific proof for the belief and it had no place in his investigations.) Psychology should return to "the things themselves," that is, it should focus on "the things" that actually appear in consciousness, not on whether what appears is what one believes should be in the mind.

The term *empirical* also distinguishes *PES*'s approach from the physiological or experimental approach advocated by Wundt's *Physiological Psychology*. The method of classification needs descriptions from the full range of appearances in consciousness and cannot be limited to the study of the subset of appearances used in experimental psychology's stimulation studies. These studies can only examine the contents that appear with stimulation of the senses; they are not able to view the activity of the mental realm. *PES* argues that what can be studied by experimentation should not define psychology's subject matter; rather the subject matter should define the method by which it is studied. Stressing experimentation to the exclusion of other empirical methods blinds one to significant aspects of the mental realm. An authentic empirical science of classification discovers much more in consciousness than mere stimulated contents.

PES's empirical standpoint refers to grounding the study of the mental realm in experiential evidence; it is not a reference to the problem of the empirical philosophers as to whether the representations in the mind are accurate reflections of the objects in the world. *PES* describes Locke's experiment of the experience of coldness and warmth. Locke warmed one hand while simultaneously cooling the other. Then he placed both hands into a pan of lukewarm water. He experienced warmth in the hand that was previously cooled and coolness in the hand that had previously been warmed. Brentano (1874/1995c) argued in *PES* that the experiment "proved that neither warmth nor cold really existed in the water" (p. 9). Although *PES* posits that conscious experience need not accurately reflect the world, the classification study of the mental realm does not depend on the resolution of the issue.

After clarifying what is meant by its *empirical standpoint*, *PES* spells out the processes involved in using a science of classification to study the mental realm. (Although not directly taken from *PES*, contemporary qualitative research makes use of these same processes.) First, examples of particular instances of mental phenomena are collected to produce a dataset to be submitted to a taxonomic or categorical analysis. From the study of these data, the researcher intuits a set of categories that partition the data into different kinds. *PES* uses terms such as *intuition, immediately evident,* and *insight* in describing the process by which the researcher identifies the categories or kinds of things that turn up in the descriptions. *PES* does not propose a formal inductive process in which claims about general truths are derived from the collection of particular examples. *PES* reminds readers that the starting point from which intuited categories arise is a "methodical, painstaking, and detailed" perception of the events and contents of consciousness (Rancurello, 1968, p. 26). The process of teasing out the various kinds of phenomena that appear in consciousness is an iterative one. Initially, intuited patterns and themes are tried on the data to see if they actually fit the data. If they do not serve to locate all the experiences into the proposed, intuited partitions, new intuited categories are tried on the data.

Having argued why psychology should be an empirical science of classification and having outlined the processes involved in conducting such a science, Book One addresses the difficult problem of how empirical descriptions (data) of the aspects of consciousness can be obtained. Before the process of classification can begin, careful and accurate descriptions are needed. Self-reflection on one's own consciousness had been the traditional means to garnering descriptions of the mental realm. However, self-reflection as traditionally practiced is problematic. The difficulty of clarifying how self-reflection could produce reliable descriptions was also a concern for Wundt and the experimental psychologists.

One of PES's important contributions is the clarity it brought to the issue of accurate self-reflection. Various terms, such as *introspection, inner sense*, and *reflection*, had been used to refer to the awareness a person has of the operations and contents of his or her consciousness. PES calls attention to the difference between inner perception and inner observation. "Until now, to my knowledge, no psychologist has drawn this distinction" (Brentano, 1874/1995c, p. 30). PES holds that access to the data of consciousness requires inner perception rather than inner observation. Inner observation is based on the error that the observation of mental phenomena takes place in the same manner as the observation of external objects. However, observation is based on the premise that there is an observer and a separate object that is observed. But access to one's own consciousness is completely different from the access and observation of physical objects. We do not look upon our consciousness; we are directly aware of it or we directly perceive it. The data for psychology are not something we direct our attention to but something immediately present to us. For example, in trying to observe one's own anger, the very act of attempting to observe the experience of anger alters one's attention away from the anger itself and thereby dissipates it.

The phenomena of consciousness that present themselves in inner perception have an unmediated quality, and (in line with the Cartesian tradition) they give knowledge that is self-evident, incontrovertible, and necessary. Thus, the exclusive source of reliable, indeed infallible, knowledge of the mental realm is inner perception; that is, the mind's simultaneous reflexive awareness of itself, which is a part of every mental phenomenon. Because what is studied by psychology is the appearances in consciousness, appearance and reality within inner perception are one and the same.

In summary, Book One argues that the scientific study of the mind must replace the theological and philosophical approaches. But the science of the mind must develop its own method that is compatible with the full range of appearances that come into view in one's consciousness. The kind of experimental procedures used in physiology's stimulation studies is inadequate to deal with the fullness of consciousness. Instead, the science of the mind needs to employ a science of classification based on careful descriptions of all features of the mental realm. These descriptions are of the inner perceptions of aspects and operations of the mind, not of attempted observations on the mind. Having established the kind of science and methods of the new psychology, which would be termed *phenomenology* by Edmund Husserl and later followers of Brentano, *PES* moves on in Book Two to give the initial results of the application of the science of classification.

Book Two: Mental Phenomena in General

Book Two presents its initial findings of *PES*'s classificatory study of consciousness, that is, to provide an articulation of what the kinds of things are that exist in consciousness. At the highest level of classification, *PES* notes that there are two basic kinds of phenomena in consciousness: mental phenomena and physical phenomena. Physical phenomena are the appearance of physical qualities such as colors, sizes, and shapes; for example, the sensory experience of the physical quality red presents itself as a physical content or phenomena in consciousness. Both of the terms *mental phenomena* and *physical phenomena* refer to aspects that appear in consciousness or the mental realm. They do not refer to two separate realms, the mental/subjective realm and the physical realm of worldly objects. Thus, of the appearances (phenomena) in consciousness, there are those that are activities, such as seeing, judging, remembering, and there are those that are sensed contents, such as red, sour, and heavy. Because both kinds of phenomena or appearances occur within consciousness, using the terms *mental* and *physical* to differentiate them can be confusing when taken out of the context of the argument developed in *PES*. *PES* uses *mental phenomena* to refer to the *acts* of consciousness because they are the primary property of the whole mental realm. Without the acts of consciousness there would be no appearance of sense content or *physical phenomena*, representing the physical realm.

Physical phenomena are the phenomena studied in the stimulation studies of experimental physiology. These studies, as described earlier, attempted to discover laws or regularities between the variation of appearances of these sensual qualities in consciousness and the variations of physical stimuli (e.g., sounds, weights, and colors). *PES* is not much interested in these studies except to point out some flaws in the mathematical relations posed in this research and to note that some physical phenomena, such as a unicorn, need not actually exist in the physical world. It is not the actual things of the world that appear in consciousness, and one cannot assume that the things in the world are the same as what appears. "We have no right, therefore, to believe that the objects of so-called external perception really exist as they appear to us" (Brentano 1874/1995c, p. 10). The primary focus in *PES* is on what is missing from these studies, the recognition of the acts of consciousness—mental phenomena.

In *PES*, Brentano argued that it is the act of experiencing or mental phenomena that is the more basic subject matter of psychology. The acts of consciousness always include contents; the act of sensing without being about something sensed is meaningless. Thus, mental phenomena are *intentional*; that is, they are always about or are directed toward some content of consciousness. Physical phenomena do not have this property of intentionality; they are not about other physical qualities. The acts of consciousness (mental phenomena) are not accessible through the experimental methods of physiological psychology but only through a classificatory science.

What distinguishes mental phenomena or mental acts is that they have the property of having reference to an object other than themselves. Thus, the mental phenomena of hearing always relate to or are about something heard, and believing relates to something believed. Hearing never appears without something being heard, and believing never appears without something being believed. Thus, mental phenomena appear as actions, such as hearing, seeing, sensing, thinking, judging, inferring, loving, and hating. These acts include the object they are about; they amount to doing something. Thus, mental phenomena are experienced as activities one is carrying out.

The recognition that only mental phenomena or the acts of consciousness have the property of intentionality is the most important and lasting idea presented in *PES*. According to Brentano (1874/1995c), "Every mental phenomenon includes something as object within itself" (p. 88). The idea that only mental phenomena have the property of intentionality has been appealed to as a restraint on those who propose that mentality can simply be reduced to physical properties. To avoid confusion in what *PES* means by the term *intentional*, its meaning needs to be distinguished from the meaning of the English word *intention*, which refers to doing something on purpose or to intend an outcome. The meaning in *PES* is derived from the Scholastic notion of *intentio*, which is the characteristic that mental operations refer to objects.

In its most famous and most quoted passage, *PES* demarcates mental phenomena from physical phenomena.

> Every mental phenomenon is characterized by what the Scholastics of the Middle Ages call the intentional (or mental) inexistence of an object, and what we might call, though not wholly unambiguously, reference to a content, direction toward an object (which is not to be understood here as meaning a thing), or immanent objectivity. Every mental phenomenon includes something as object within itself, although they do not all do so in the same way. In presentation something is presented,

in judgment something is affirmed or denied, in love loved, in hate hated, in desire desired and so on. (Brentano, 1874/1995c, p. 88)

Having first identified that what appears in consciousness is of two basic types—mental phenomena with intentionality and physical phenomena without intentionality—PES moves to differentiate the various kinds of mental phenomena. There are three ways in which one may be intentionally related to an object: presentation, judgment, and emotion. These three kinds are the different ways in which mental actions may refer to, or be directed on, their objects. In presentation, the basic mental act, something makes an appearance in consciousness. For example, in the act of seeing a color is presented, in hearing a sound is presented, and in imaging an image is presented. Describing presentation, Brentano (1874/1995c) noted, "When I hear and understand a word that names something, I have a presentation of what that word designates; and generally speaking the purpose of such words is to evoke presentations" (p. 198). In judgment, one takes an intellectual stand toward an object that has been presented. Judgment relates to an object by affirming or denying the reality of the object. Thus, if a blue sweater is presented in my consciousness, I can judge that the sweater is "really" present in the world or is "really" not in the world. The third mode of relating to objects is emotional, that is, the object is related to as desirable or undesirable. Also included under this category are evaluative relationships in which the object that appears is experienced as good or bad.

THE IMPACT OF PSYCHOLOGY FROM AN EMPIRICAL STANDPOINT

As a historical text, PES has had phases during which it has had high impact in philosophical and theoretical psychology and phases from which it was lost from view. After the period of fading influence, PES has been revived in recent decades by philosophers of the mind.

The Early Impact

In the decades after its publication, PES's impact was high. Its initial impact was in three areas: (a) act psychology, (b) phenomenology, and (c) Freud's psychoanalysis.

Act Psychology

PES was the basic text of act psychology. Act psychology stressed that the primary focus of psychology should be on the mental processes of acts rather than on the contents or "objects" that appeared in the mind. The competition for what kind of science the new psychology was to be was between *PES* and Wundt's experimental psychology. Boring (1950) wrote, "[the] dilemma for systematic psychology in the late nineteenth century lay between act and content, between Brentano and Wundt" (p. 361). The act psychologists, such as Theodore Lipps, James Ward, and the Danish psychologist Harald Höffding, approached the person as a psychically active subject rather than a passive receptacle for sense impressions. They used *PES*'s classificatory method instead of experimentation for its method of investigation.

Although *PES* created Brentano's reputation, it is difficult to separate its impact from the impact of Brentano on his students. He had "a peculiar appearance, attractive philosophical personality, solemnity in his speech, and at the same time, he managed to keep a special glitter and charm" (Kraus, 1976). While a professor at Würzburg, Brentano developed close lifelong relationships with two of his students—Carl Stumpf and Anton Marty—who went on to make important contributions to psychology and philosophy. Stumpf, who had come to Würzburg to study law, changed to the study of philosophy under the influence of Brentano (Stumpf, 1976). Stumpf's area of research was in auditory phenomena. Marty became a professor at the German University of Prague and wrote on the philosophy of language and the theory of meaning. He remained a close associate of Brentano's for 40 years. Three of Stumpf's students—Max Wertheimer, Kurt Koffa, and Wolfgang Köhler—were the developers of Gestalt psychology. They appropriated two ideas from *PES*: (a) the notion that the study of the mind should produce descriptions of inner perception rather than an experimental search for mental elements and (b) the idea that the mind is an active contributor to what appears in it.

Brentano's impact on students continued after he moved to Vienna. Even though he held a professorship at the University of Vienna for only 6 years, he continued to produce scholars who went on to make their own strong contributions to theoretical psychology. Blackmore (1998) noted the significance of Brentano's participation in the University of Vienna's philosophical society after he had lost his professorship. He continued to influence students and draw them toward the study of philosophy. His most famous students from the University of Vienna—Edmund Husserl and Alexius von Meinong—remained corresponding members of the society for some years after they had completed their studies at Vienna. Husserl had come to Vienna to study mathematics but changed to philosophy because of Brentano. Husserl wrote,

> At a time when my philosophical interests were increasing and I was uncertain whether to make my career in mathematics or to dedicate myself totally to philosophy, Brentano's lectures settled the matter. Brentano's lectures gave me for the first time the conviction that philosophy too was a serious discipline which also could be and must be dealt with in the spirit of the stricted science. (quoted in Hill, 1998, p. 154)

Meinong studied under Brentano from 1875 through 1878. He became a professor at the University of Graz and established the first psychology laboratory in Austria in 1894. Most of his work followed the ideas of a descriptive psychology developed in *PES*. Another of Brentano's students, Kasimir Twardowski, became a leading scholar in Poland and transformed philosophy in that country. All of these scholars "exerted a strong impact on the fields of study" (Albertazzi, Librardi, & Poli, 1996, p. 8). Brentano produced a network of students he had trained across Eastern Europe. The network included leading scholars and professors of philosophy who taught in many of the major European universities. Although they worked in various areas of psychology and philosophy, they followed the classificatory method of investigation outlined in *PES*; that is, (a) develop an accurate description of the phenomena, (b) gather examples and counterexamples, (c) put together a complete list of all the existing theories, and (d) eliminate the theories that do not match the data. Albertazzi et al. argued that the network of Brentano's students as well as their shared view of how psychological inquiry was to be conducted entitles one to talk about the "School of Brentano."

Phenomenology

Husserl is perhaps the most well-known student of Brentano's. He used *PES*'s method of describing and classifying what appeared in consciousness, and his notion of the reductions follow from *PES*'s development of inner perception. Husserl's writings came to overshadow *PES* in the promotion of phenomenology. Husserl's student, Martin Heidegger, who further developed phenomenology, was a second-generation follower of Brentano. Heidegger told that it was his reading of Brentano's *On the Several Senses of Being in Aristotle* that changed his philosophical life and was the seed for his *Being and Time* (Hearnshaw, 1987). The lineage of phenomenology begins with Brentano and his *PES*, moves through Husserl, and then Heidegger, and crossed to the United States as the philosophical ground for the writings of Abraham Maslow and other humanistic psychologists. The Wundt–Brentano competition between experimental and classificatory psychology reappeared in the United States in the Skinner–Rogers debates on whether psychology should be an experimental or phenomenological science (Wann, 1964).

Freud

Another person who felt the impact of *PES* and Brentano's teaching was Sigmund Freud (Wertz, 1993). Freud attended lectures by Brentano in Vienna between 1874 and 1876. About these classes, Freud wrote,

> I have never before enjoyed the feeling one calls academic bliss and which, for the most part, consists in the awareness of sitting at the source from which knowledge pours forth in its greatest purity and taking a good, deep drink of it. (quoted in McGrath, 1986, p. 110)

While a student in Vienna, Freud also translated a volume of John Stuart Mill's works under Brentano's supervision. Even though *PES* does not support the notion of an unconscious, its ideas that mental phenomena are active and have the property of intentionality are recognizable in Freud's theories. Wollheim (1971), a biographer of Freud, wrote,

> The underying philosophical assumption that Freud retained through out his work, and which probably derives from the Viennese philosopher Franz Brentano, . . . that every mental state or condition can be analyzed into two components: an idea, which gives the mental state its object or what it is directed upon; and its charge of affect, which gives its measure of strength or efficacy. (p. 20)

Lessening Impact

The substance of Brentano's and Wundt's ideas began to fade from view after their and their students' deaths. Both their positions came under criticism by later developments; for example, the German Gestalt psychologists accused Wundt of not being synthetic enough, and physiologists accused Brentano of being solipsistic. Brentano's reputation became reduced to that of the teacher of Husserl. Then, with the coming of the Nazis into power in Germany in the 1930s, followed by World War II, Brentano's and Wundt's views, along with those of many other members of the German intellectual community, perished (Leahey, 1980). In the United States, psychology turned away from the study of consciousness and limited the field to the observation of behavior. Experimental psychology no longer concerned itself with stimulus-initiated changes in consciousness; instead, it focused on stimulus-initiated and publicly observable behaviors.

The Disappearance of PES

In spite of the range and importance of its contributions, scholars in philosophical and theoretical psychology did not often acknowledge the impact of *PES* on the field. The central role it played in the development of our field was unnoticed and unobserved in the United States for a number of decades. It reached the point where Poli (1998) could puzzle over the invisibility of *PES* in the field. Poli offered several explanations for why *PES* lost its impact on scholars as one of the most important texts of the 19th century. First, other than *PES*, Brentano published very little during his lifetime, and posthumous attempts by others to publish his notes were improperly put together, thus making it difficult to clearly understand the intended meaning of his ideals. Second, for many years the principal sources of Brentano's other ideas were notes made by students of his lectures; however, these notes have been lost and are no longer available. Third, Brentano laid great emphasis on oral teaching, which he regarded as more important than his written works.

Fourth, a number of Brentano's students were successful in their own right and founded their own schools, and attention became focused on their interpretations of Brentano's ideas rather than on the original formulations of them in *PES*. Simons (1992) dated the loss of recognition of Brentano's importance to the death of those who had studied directly with him: "It is fair to say the Brentano tradition effectively died with the First World War. This was simply because the first two generations lost most of their members. Brentano died in 1917, Marty in 1914, and Meinong in 1920" (p. 156).

Brentano and Wundt in American Psychology

The Wundt as presented by Titchener was the one who made an impact on American psychology. This was the Wundt who was the experimental psychologist of the *Physiological Psychology*. Titchener depicted Wundt as focused on the discovery and cataloguing of the basic sensation elements to which all complex conscious processes could be reduced. In the United States, although Wundt has been held out as the father of psychology, Brentano has been relegated to the position of a minor contributor. The continued presence of Wundt's name and the absence of Brentano's name and references to *PES* in American psychology can be largely attributed to the promotion of Wundt by Titchener, one of the most influential early American psychologists. Titchener, who was an Englishman, went to Leipzig for 2 years to study with Wundt after his studies at Oxford. In 1892, following his stay in Leipzing, he took a position in the United States at Cornell University, where he established a Wundt-like psychological laboratory. While there, he developed the largest doctoral program in psychology in the United States and remained a significant voice in psychology until his death in 1927. Titchener presented himself as the representative in America of Wundt's ideas. (Recent historical scholarship, for example, Danziger, 1980b, has questioned how reliably Titchener actually represented Wundt's positions.)

Titchener translated into English several of Wundt's books, including his 1904 translation of the *Principles of Physiological Psychology*. Titchener was also an advocate of his version of Wundt's psychology against the psychology of Brentano. In his 1921 article, Titchener said that there is "no middle ground between Brentano and Wundt" (p. 108). He said that psychology students had to make a choice for either one or the other; however, as he made clear, the correct choice was Wundt. Titchener held Wundt up as the father of psychology. Boring, who was a devoted student of Titchener's and one of the first historians of psychology, wrote one of the first American histories of psychology in 1923, *A History of Experimental Psychology* (1950). Boring dedicated his book to Titchener and wrote in the preface: "Titchener was the historian par excellence. He should have written this book, and it is with great diffidence that I offer a poor substitute" (p. xii). In his *History*, which became the accepted American version of psychology's history, Boring repeated his teacher's proclamation that Wundt was the father of psychology. Boring (1950) wrote,

> Wundt is the senior psychologist in the history of psychology. He is the first man who without reservation is properly called a psychologist. Before him there had been psychology enough, but no psychologists. . . . When we call him [Wundt] the "founder" of experimental psychology, we mean both that he promoted the idea of psychology as an independent science and that he is the senior among "psychologists." (p. 316)

Although Wundt may have been the "father" of the kind of "structuralist" psychology practiced by Titchener, Wundt's parenthood did not extend to all the versions of American psychology that were being practiced during its nascent period. More widely practiced was "functionalist" psychology, whose parenthood should more likely be attributed to Darwin. Although many American students of psychology went to Leipzig to study with Wundt, unlike Titchener, they did not attempt to practice a version of Wundt's psychology on their return to the United States. "Wundt's American students happily got their degrees in Leipzig, but pursued a thoroughly American psychology, functionalism, when they returned home, and psychology quickly became an American science" (Leahey, 1980, p. 267). Functionalism, which was linked to the work of psychologists such as William James, John Dewey, and James R. Angell, advocated studying mental processes from the evolutionary perspective of how they aided organisms in adapting to their environments.

The structuralist and functionalist versions of early American psychology maintained their focus on the study of consciousness. However, beginning in the 1920s, they were overwhelmed and replaced by the advent of the behavioral version of psychology. American psychology came to look less and less like a progeny of Wundt's and more and more like a mutation of the science of mechanics. As behaviorism came to dominate the definition of psychology, structuralism and functionalism disappeared from mainstream American psychology. John B. Watson's definition of behaviorism was itself a clear rejection of the view of psychology proposed by Wundt and *PES*, which held that psychology is the study of consciousness by methods of inner perception. Watson stated,

> Psychology as the Behaviorist views it is a purely objective experimental branch of natural science. Its theoretical goal is the prediction and control of behavior. Introspection forms no essential part of its methods, nor is the scientific value of its data dependent upon the readiness with which they lend themselves to interpretation in terms of consciousness. The Behaviorist . . . recognizes no dividing line between man and brute. (Watson, 1913, p. 158)

The ascendancy of behaviorism brought with it a change in the subject matter and investigative approaches used in American psychology. Psychology was changed from a discipline whose purpose was to study consciousness to a discipline that studied behaviors. Its data changed from descriptions of people's first-person awareness of the operations and contents of their consciousness to third-person observations and measurements of behavioral movements (Hornstein, 1988). Its analysis changed from explicating and developing taxonomies of aspects of consciousness to relating mathematically groups of instrumentally produced scores. Brentano and Wundt had understood that psychology was the discipline that studied what was particularly unique about human beings, that is, human consciousness. Behaviorism, by limiting the discipline to what could be publicly observed, abandoned this original purpose. Thus, psychology was transformed from the investigation of human consciousness and experience to investigations of the responses of rats and pigeons to various stimuli patterns.

During the half-century of its commitment to behaviorism, mainstream American psychology bore little resemblance to the psychology prescribed by Brentano and Wundt. It made an alliance with logical positivism (L. D. Smith, 1986) and in service to methodological purity replaced the original methods of Wundt and Brentano with a different kind of experimentalism. In spite of Titchener's earlier championing of Wundt and Boring's perpetuation of him as the father of psychology, American interest in the English translations of Wundt's actual texts diminished and translations of Brentano's works were not undertaken. It was not until the 1970s that American psychology began again to study the original subject matter of psychology, the mind. In that context, there has been a renewed interest in PES but not in *Physiological Psychology*.

The Revival of PES

A revival of interest in PES occurred first by the analytic philosophers in the 1960s and 1970s. Their interest in the philosophy of mind led them to PES's notion that mental phenomena are characterized by intentionality. Chisholm (1976) gave a linguistic turn to PES's idea of intentionality: "[Brentano's] descriptive psychology is . . . very close to the 'philosophy of mind' or 'philosophical psychology,' that is now [1976] of concern to philosophers in the analytic tradition" (p. 91). Chisholm adapted PES's intentionality to his own notion on intentionality as a linguistic relation to objects or states of affairs of the external world; that is, external to the mind (Dupuy, 1994/2000). In PES, however, Brentano had understood intentionality as the unique property of mental activities in that they relate to mental contents immanent in consciousness. In spite of Chisholm's linguistic revision of PES's concepts, he did introduce these concepts into the analytic discussion of the theory of mind.

Beginning in earnest in the 1970s, American psychology returned its attention to mental operations, such as cognition, conation, and emotion. With this turn came a growing appreciation of the importance of Brentano's contribution, through the publication of PES, to understanding human consciousness. A secondary literature on *PES*, which had been practically non-existent until recent decades, began to appear, for example, B. Smith's *Austrian Philosophy: The Legacy of Franz Brentano* (1994), Albertazzi et al.'s *The School of Franz Brentano* (1996), Poli's *The Brentano Puzzle* (1998), and Velarde-Mayol's *On Brentano* (2000). *PES*, which had not been translated into English until 1973, was reissued by Routledge with a new introduction in 1995 (Brentano, 1874/1995c), and a translation was published of a collection of Brentano's lectures under the title *Descriptive Psychology* (Brentano, 1982/1995b). This recent flurry of publications about *PES* is a consequence of the importance of its ideas for contemporary psychology's theory of mind.

The ideas in *PES* have special relevance for contemporary areas of theoretical psychology. For philosophy of mind, the idea of intentionality, sometimes referred to as the Brentano's "irreducibility thesis," holds that mental phenomena cannot be a species of physical phenomena. Petitot, Varela, Pachoud, and Roy (1999) pointed out that there remains a gap between the descriptions of experience, such as those developed in *PES*, and the computerized and naturalized models of the mind. One of the current texts that makes use of the concept of intentionality is Searle's *Intentionality* (1983). Searle wrote,

> Intentionality is that property of many mental states and events by which they are directed at or about objects and states of affairs in the world. . . . I follow a long philosophical tradition in calling this feature of directedness or aboutness "Intentionality." (p. 1)

Searle also follows *PES* in arguing for first-person (*PES*'s inner perception) reports as appropriate data for the scientific study of the mind. Other authors (e.g., Dreyfus, 2000) have worked to refine the idea of intentionality as originally laid out in *PES*; nevertheless, the original notion that intentionality is the defining property of the mental is being used to confront the limitations of computerized views of the mind.

Another contemporary use of the ideas developed in *PES* is in the upsurge of qualitative research designs. These designs, with rare acknowledgment of *PES* as their original source, were early termed *phenomenological* research. They use the classificatory method for the study of human experience. They make use of descriptions from participant's self-reflections, and their analysis consists in deriving the classes or themes into which the descriptions fall. However, much of the literature on qualitative research lacks the sophistication given to the process of self-reflection as inner perception laid out in *PES*.

WRITING A TEXT THAT MAKES AN IMPACT

A close study of Brentano's *Psychology From an Empirical Standpoint* provides current writers with a number of important suggestions about producing a text that will make a significant impact on the field of psychology. Such texts need to include an original idea that offers a timely solution to an important problem in the field. These texts are often the result of extensive scholarly preparation, and they provide timely solutions to important problems in the discipline. They require taking a bold approach that risks rejection and criticism.

Perhaps the most important thing to be learned from the study of *PES* about writing a text that makes an impact is to have a new idea that addresses a critical issue in the discipline. The new ideas in *PES* were the product of creative, insightful, and synthetic thinking. However, coming up with ideas that solve issues in a discipline is not simply a matter of natural ability. New ideas occur as the result of long and hard study rather than the result of hoping and waiting for them to happen. Brentano was an experienced scholar of 36 before he wrote *PES* and had researched and lectured on philosophy and psychology for more than a decade. He had written two previous books, both on Aristotle—neither of which had much impact or lasting influence. (It is only because of Heidegger's citation of Brentano's *On the Several Senses of Being in Aristotle* in *Being and Time* that there is any current awareness of the books.) Thus, writers can learn from Brentano's experience that writing a book with impact requires preparation and grows out of years of scholarly activity.

PES was an answer to the crucial concern of how to develop a scientific study of consciousness. The zeitgeist of the day made traditional theological and metaphysical approaches no longer acceptable. The emerging, but limiting, approach to answering the need for a scientific psychology was physiological experimentation. The timing of a publication affects the impact it can have. Something published before the problem that it is intended to solve has generated interest may fail to gain an audience, as does something published after the problem has been passed over and the field has moved on to new issues. *PES* made its appearance at the apex of interest in determining the subject matter of the new psychology and the method that would be used to study this subject matter.

The next thing to be learned from *PES* is to think beyond what appears obvious. To do this, one has to draw on knowledge from outside the immediate field. Brentano had a vast fund of knowledge of philosophy and science. He was able to take ideas from this fund of ideas and adapt, reconfigure, and merge them into a unique and original formulation. Wundt, in his early experimental work, simply accepted a developing method from physiology, to which he simply contributed refinements.

PES first examined the area to be studied and then developed a method for its study. Writing that has an impact ventures beyond what is assumed to be the only valid way to study an area. The area itself informs what the appropriate method of study is. Approaching already-studied topics with a new method can show aspects of the topic that have been overlooked by the traditional way in which it was studied. Writing that makes an impact shows topics in a way they have not been seen before.

Writers can also learn that not every book they write will have wide impact. Brentano intended, however, that unlike his Aristotle books, *PES* was to make an impact and to establish a new field of scientific study—psychology. Thus, books that make an impact are not those addressed merely to the other members of the author's narrow niche in a field. Publishing a book addressed primarily to a small group of fellow specialty experts is not likely to make an impact on the whole field. Addressing the technical problems that concern only a limited number of experts and writing in a jargon used exclusively by those interested in these niche problems will produce only a limited readership. Like Brentano's books on Aristotle, these kinds of books will not often reach or affect the broader community of scholars in a field.

PES laid the groundwork on which others built. Books that make an impact open up new areas of inquiry. They set new directions and trajectories. They are not simply critiques of what is wrong with the field and the ideas of other scholars. *PES*, while noting the limitations of previous approaches to the study of the mind, went beyond critique and offered a new solution. Also, it did not simply reject what had been done before but took from it what seemed helpful and adapted ideas from others and fashioned them with its own contributions into an original contribution. *PES* addressed the ideas of the Greek philosophers, particularly Aristotle, the views of the empirical philosophers, such as Locke, and the German philosophers, such as Kant. The book engages these scholars in dialogue and, out of the dialogue, works out its own position. To make an impact, a book needs to do more than criticize traditional views; it needs to present a positive alternative to what it holds out to be the limitations of other views.

Lastly, *PES* is a courageous book. It was a bold and risky undertaking in that it proposed a new method and a new area of investigation. The book was heavily criticized by the experimental physiologists. I think writing a book that will impact a field by opening new ground for exploration takes courage. It needs to be an expression of one's deeply held beliefs. Impacting a field is not work for the faint-hearted. The proposal of new and different ways of thinking about a subject matter is usually met with rejection and criticism by those committed to the traditional way of thinking. But those who want to make an impact are not deterred by opposition.

REFERENCES

Albertazzi, L., Librardi, M., & Poli, R. (1996). Brentano and his school: Reassembling the puzzle. In L. Albertazzi, M. Librardi, & R. Poli (Eds.), *The school of Franz Brentano* (pp. 1–23). Dordrecht, The Netherlands: Kluwer.

Blackmore, J. (1998). Franz Brentano and the University of Vienna philosophical society 1888–1938. In R. Poli (Ed.), *The Brentano puzzle* (pp. 73–92). Aldershot, England: Ashgate.

Boring, E. G. (1950). *A history of experimental psychology* (2nd rev ed.). Englewood Cliffs, NJ: Prentice-Hall.

Boring, E. G. (1953). A history of introspection. *Psychological Bulletin, 50,* 169–189.

Brentano, F. (1995a). Additional essays from Brentano's *Nachlass* concerning intutions, concepts, and objects of reason. In O. Kraus (Ed.), *Psychology from an empirical standpoint* (A. C. Rancurello, D. B. Terrel, & L. L. McAlister, Trans.) (pp. 311–368). New York: Routledge. (Original work published in 1924)

Brentano, F. (1995b). *Descriptive psychology* (B. Müller, Trans.). New York: Routledge. (Original work published 1982)

Brentano, F. (1995c). *Psychology from an empirical standpoint* (A. C. Rancurello, D. B. Terrel, & L. L. McAlister, Trans.). New York: Routledge. (Original work published 1874)

Chisholm, R. (1976). Brentano's descriptive psychology. In L. L. McAlister (Ed.), *The philosophy of Brentano* (pp. 91–100). London: Duckworth.

Chisholm, R., Baumgartner, W., & Müller, B. (1995). Introduction. In F. Brentano (Ed.), *Descriptive psychology* (pp. x–xxvi). New York: Routledge.

Danziger, K. (1980a). The history of introspection reconsidered. *Journal of the History of the Behavioral Sciences, 16,* 241–262.

Danziger, K. (1980b). Wundt and the two traditions of psychology. In R. W. Rieber (Ed.), *Wilhelm Wundt and the making of a scientific psychology* (pp. 73–87). New York: Plenum.

Danziger, K. (1990). *Constructing the subject.* Cambridge, England: Cambridge University Press.

Dreyfus, H. L. (2000). Merleau-Ponty's critique of Husserl's (and Searle's) concept of intentionality. In L. Hass & D. Olkowski (Eds.), *Rereading Merleau-Ponty: Essays beyond the continental-analytic divide* (pp. 33–51). Amherst, NY: Humanity.

Droysen, J. (1893). *Outline of the principles of history* (E. B. Andrews, Trans.). Boston: Ginn. (Original work published 1858)

Dupuy, J.-P. (2000). *The mechanization of the mind: On the origins of cognitive science* (M. B. DeBevoise, Trans.). Princeton, NJ: Princeton University Press. (Original work published 1994)

Fechner, G. T. (1966). *Elements of psychophysics.* New York: Holt, Rinehart, and Winston. (Original work published 1860)

Hearnshaw, L. S. (1987). *The shaping of modern psychology: An historical introduction.* New York: Routledge & Kegan Paul.

Helmholtz, H. (1867). *Hundbuch der physiologischen Optik* [Handbook of physiological optics]. Leipzig, Germany: Voss.

Hill, C. O. (1998). From empirical psychology to phenomenology: Edmund Husserl on the "Brentano puzzle." In R. Poli (Ed.), *The Brentano puzzle* (pp. 151–167). Aldershot, England: Ashgate.

Hornstein, G. A. (1988). Quantifying psychological phenomena: Debates, dilemmas, and implications. In J. G. Morawski (Ed.), *The rise of experimentation in American psychology* (pp. 1–34). New Haven, CT: Yale University Press.

Kraus, O. (1976). Biographical sketch of Franz Brentano. In L. L. McAlister (Ed.), *The philosophy of Brentano* (pp. 1–9). London: Duckworth.

Leahey, T. H. (1980). *A history of psychology: Main currents in psychological thought.* Englewood Cliffs, NJ: Prentice-Hall.

Lotze, H. (1886). *Outlines of psychology* (G. T. Ladd, Trans.). Boston: Ginn. (Original work published 1881)

Lyons, W. (1986). *The disappearance of introspection.* Cambridge, MA: MIT Press.

McGrath, W. J. (1986). *Freud's discovery of psychoanalysis: The politics of hysteria.* Ithaca, NY: Cornell University Press.

Mendeleev, D. I. (in press). *Principles of chemistry* (T. H. Pope, Ed.). Periodicals Service. (Original work published 1869)

Mohanty, J. N. (1972). *The concept of intentionality.* St. Louis, MO: Warren H. Green.

Peters, R. S. (Ed.). (1962). *Brett's history of psychology* (rev ed.). Cambridge, MA: MIT Press.

Petitot, J., Varela, F. J., Pachoud, B., & Roy, J. -M. (Eds.). (1999). *Naturalizing phenomenology: Issues in contemporary phenomenology and cognitive science.* Stanford, CA: Stanford University Press.

Poli, R. (1998). The Brentano puzzle: An introduction. In R. Poli (Ed.), *The Brentano puzzle* (pp. 1–14). Aldershot, England: Ashgate.

Polkinghorne, D. E. (1983). *Methodology for the human sciences: Systems of inquiry.* Albany: State University of New York Press.

Rancurello, A. C. (1968). *A study of Franz Brentano.* New York: Academic Press.

Searle, J. R. (1983). *Intentionality: An essay in the philosophy of mind.* Cambridge, England: Cambridge University Press.

Simons, P. (1992). *Philosophy and logic in Central Europe from Bolzano to Tarski.* Dordrecht, The Netherlands: Kluwer.

Smith, B. (1994). *Austrian philosophy: The legacy of Franz Brentano.* La Salle, IL: Open Court.

Smith, L. D. (1986). *Behaviorism and logical positivism: A reassessment of the alliance.* Stanford, CA: Stanford University Press.

Spiegelberg, H. (1976). *The phenomenological movement: A historical introduction* (2nd ed., Vol. 1). The Hague: Martinus Nijhoff.

Stumpf, C. (1976). Reminiscences of Franz Brentano. In L. L. McAlister (Ed.), *The philosophy of Brentano* (pp. 10–46). London: Duckworth.

Thinès, G. (1987). Brentano, Franz. In R. L. Gregory (Ed.), *The Oxford companion to the mind* (pp. 117–118). Oxford, England: Oxford University Press.

Titchener, E. B. (1921). Brentano and Wundt: Empirical and experimental psychology. *American Journal of Psychology, 32,* 108–120.

Velarde-Mayol, V. (2000). *On Brentano.* Belmont, CA: Wadsworth.

Vico, G. (2002). *The new science.* (L. Pompa, Trans.). Cambridge, England: Cambridge University Press. (Original work published 1725)

Viney, W. (1993). *A history of psychology: Ideas and context.* Boston: Allyn & Bacon.

Wann, T. W. (Ed.). (1964). *Behaviorism and phenomenology: Contrasting bases for modern psychology.* Chicago: University of Chicago Press.

Watson, J. B. (1913). Psychology as a behaviorist views it. *Psychological Review, 20,* 158–177.

Weber, E. H. (1978). *Sense of touch* (J. D. Mollon, Trans.). New York: Academic Press for Experimental Psychology. (Original work published 1846)

Wertz, F. J. (1993). The phenomenology of Sigmund Freud. *Journal of Phenomenological Psychology, 24,* 101–129.

Wollheim, R. (1971). *Sigmund Freud.* New York: Viking.

Wundt, W. (1900–1920). *Völkerpsychologie* [Cultural psychology] (Vols. 1–10). Leipzig, Germany: Engelmann.

Wundt, W. (1904). *Principles of physiological psychology* (E. B. Titchener, Trans.). London: Swan Sonnenschein. (Original work published 1874)

4

THE IMPACT OF SIGMUND FREUD AND *THE INTERPRETATION OF DREAMS*

STANLEY B. MESSER AND NANCY McWILLIAMS

The Interpretation of Dreams is regarded as Sigmund Freud's seminal work—certainly, he considered it so. Not only did it bring together some hitherto isolated ideas about the meaning of dreams, but it also presented a novel theory of psychopathology and human functioning more generally. The title itself was provocative in that the German title *Traumdeutung* referred to the popular interpretation of dreams by fortune-tellers. Even the book's motto (borrowed from Vergil's *Aeneid*) was somewhat intriguing and shocking to contemporary scientists: "If I cannot bend heaven, then I will arouse hell!" Other features contributed to the effect the book had on its readers. It was intimately connected with Freud's life and personality, it had many humorous allusions to life in *fin-de-siecle* Vienna, and it was written in high literary style (Ellenberger, 1970).

In this post-Freudian era, it is perhaps hard to imagine a pre-Freudian intellectual world. *The Interpretation of Dreams* was the original work by which Freud's ideas gradually but dramatically permeated the intellectual climate of the last century. In this chapter, we explore some of the complex and overlapping reasons why this first psychoanalytic book to be aimed at a broadly educated audience had such a remarkable impact.[1] We then present two dreams (one a friend's dream and another that of a therapy patient's), which we analyze by drawing on Freud's dream theory. In this way, we hope to give the reader a more direct sense of why the theory's impact has been so great. On the basis of our historical analysis, we offer advice to aspiring psychologists in their effort to have an impact on the field.

Freud's initial and persisting belief in the centrality of *The Interpretation of Dreams* to his developing theory of the mind has been at least partially supported by its documentably seminal role in what eventually has become the vast *oeuvre* of psychoanalysis and psychoanalytically influenced scholarship. In addition, it is at least arguable that Freud's conviction about its importance worked like a self-fulfilling prophecy. The fact that Freud could set such a prophecy in motion, while comparably original thinkers have not been so lucky, can be accounted for by both personal and contextual factors.

FREUD'S DEBT TO THE ENLIGHTENMENT

At the time Freud published his ideas about a new, *scientific* approach to the understanding of dreams (1900/1971), Enlightenment-era attitudes pervaded the European community of intellectuals and scholars. The expectation of social progress, intimately connected with the progress of science, was an article of secular faith. "Civilization" was transforming the world of the "savage." Still awaiting the disillusionment attending the more destructive applications of science in the Great War and subsequent catastrophes, the intellectual centers of Europe were awash in optimism about the future. The prospect of applying the power of science to a subject so ephemeral, elusive, and inherently fascinating as dreaming was a compelling idea in itself. In this connection, Freud applied the methods of science even if not those of today's controlled clinical trials. He paid meticulous attention to the details of psychological phenomena, not disregarding or overlooking that which appeared trivial to the casual observer.

Prior to *The Interpretation of Dreams* there had been a few scholarly treatises on dreams; for example, Freud mentions, among others, Sir John Lubbock, Herbert Spencer, and E. B. Taylor. Most of these attempted to understand sleep as well and gave more attention to the physical determinants of dreaming than to the possible meanings of dreams. By the 1890s, prevailing scientific theories about the nature and function of dreams construed them as by-products of the random release of stored neural excitations, whereas popular theories about dreams invoked spiritual and super-

---

[1]*Studies in Hysteria*, an 1896 work for which Freud was second author to his then-mentor Josef Breuer, attracted considerable attention in the psychiatric community but attained nothing like the cross-disciplinary attention claimed eventually by *The Interpretation of Dreams*.

natural forces as explanatory principles. Freud embodied typical 19th-century rationalism in approaching his subject with the assumption that dreams are neither accidental discharge phenomena nor products of divine visitation; the scientific determinism of his day held that all natural phenomena are potentially explainable. In the wake of Galileo, Sir Isaac Newton, and Charles Darwin, all kinds of phenomena that previously had been considered essentially mysterious were revealing their secrets to the searchlight of scientific investigation.

FREUD'S PERSONAL MYTH

Freud proposed to examine a phenomenon that is perhaps even more daunting than the solar system, gravity, or the origin of the species and to make scientific sense of it. In this ambition, he took great pride, minimizing the fact that many of his conclusions about dreaming had been anticipated by others (see Parcifal-Charles, 1986; Sand, 1999). In fact, much of Freud's success in reaching a large and diverse community of readers can be attributed to the convincing way in which he presented himself as a fearless explorer, a conquering hero, an illusion-free archeologist of the depths of the mind. These romantic images were highly appealing to early 20th-century sensibilities, and Freud's own personal mythology about being a kind of scientific conquistador (see Breger, 2000; Sulloway, 1979) positioned him perfectly to appeal to such images. His childhood hero was Hannibal. He repeatedly cast himself as a conqueror defying great odds to vanquish enemies, a pioneering explorer defying Nature to withhold her secrets, a Man of Reason who could remain uncowed before the scathing glare of Religion and Convention. "We may leave on one side pietistic and mystical writers, who," he magnanimously declared, "are perfectly justified in remaining in occupation of what is left of the once wide domain of the supernatural so long as that field is not conquered by scientific explanation" (Freud, 1900/1971, p. 4).

Freud also had a knack for presenting himself as misunderstood, unappreciated, even persecuted, and there has always been a compelling disposition in Western culture to take David's side against Goliath's. Certainly, there was some truth to Freud's claim that his detractors could be vehement and *ad hominem* in their criticism (see Gay, 1988). And yet recent scholarship (e.g., Breger, 2000; Hale, 1995) has revealed that Freud frequently exaggerated the degree of rejection with which the scientific community greeted his pet theories. He seems to have been easily wounded and unforgiving of colleagues who reacted to his "discoveries" with anything less than unambivalent enthusiasm. He often viewed disagreement or questioning as equivalent to personal attack, and he avoided opportunities to converse thoughtfully with people of differing opinions.

When other scholars offered competing interpretations of phenomena Freud believed he had convincingly explained, he tended to dismiss them as victims of the defense mechanism of repression or, if he had previously seen them as insiders, as heretics. This attitude did not make him many friends outside his own circle of adherents. Perhaps some of this disposition not to spend his energy defending or rethinking his ideas in the light of others' objections involved the simple economics of managing his time: He was much more interested in pursuing his own thinking than in stopping to take account of others' critiques. However, Freud's hostility to those who refused to take in his arguments uncritically also seems to have reflected aspects of his personality and sense of personal mission.

Freud insisted on making psychoanalysis a *movement*, not just a theory. In addition, as is characteristic of movements, psychoanalysis tended to elicit either devotion or skepticism, with very little in between. When he received news that American experimental psychologists had found empirical support for some of his ideas, Freud was memorably unimpressed, taking the stance that his propositions had already been demonstrated to the satisfaction of anyone who would entertain them without defensiveness. In the long run, his indifference to and "splendid isolation" from the larger scientific community, a position embraced uncritically by many of those he inspired, contributed to the ignoring or marginalizing of valuable ideas that have emerged from the psychoanalytic tradition. Nevertheless, in the short run, the status of psychoanalysis as a movement—a radical rethinking of the status quo, a haven for truly courageous, unconventional cognoscenti—made it highly attractive to 20th-century intellectuals. Evidently, one way to attract attention to one's ideas is to present oneself as a lonely crusader for truth, heroically battling the entrenched and unimaginative establishment.

FREUD'S ORIGINALITY, CONVICTION, AND APPEAL TO 20TH-CENTURY IDEALS

Quite aside from Freud's penchant for personal legend-making, his ideas were uniquely innovative and challenging to existing Edwardian and Victorian habits of mind. To portray children as more sexually interested than popular sentiment would admit was a genuinely brave position to take in the late 19th century. To argue that women were as entitled as men to sexual gratification was a stance comparably alien to most of his peers. To claim that all human beings are inherently bisexual (an idea Freud appropriated from his once intimate and later rejected friend Wilhelm Fliess) was certainly jarring. To insist on the coexistence of hatred with love, selfishness with generosity, the enjoyment of depravity in the guise of righteous indignation—in short, to expose ambivalence in virtually every aspect of mental and emotional life—required a genuinely independent, intrepid intellect.

Although many of these ideas, contrary to the Freudian myth, had been considered by others, Freud's way of putting them together was unique.

When Freud became convinced of something that had been counterintuitive, to him as well as to others, he held on to it the way a dog grips a bone, daring competitors to try to take it away. There is something enviable and compelling about a writer who was so sure of so much that defied the "common sense" of his era and culture. Moreover, Freud's determination to produce a "science of the mind" was the kind of project that appealed to 20th-century appetites for grand theories and universal, far-reaching explanations of complex human dilemmas. Thinkers as diverse as Albert Einstein, Karl Marx, and Mahatma Gandhi extracted comparable reverence from significant segments of an intellectual community that was in love with controversial ideas that seemed both new and larger than life.

One aspect of the content and tone of Freud's work that had great appeal to his own generation and those that followed is his relative egalitarianism. This attitude is certainly discernible even in *The Interpretation of Dreams* and may account for its resonance to the literate public. It is a quality that we have not seen discussed much in the literature on psychoanalytic theory but one that was critical to the sensibilities of his era. Although often portrayed as either personally authoritarian or hopelessly petit-bourgeois, Freud was, at least as he presented himself in his writing, committed to the idea that ultimately, "civilized" people are no different from "savages," wealthy people struggle with the same conflicts that poor people do, and individuals living in the most far-flung and alien cultures can be found to struggle with the same human problems their European counterparts confront. For all of his much (and appropriately) criticized misunderstanding of women, Freud treated his female colleagues respectfully and encouraged women into the profession as equals to men. The tone of most of his writing about female patients accords them the dignity of people whose problems may be taken seriously rather than scorned as feminine weakness, an attitude all too common among Victorian-influenced physicians. He took children seriously as well, listening to them carefully at a time when they were famously advised to be seen and not heard.

FREUD'S WRITING STYLE

Freud was a brilliant stylist and a master of argument. Even in translation, his writing is eloquent, evocative, and persuasive. His case studies have been heralded as literary jewels. And not since Jesus has there been such a master of the use of the parable. Freud's analogies are so varied and arresting that the *Standard Edition* of his works has a whole index devoted to them. Numerous scholars have studied his manner of marshaling evidence for his propositions and concluded that his effectiveness in conveying his ideas has very little to do with their evidentiary status. We believe that his persuasiveness came as much from emotional attunement as from the clarity of his reasoning and the appealing inner consistency of his theory. That is, there is something in the way Freud wrote that kept his audience with him, that made them want him to be right.

Freud was a good teacher. He knew how to tell a joke. He sprinkled even his most scientific writing with homey and often droll illustrations and quips. He seems to have known how to meet the reader's need to be respected, to be understood, to feel directly addressed and embraced by the writer, to be given credit for intelligence and open-mindedness. He made complex ideas accessible. Unlike so many psychoanalysts who succeeded him, he could make difficult concepts understandable through prose of extraordinary beauty and lucidity. Consider, for example, his poetic phrasing for the subtle process by which someone suffering from clinical depression has identified with the love object who has rejected her: "the shadow of the object fell upon the ego" (Freud, 1917/1971, p. 249). Freud did not talk down to his readers or obscure his concepts in arcane jargon and complicated sentence structure.

FREUD'S PROLIFIC OUTPUT

Freud wrote a lot. From 1900 on, he turned out a major essay or book-length work at the rate of at least one a year. It is hard to be ignored when one is so prolific, when one applies a comprehensive theory to subject matter as diverse as human sexuality, creativity, destructiveness, loss, guilt, anxiety, and the tendency to repeat traumatic experiences. From considering the specific origins of hysterical psychopathology to speculating on the role of Moses in establishing monotheism, Freud instituted psychoanalysis as an all-purpose, general theory. Much to the irritation of those who saw him as a self-promoting ideologist, he made himself a force to be reckoned with for any educated person. When mainstream publications rejected his articles, he developed his own avenues for getting them into print, founding a journal and encouraging his colleagues to write and publish.

Perhaps it is also worth noting that Freud's writing was not limited to the formal. From at least his adolescence on, he spent literally hours each day on his correspondence. Volumes of these letters to friends and colleagues are extant; in fact, their sheer extensiveness is somewhat overwhelming, even to Freud scholars. Volumes more have been lost, some of them the victim of Freud's determination to leave his biographers in the dark about some aspects of his history. Decades before the Internet, Freud established a web of connections throughout Europe and the United States with people who felt affectionately and personally connected to him and to his movement. In contemporary parlance, he was good at networking. He cultivated people who could give him support, including financial support for his projects. These international connections not only contributed to the spread of psychoanalytic theory beyond Vienna but also played a role in saving Freud from the Nazis in the last years of his life, when Princess Marie Bonaparte arranged for his move to London.

FREUD'S ELEGANT THEORIZING

Many of the ideas that Freud pursued were already in the air of mid- to end-of-century Vienna (Ellenberger, 1970; Henry, 1993). Friedrich Nietzsche, for example, talked of how dammed up psychic energy could be contained until utilized and even transferred from one instinct to another. Like Freud, he envisioned the human mind as a system of drives and showed how every kind of feeling, opinion, or behavior was rooted in self-deception or an unconscious lie. Furthermore, he talked of sublimation, of repression, and of how the origin of civilization depended on renouncing gratification of our instincts. The familiarity factor undoubtedly helped a readier acceptance of Freud's theory by the educated public.

Freud's impact on psychology, however, was far greater than that of his like-minded contemporaries, in part because he was able to discern the common, underlying structure of a variety of everyday phenomena. Here his originality and creativity shone. Consider the apparently disparate appearance of psychiatric symptoms, dreams, jokes, forgetting, and slips of the tongue or pen. All have a surface content, which, according to Freud, effect a compromise between a repressed memory, event, or trauma, and a current experience. Surface and depth are connected by a chain of memories or associations that reveal the unconscious elements contained in the symptom, dream, or joke. The compromise formation represented in the surface content was said to be the result of a conflict between an unconscious sexual or aggressive impulse pressing for expression and the defensive processes (such as repression) that keep it at bay. In other words, psychological life was viewed as proceeding on two levels—one conscious, one unconscious, the two being quite different from one another and often in conflict. The manifest content presents clues to the underlying text in which the true explanation of the surface phenomenon is contained. Extending his theory across such a wide domain of human functioning gave it a strongly integrative thrust.

FREUD'S IMPACT COMPARED WITH THAT OF
A COMPARABLE COLLEAGUE

It is instructive to contrast the fate of Freud's ideas with those of Pierre Janet, a contemporary whose extraordinarily humane, creative, ambitious, and scholarly work was in many ways equivalent in scope and vision. Born only 3 years after his Viennese colleague, Janet outlived Freud by almost 10 years. Working at the Salpêtrière hospital in France where Freud was inspired by Jean-Martin Charcot, Janet published careful and moving case histories of patients with hysterical neuroses; wrote major works on philosophy and psychology; and even shared some nonclinical interests with Freud, such as his fascination with the origins of religion and culture. It was Janet who coined the term *subconscious*. In recent years, scholars in trauma and dissociation (e.g., Herman, 1992) have tended to regard Janet's ideas about those conditions as more accurate than were Freud's. Yet few contemporary intellectuals even know Janet's name.

Ellenberger (1970), while documenting Janet's influence, spent several paragraphs on the riddle of his relative obscurity, speculatively attributing it to his lack of an official post or ward at the Salpêtrière that would have provided regular audiences of medical students; to his close association with Charcot, whose work was generally devalued after his death in 1893; to the fact that Janet's lectures on psychotherapy, given in 1909 and 1910, were seen as dated in the changed climate after World War I; and to his temperamental reserve, especially the fact that "any kind of proselytism was absolutely alien to him" (p. 408). Given that Freud also lacked a prominent institutional training role, was also associated with Charcot, and published his main teachings on psychotherapy at roughly the same time, Freud's talent for proselytizing, along with the other qualities we have described, must be given the most weight in understanding his exponentially greater impact.

FREUD'S WILLINGNESS TO CHANGE AND CORRECT HIS THEORIES

An additional, intriguing component of Freud's success is the humility that coexisted with the self-importance and stubbornness we have already noted under the topic of his myth making.[2] Albeit prickly when others questioned his theories, Freud was his own harshest critic. He often announced that he had been wrong previously, or that he had developed a better way of accounting for something than he had in a prior work. Something about this ongoing revision of his theory made his admirers feel a vitality, an inquisitiveness, a preference for painful truths over earlier, more comforting illusions. Freud's willingness to change his ideas when the data failed to support

---

[2]A Freudian would say that the coexistence of great humility and great arrogance in Freud illustrates the psychoanalytic principle that individuals are psychologically organized around particular *dimensions* of behavior. For example, obsessional people are preoccupied with the issue of control and tend to have areas of both overcontrol and dyscontrol; histrionic people are preoccupied with gender and power and tend to have both seductiveness and sexual inhibition; narcissistic people alternate between feeling superior to and inferior to others. What appear to be incompatible traits are actually coexisting ends of a continuum that is salient in a given individual.

them certainly enhanced his reputation as a clear-eyed, open-minded scientist, a man who put knowledge above his narcissistic investment in prior beliefs.

In an age captivated by the myth of scientific progress, the atmosphere that Freud and his colleagues emitted of an ongoing project of discovery, application, revision, reapplication, and evaluation rang true to an intellectual ideal of open-minded inquiry and hypothesis testing. And Freud was, personally and in his written citations, generous in his praise to those of his close colleagues who contributed new ideas to the psychoanalytic effort—at least when he felt that those ideas were not inconsistent with his own. The fact that he ostracized and then ignored the theories of erstwhile intimates whose work began to drift too far from what he considered the sexual and oedipal bedrock of psychoanalytic theory was less evident to outsiders than the more welcoming, inclusive tone he tended to take in his published writing.

FREUD'S CASE STUDY AND FREE ASSOCIATION METHODS

As in any domain of science, one needs an instrument or technique with which to explore the phenomenon of interest. For Freud that technique—in his mind akin to the biologist's microscope—was free association in the presence of the analyst's neutral, evenly hovering attention. In this way, clinical practice became an excellent source of ideas, hypotheses, and clinical propositions. Psychoanalysis offered special conditions that allowed for observation of fantasies, wishes, fears, and all sorts of psychopathology that people did not normally share even with good friends or family. Psychoanalytic therapy remains a fertile laboratory for generating ideas about human nature.

Freud's focus on clinical phenomena in individuals led to an emphasis in psychoanalysis on case studies that brought life to scientific abstractions. Freud's cases have been a source of people's fascination with his work and have undoubtedly been an important source of his impact. One advantage, among many others, of case studies is their ability to present psychological phenomena in context. For example, to understand a dream in the context of a person's life, as we illustrate next, is quite different from studying it as an isolated, disembodied psychological variable.

THE PERSONAL AND THERAPEUTIC RELEVANCE
OF FREUD'S THEORY OF DREAMS

A final and critical feature of the appeal of Freud's writing about dreams was its practical applicability to the nascent professional hope of developing therapies that would reliably relieve neurotic suffering. At the turn of the 20th century, there was a growing optimism in psychiatric circles that the debilitating and thus far treatment-resistant "neuroses" could be significantly mitigated with enough attention to the unconscious processes that might be creating and maintaining them. In the nosology of the day, fathered by the preeminent psychiatrist Emil Kraepelin, the neurotic conditions included the hysterical disorders (dissociative reactions, conversions, and neurasthenic or somatizing tendencies), obsessions, compulsions, phobias, and nonpsychotic depressions—not an insignificant catalogue of human miseries. Any procedure that held some promise to relieve these conditions aroused great excitement.

Before we delve into the clinical use of Freudian dream theory and its more contemporary relatives, we give an account of Freud's central ideas about dream interpretation. First, we apply them to the dream of a friend of one of us, a man we call Jack, who described a dream and its associations that Freud would have found perfectly suited for demonstrating his theory. This exercise is intended to help the reader get an immediate sense of why Freud's dream theory continues to have such wide impact on practicing clinicians and the general public.

Jack's Dream

Jack, 29, had been married just 3 months previously to Linda, 21, a very attractive woman with an hourglass figure—the kind that attracts rapt attention from most men. Jack and Linda were visiting from out of town at the home of one of us, when Jack (in Linda's absence) spontaneously related the following dream:

> Linda and I are in our apartment, and Linda is doing a belly dance in the nude. I am concerned because the shades aren't drawn, and there is a keyhole in the door through which someone could peep. Linda is completely unconcerned, laughs at my worry and continues to dance.
>
> To show me that there is no one in the hallway, Linda goes to the door, opens it, and sure enough, there is a man there, who, it would seem, has been watching all along. She slams the door and tells me that there is someone in the hallway on the other side of the door. I go to the door, open it, and try to push the man away, but I can't manage to get the door closed.

Associations to the Dream

Jack was asked to say whatever came to his mind about the dream— that is, to associate as freely as possible to it. (Freud considered associations to be the key to arriving at the true or "latent" meaning of a dream.) Linda, he said, loves to dance naked around the house. In addition, she frequently tends to think that she may have left the key to their apartment door in the outside lock. So, before she goes to bed, and while in her nightclothes, she goes to the door to see if the key is in the lock. She then opens the door to check, a practice that annoys Jack and makes him anxious because she is in her nightclothes, and someone could be there.

Jack was then asked what came to mind about the man at the door. He thought the man was a salesman, roughly 30–35 years old. He reminded Jack of his father, who he felt was interfering with his life in various ways. Jack's father is the prime salesman for a business that he owns and presides over.

The Day Residue

Another feature that Freud considered of some importance to understanding a dream is what he called the *day residue*, the events of the previous day that may have stimulated the dream. Jack explained that he and Linda had been in New York City the day before he had had the dream. In their hotel lobby, Linda had been counting out a considerable amount of money from her wallet while facing the lobby, where several people were nearby. Jack had made her turn around and count it more discreetly. Later in the day, they had been on a Manhattan street and had wanted to take a bus for which they needed exact change. Linda had opened her purse, taken out her wallet, and begun counting her money while facing the street. Jack had gotten worried that her purse or wallet could be snatched by someone who might be watching them, and he had asked her to close the purse and count her money in a more cautious way. Linda had seemed oblivious to, and annoyed by, his concerns.

Freud's Theory of Dreams

For Freud, the *manifest content* is the dream as remembered and related. Underlying the manifest content is the *latent content*, which is disguised by a mental function that Freud anthropomorphized as the *dream censor* (after 1923, he subsumed this function under the concept of the superego). The censoring process was understood to protect the dreamer from awakening and becoming aware of the problematic unconscious content or conflict. It is for this reason that Freud considered dreams to be the guardians of sleep. The process of disguising the dream is known as the *dream-work*, which occurs through *symbolization*, *displacement*, and *condensation*. The latent content was said to express, in disguise, a *childhood memory* involving the expression of libidinal energy—such as a repressed sexual wish, often one of Oedipal origin. Among the many events of the day, the dream "chooses" one that shows some relationship to the childhood memory, which Freud called the *day residue*, as previously noted. According to Freud, then, the dream has one foot in the present and one in the past. Three levels of *regression* take place in the dream at the same time: from the conscious to the unconscious, from the present to childhood, and from the level of everyday language to that of symbolic and pictorial representations.

Although some of these ideas about dreams had been suggested by others, Freud introduced five innovations: (a) the distinction between the manifest and latent content of a dream; (b) its being lived in both the present and the past simultaneously; (c) the manifest content as a distortion of the latent content, resulting from the dream-work of the censor; (d) the use of free association to analyze the dream; and (e) dream interpretation as a tool of psychotherapy (Ellenberger, 1970).

Dream Interpretation

With this much theory in hand, let us go back to Jack's dream and consider its structure and possible meaning. Focusing for the moment on the manifest dream only, Jack seems to be anxious about his wife's exhibitionistic ways and her indifference to his concern about them. Specifically, Jack does not want others to see Linda dancing in the nude. There is the threat of another man watching Linda and forcing his way into the apartment—a realization of Jack's worst fears. Jack, newly married to an attractive, uninhibited woman, seems concerned that another man may gain access to her and that he will be helpless to prevent it.

As an aside, with the development of ego psychology and its enhanced respect for conscious and adaptive processes has come a greater interest in the manifest material of dreams and their conscious import. In light of ongoing clinical experience and empirical research on dreaming, contemporary psychoanalytic therapists have questioned many of Freud's conclusions about dreams, but they remain convinced of Freud's position that dreams are meaningful and understandable (see Greenberg & Pearlman, 1999). There is good empirical support (Fisher & Greenberg, 1996) for the existence of a relationship between the manifest content of dreams and the dreamer's current life concerns. Dreams may be seen as an effort at problem solving, for example, which in this case would be Jack's effort to get rid of his imagined male competitor.

Although there is much material of interest in Jack's manifest dream, it is the latent content that Freud considered most telling. To gain access to the latent meaning, interpreters rely on the dreamer's free associations and whatever else is known about him or her. Consider the process of symbolization, which Freud viewed as the censor's effort to disguise the dream. An apartment or house is a symbol that Freud saw as frequently standing for a woman's body. The door and/or the keyhole, then, would symbolize her vagina into which a man is trying to intrude. In other words, Jack's deeper concern is the danger of another man's possessing his wife sexually. Supporting this way of understanding the dream is Jack's preoccupation with Linda's exposing her purse or wallet (common symbols for the uterine cavity, according to Freud) and its contents to others in the hotel lobby or on the street. Jack is afraid and upset that Linda, in her naiveté, may be offering herself sexually to another man.

Who might this man be? In his associations, Jack said that the man at the door reminded him of his father. His father, however, is 60, and this man is 30–35 years old. Extrapolating backward, we note that Jack would have been between ages 1 and 6 at the time that his father was in his early 30s. Therefore, the intruder/competitor could be understood as representing his father at the time that Jack was in the Freudian Oedipal stage of 3–6. What we know about Linda is that she has many of Jack's mother's characteristics and even appearance. Furthermore, Jack married her at the same age (29) that his father had married his mother who, in turn, was the same age as Linda when she married Jack's father. Jack was the youngest of three children and the only boy, doted on by his mother. According to Freud's theory, the day residue of the events in New York connected with the struggles of Jack's repressed but not resolved Oedipal complex when he was in competition with his father for sexual possession of his mother. As much as he tried, and as intrusive as he found his father, he could not "close the door" on him and keep him away from his mother. Freud would have said that the guise of the 30-plus-year-old salesman is a displacement for Jack's father and that Linda is a displacement for his mother.

Mindful that this was not a therapy session, the listener in this case simply commented to Jack, "It appears that you are afraid of losing Linda to another man." Jack nodded in agreement and remarked that the comment immediately brought to mind something else that had happened the day before as he and Linda had been strolling in New York. He had felt that Linda was wearing a sweater that was too tight. He had noticed how much men turned to look at her and had felt that if he did not show that she belonged to him, someone else might step in. Therefore, he had grabbed her close to him by putting his arm around her quite forcefully. Linda had been annoyed, feeling that this was an unnecessary gesture.

Freud would have regarded Jack's response to this one-line dream interpretation as confirmation of the correctness of the analysis. He held that the criterion for judging whether an interpretation is valid is not the dreamer's agreement with it, but whether he or she spontaneously generates subsequent associations that are confirmatory to the theme of the analysis. As Freud believed that the ultimate instigator of every dream is a wish (a generalization not well supported by recent empirical investigations, incidentally, though probably applicable to many dreams; see Hartmann, 1998), he would have assumed that Jack's dream was nicely fulfilling his wish to be *right* in his arguments with Linda about her tendencies to expose herself and her resources. In the dream, there *was* danger, and Linda's cavalier attitude was demonstrated to be mistaken. Freud would also have regarded as significant the fact that Jack chose to relate this particular dream to someone else. Contemporary clinical practice in the psychoanalytic tradition (e.g., Altman, 1975; Bonime, 1986; Delaney, 1993; Reiser, 1997) puts considerable emphasis on the communicative aspect of dreams and the reporting of them to the psychotherapist.

Kate's Dream

The next dream was told in therapy, giving us access to more information about the inner life of the dreamer. The patient, Kate, was a 30-year-old graduate student in treatment for depressive symptoms. She had been referred by her husband, a reputedly brilliant law student who, it was quickly becoming apparent, was quite abusive to her. He was newly in psychoanalysis and had insisted, with the fervor of the new enthusiast, that she "get analyzed." Kate's mother was described as critical and controlling, and her father as an ineffectual alcoholic; the two also seemed poorly matched. The mother had converted to the father's Roman Catholicism and was seen by her daughter as "holier than the Pope." Although raised as a strict Catholic, Kate herself was agnostic and religiously unobservant. She was the oldest of five siblings, for whom she had been given much responsibility. By the time Kate was a teenager, one younger sister had died from leukemia, and a brother had died in a car accident. The family had never mourned their deaths. Kate had been in treatment only a few weeks when she identified the following as a "fragment" of a larger dream that she could not remember: Someone was smashing religious statues on the floor.

The Day Residue

Kate had had a difficult time at the dentist on the day when she had this dream. She had had to endure a procedure involving the replacement of a bridge that took much longer than expected, and to her embarrassment, she had suffered a panic attack while in the dentist's chair. On telling her husband about it, she was shamed further by his patronizing response that once she was well enough analyzed, she would not have reactions like that. When asked how she had felt about this interaction, she protested her husband's good intentions and denied any irritation at his lack of empathy.

Associations to the Dream

Kate first commented that there was something about the breaking of religious statues that was equivalent in her mind to "all hell breaking loose." She went on to remember a time when she had been upset that her sister had knocked a then beloved religious statue of her own off a dresser, "and I got lectured at for not being tolerant of younger children." Then she recalled an incident in which a different sister had knocked over some vases, "and I got blamed for not watching her more carefully." These associations led to a general exploration of her chronic feelings of guilt and responsibility as a child and of her constant fear of her mother's arbitrary and unpredictable tendency to blame her for anything that went wrong. Toward the end of the session, she was becoming aware of some feelings of resentment about her husband's ubiquitously critical attitude; she felt that, like her mother, he was a "convert" to a "religion" (psychoanalysis) that he intended to push on her whether or not it suited her own needs or appealed to her sensibilities.

Dream Interpretation

Much could be said about this dream, despite its brevity. Freud would have seen in it Kate's wish to attack her mother's cherished religious images, and by extension, her mother and any similarly critical love object/competitor. Certainly, the constant criticism from her husband was reawakening in Kate many of the feelings she had had as a little girl. His messages, on the theme that she was not grown up enough to avoid childish reactions like panic at the dentist, replicated frequent childhood injunctions to be more mature. Kate had protected herself from knowledge of her hostile wish by displacing the crime to an anonymous "someone." Her therapist's understanding of her probable feelings of guilt over normal aggressive attitudes toward her siblings—guilt that was exacerbated by their deaths, in the context of her own inculcation with a sense of responsibility—made the therapist wary of plunging immediately into speculations about disowned aggression. It was also likely that Kate's hostility toward zealots and judgmental authorities extended to the clinician, but an explicit interpretation of her unconscious wish to destroy the therapist would probably have been experienced as an attack, even if it had been right.

Among other things, the therapist was attuned to the probability that Kate was experiencing her therapy as an attempt at conversion similar to her mother's efforts to turn her into a "good Catholic girl." Although outwardly compliant with the demands of her role as patient (just as she had been outwardly compliant with her mother's religious strictures), Kate was, in this early phase of treatment, talking a lot about her distaste for orthodoxy. The idols that were being destroyed in the dream, the therapist suspected, represented icons of psychoanalysis (in fact, in the consulting room, a small bust of Freud was visible from the client's chair).

The therapist was also wondering whether Kate's uncharacteristic response to the invasion of her mouth by the dentist was a displacement of her panic about "opening up" to psychoanalytic intrusion. The therapist therefore chose to focus, toward the end of the session in which the dream was reported, on Kate's fears of all hell breaking loose because she was newly in psychotherapy. When Kate gave some confirmatory associations to the effect that she was afraid that, as with the dentist, she would become regressed and disoriented, the therapist went on to comment empathically on her self-protective resistance to complying, at least internally, with authorities, religious or otherwise. Kate was told she would probably find herself with mixed feelings about whether to go along with what she assumed to be the therapist's orthodoxies.

Kate seemed to feel relieved by this choice of emphasis. Although the session ended before she generated further associations to the therapist's interpretive comments, her relaxation in the subsequent session, in which she reported having for the first time confronted her husband about his unhelpful tendencies to criticize her, suggested to the therapist that their work together on the dream had made her feel less "pathologized," braver, and more entitled to express appropriate aggression even in the absence of the direct interpretation of it. The communication to the therapist here of both her wish to attack orthodoxy and her fear that if she did so, she would suffer devastating attacks herself, was the primary therapeutic concern.

Before leaving the topic of Freud's dream theory, we note that both academic and clinical interest in it continues unabated (e.g., Hartmann, 1998; Hill, 1996; Sloane, 1990). Perhaps most innovative have been efforts to correlate brain structures and states with elements of the theory (e.g., Solms, 1997). Solms (2000) concluded that recent neuropsychological work, while not definitive, suggests that Freud was on the right track. Apparently, dreaming is obliterated by damage to only two brain structures: one responsible for visuospatial perception and cognition (the one creating the manifest dream) and the other for instigating goal-seeking behavior and appetitive interactions with the world (the one contributing to the latent content). About the latter, Solms remarked, "No single brain system comes closer in its functional properties than this one to the 'libido' of Freudian dream theory" (p. 619). In brief, there is a "close link between brain structures responsible for dreaming and those responsible for biological emotions and motivations" (p. 619).

OUR ADVICE TO ASPIRING ACADEMICS

Despite his remarkable public relations coup, Freud paid an eventual price for the strategies we have discussed. Although he succeeded in evoking an idealization of his theories, psychoanalysis later became associated, in both public and academic realms, with smugness and dogmatism. Because this fate has not befallen all provocative and seminal writers, it cannot be ascribed entirely to ordinary scientific processes of questioning and rejecting flawed ideas. Like all idealizations, enthusiasm for Freudian theory soon begged a compensatory devaluation, something from which psychoanalysis as a scholarly discipline continues to suffer. The following advice to authors striving to influence the field, based on our study of the reasons for Freud's success, should therefore be taken with a dose of caution about using Freud uncritically as a role model for making an impact.

- Write about something inherently interesting to a wide audience.
- Keep that audience in mind, and treat it with respect.
- Present yourself as heroically challenging established conventions and ideas.

- Perfect your writing style: Keep it clear, avoid obfuscation, and seek beauty and elegance in your turns of phrase.
- Write copiously, and don't let criticism or rejected manuscripts reduce your spirits or output.
- Cultivate supporters who publicize and expand on your work; in other words, network!
- Be creative and original, even while drawing on the work of others.
- Develop an instrument or technique that allows you to view behavior from a new angle.
- Stretch your theory to encompass and account for as wide a range of phenomena as possible.
- Admit your errors and areas of ignorance, always being prepared to modify your theory.
- Give lavish credit to your collaborators.
- Use case studies to illustrate your work, including examples from your own life.
- Be scientific while keeping in mind that this can mean using a variety of methods.

REFERENCES

Altman, L. L. (1975). *The dream in psychoanalysis* (rev. ed.). New York: International Universities Press.

Bonime, W. (1986). Collaborative dream interpretation. *Journal of the American Academy of Psychoanalysis, 14*, 15–26.

Breger, L. (2000). *Freud: Darkness in the midst of vision: An analytical biography.* New York: Wiley.

Delaney, G. (Ed.). (1993). *New directions in dream interpretation.* Albany: State University of New York Press.

Ellenberger, H. (1970). *The discovery of the unconscious.* New York: Basic Books.

Fisher, S., & Greenberg, R. P. (1996). *Freud scientifically appraised: Testing the theories and the therapy.* New York: Wiley.

Freud, S. (1971). The interpretation of dreams (J. Strachey, Trans.). In *Standard edition* (Vol. 4). London: Hogarth Press. (Original work published 1900)

Freud, S. (1971). Mourning and melancholia (J. Strachey, Trans.). In *Standard edition* (Vol. 14, pp. 243–258). London: Hogarth Press. (Original work published 1917)

Gay, P. (1988). *Freud: A life for our time.* New York: Norton.

Greenberg, R., & Pearlman, C. A. (1999). The interpretation of dreams: A classic revisited. *Psychoanalytic Dialogues, 9*, 749–765.

Hale, N. G. (1995). *The rise and crisis of psychoanalysis in the United States: Freud and the Americans, 1917–1985.* New York: Oxford University Press.

Hartmann, E. (1998). *Dreams and nightmares: The new theory on the origin and meaning of dreams.* New York: Plenum Press.

Henry, M. (1993). *The genealogy of psychoanalysis.* Palo Alto, CA: Stanford University Press.

Herman, J. L. (1992). *Trauma and recovery: The aftermath of violence—From domestic abuse to political terror.* New York: Basic Books.

Hill, C. E. (1996). *Working with dreams in psychotherapy.* New York: Guilford Press.

Parcifal-Charles, N. (1986). *The dream, 4000 years of theory and practice.* West Cornwall, CT: Locust Hill Press.

Reiser, M. (1997). The art and science of dream interpretation: Isakower revisited. *Journal of the American Psychoanalytic Association, 45,* 891–906.

Sand, R. (1999). The interpretation of dreams: Freud and the Western dream tradition. *Psychoanalytic Dialogues, 9,* 725–748.

Sloane, P. (1990). *Psychoanalytic understanding of the dream.* Northvale, NJ: Jason Aronson.

Solms, M. (1997). *The neuropsychology of dreams.* Mahwah, NJ: Erlbaum.

Solms, M. (2000). Freudian dream theory today. *The Psychologist, 13,* 618–619.

Sulloway, F. J. (1979). *Freud, biologist of the mind: Beyond the psychoanalytic legend.* New York: Basic Books.

5

ALFRED BINET'S CONTRIBUTIONS AS A PARADIGM FOR IMPACT IN PSYCHOLOGY

ROBERT J. STERNBERG AND LINDA JARVIN

Alfred Binet was one of the most influential psychologists in the history of psychology. An updated edition of his test of intelligence, the version known in the United States as the Stanford–Binet–IV, is still one of the most widely used intelligence tests. Binet's ideas about intelligence also have given rise to other related tests of intelligence, such as the Wechsler series. And Binet's ideas about the modifiability of intelligence are still influential in numerous programs for developing intellectual skills.

The remainder of this chapter is divided into four sections. First, we provide a brief biography of Binet. Second, we discuss his work in the field of education and cognitive assessment. Third, we review what we believe to be his most outstanding and lasting contributions. Finally, we consider why these contributions were so influential.

A BRIEF BIOGRAPHY

Alfred Binet was born in the French town of Nice on July 11, 1857. According to his daughter Madeleine (Avanzini, 1974), Alfred was a bright child who succeeded so well in school that his mother decided to send him away to the capital when he was barely 12 years old, in order that he might study at one of the best schools of the country. In his own words, Binet was "born to work," and he increased his efficiency by maintaining many fruitful, and often interdisciplinary, professional collaborations. Throughout his career, Binet's prolific scientific production was complemented with more literary work on famous writers and artists, as well as with the creation of nine plays written in collaboration with André de Lorde.

Binet studied many diverse topics, some largely unnoticed (Siegler, 1992), and a chronological account of his bibliography shows that his research interests included but were not limited to perception, hallucinations, reasoning, animal magnetism, hysteria, mental images, fetishism in love, moral responsibility, court witnessing, double consciousness, movement, inhibition, language, audition, chess players, memory, physiology, anatomy, graphology, intellectual exhaustion, craniometry, suggestibility, pedagogy, intelligence, literary creation, retardation and academic underachievement, the soul, abnormality, mental alienation, and measurement of intelligence. A complete bibliography can be found in Avanzini's (1974) collection of Binet writings or in Zuza (1948). To simplify, one can distinguish three phases in his career as a psychologist, although his publications prove that they were overlapping rather than strictly separate (Delay, 1958): psychopathology, experimental psychology, and child psychology.

French psychology in the second half of the 19th century was mainly focused on psychopathology, and Binet's early interests were not an exception. In 1891 Binet obtained a position in the Physiological Psychology Laboratory at the Sorbonne University in Paris, where his research focus switched from clinical to physiological and experimental psychology (Robinson, 1977–1978). The main contemporary influences in psychophysiology and experimental psychology were German, namely Wilhelm Wundt, whose laboratory in Leipzig served as a model for the one created in Paris. Like many researchers of his time, Binet decided to follow in the footsteps of the neurologist Paul Broca and explored intelligence through phrenology, believing that there is a direct relation between the size of the cranium and a person's level of intelligence (see, e.g., Binet, 1901; Gould, 1981). Binet also used hypnosis. He eventually abandoned both hypnosis and phrenology and pursued the exploration of the human psyche through new tests and puzzles that he initially developed for and tested on his two daughters (Binet, 1890, 1903). As was the case with Jean Piaget several years later, most of his theoretical ideas on cognitive development sprung from the observation of his own children.

After a first period devoted to psychopathology and a second centered on experimental psychology, a third period can be distinguished in Binet's professional life, mainly dedicated to child psychology. The starting of this period can be dated to 1905, the year in which Binet and Theodore Simon published an article on the diagnosis of abnormality and the year of the opening of a laboratory of experimental pedagogy, where Binet worked closely with teachers. It was during this period that Binet made his major contributions to the study of academic underachievement and also to psychometrics. In addition to these contributions, a further major contribution of Binet to child psychology was the view that children are not, as previously thought, miniature adults but rather obey different rules of cognitive functioning (Zazzo, 1958). On October 30, 1911, Binet passed away unexpectedly at the age of 54. The rest of this chapter focuses on the important contributions Binet made to educational psychology, as applied to both normal and low-functioning students.

THEORY AND RESEARCH IN THE FIELDS OF EDUCATION AND COGNITIVE ASSESSMENT

Binet's first writing on pedagogy appeared in 1898, in a volume titled *Mental Fatigue*. Among Binet's contributions to educational psychology, *Mental Fatigue* (Binet & Henri, 1898) can be seen as a manifesto, and *Modern Ideas on Children* (Binet, 1909) as his testament. In these volumes, he criticized the widespread lack of a rigorous experimental method and stressed the fact that pedagogical choices were all too often arbitrary or based on hastily collected empirical results without any theoretical framework (Reuchlin, 1957–1958). We focus our description of Binet's research on two main topics: the use of an experimental method to investigate learning related issues and the development of a cognitive assessment tool, the Metric Intelligence Scale.

Applying the Experimental Method to Educational Psychology

Binet's contribution to educational psychology was not so much a new theory of pedagogy as it was the use of new, experimental methods in the field of educational research. Whereas much work at the time focused on the "moral effects" of teaching, Binet, deeming it more appropriate for rigorous scientific study, focused on instruction, that is, on all that would be taught by the teacher and learned by the student. In pedagogy as well as in psychology, it is imperative to observe and experiment (Binet, 1904, cited in Avanzini, 1974).

In 1898, Binet and Victor Henri published *Mental Fatigue*, the first volume in a collection of books[1] created to promote recent research in psychology relevant to educators. Their aim was not to "reform the old pedagogy" but rather to "create a new pedagogy" (p. 1). This new pedagogy must be based on observation and experimentation. In *Mental Fatigue*, Binet and Henri

---

[1]*Pedagogy and Psychology* collection.

gave a first description of the experimental method as applied to education. Let us look at their description of the method and an illustrative example of its application.

Binet and Henri distinguished two types of educational experimentation: experiments conducted in the laboratory and experiments carried out in the classroom. They felt that the researcher ought to start with experiments of the first kind, studying processes in detail and at length with volunteer participants. Most methodological problems could be solved that way, and the important research questions established. On the basis of these first results, a practical plan for continuing experimentation in school settings could be elaborated. The plan was that experimentation in schools should not disrupt the class for more than 15 minutes, and a given classroom should not be visited more than twice a month. If one respects these two conditions, the authors saw little reason for teachers not to cooperate, and data could thus be collectively gathered and subsequently analyzed on the researcher's return to the laboratory.

An illustration of an experimental investigation by Binet and his collaborators is that of mental fatigue (Binet & Henri, 1898). The question of mental fatigue, of whether the workload imposed on children in school was too heavy and exhausting for students, was first raised in the French Academy of Medicine in 1886. At around the same time, politicians in Germany debated the same issue and commissioned a psychologist to investigate the phenomenon. The phenomenon of mental fatigue had important potential consequences on several educational choices, such as the length of instructional programs and exams; the age limit for certain programs and exams; and the way time was divided among instruction, free periods, physical education, and sleep.

In *Mental Fatigue*, Binet and Henri (1898) gave a slightly ironic account of the manner in which the issue was debated in the French Academy of Medicine: The questions were raised in very general terms, and doctors expressed their opinions without providing any evidence or even referring to relevant experimental results. Binet and Henri pointed out that the only means to establish that mental fatigue is widespread and that measures to reduce the phenomenon should be taken is through experimental investigation. Binet and his collaborators thus proceeded to measure the impact of intellectual activity (i.e., an activity involving mainly concentration, attention, and, in their words, "intelligence"—as opposed to a physical activity involving mainly muscular effort) on various physiological and psychological characteristics. Physiological measures included heart rate and heart rhythm, blood circulation, quantity of blood in the brain, blood pressure, body temperature, breathing rhythms, muscular strength, and digestive functions. The psychological effects of mental fatigue were explored in two settings, first in the laboratory and then in the classroom. The main experimental results showed that mental fatigue decreased mental activity and reduced mnemonic capacities. This effect, however, varied depending on the duration of the sustained effort and on the number and the length of pauses during the activity. Indeed, research studies conducted in school settings showed that the moment of the day during which students were assessed had an effect on their performance (performance levels decrease as the day goes on) and that a break for physical activities did not, contrary to what was generally thought, restore performance levels. These results were obtained with both language- and math-based assessments, by both Binet and colleagues working in other countries.

Binet and Henri (1898) drew three main conclusions from this body of research: (a) No intellectual effort can be undertaken without affecting the organism; (b) during the first 30 minutes of the effort, there is an increase in heart beat, rhythm, blood pressure, concentration, speed of execution, and so on, but when the effort is sustained for more than an hour a general decrease can be noted; and (c) the distinctive trait that differentiates mental fatigue from nonpathological weariness is the amount of rest needed to repair it. Whereas "normal" weariness will be overcome with sleep and rest, mental fatigue will not be restored as easily.

The above account serves to illustrate what Binet defined as experimental psychology. According to Binet, the ideal for scientific method must be "a collaboration between theory and experimentation," that is, a sustained effort to collect facts firsthand rather than to gather them from readings (Binet & Simon, 1908, p. 1). Modern pedagogy is a positive science insofar as it seeks to furnish proofs of what it advocates. Binet advocated that all experimental research in education should follow four steps: statement of a hypothesis, collection of facts, interpretation of data, and replication. The hypotheses are often provided by "old pedagogy." For the data gathering, Binet stressed that the use of complicated instruments should be avoided. The best collection tool is the one that requires the least knowledge on behalf of the person administering the instrument. Binet also stressed that the quality and depth of the investigation count more than the number of investigations. Quantitative data must be gathered with care, preferably using statistics such as rank or majority. The last step of a study should always be a replication of one's findings.

Binet's will to apply a scientifically sound study method to pedagogical issues also brought him to develop new statistical tools and to make a systematic use of control groups. Among the statistical inventions were the use of rank correlation coefficients to investigate the relations between academic results and socioeconomic background.

Cognitive Assessment

Binet's main research contribution to the field of educational psychology was arguably in the area of cognitive assessment. Starting at the beginning of the 20th century, Binet showed great interest in the study of "abnormal children" (Binet & Simon, 1907), and the Free Society for the Psychological Study of Children, of which he became the president in 1902, pushed the French government to start evaluating students with the aim of early identification of abnormal children and the provision of special education for them. In 1904, Binet was officially appointed by the Minister of Public Education in France to a commission charged with devising a means of identifying retarded school children. It was based on this interest in abnormal children that Binet created the Metric Intelligence Scale during the first 6 months of 1905 (Avanzini, 1974), with the help of his doctoral student Theodore Simon (Minton, 1998). By means of this scale, children with learning impairments, who nevertheless were thought to be able to profit from education, were selected and put into special education classes. The first "perfectioning class" was opened in 1907, and two more followed that year. Although he himself was convinced that abnormality could to some extent be overcome, Binet always stressed the importance of empirically assessing the correctness of his ideas and, although mainly working on applied problems, he never forgot strict experimental methodology. Binet insisted that, before any legislative measures are taken to make these special education classes available for all retarded children, their positive impact must be assessed experimentally.

Before further describing the Metric Intelligence Scale and its most widespread American adaptation, the Stanford–Binet Scale of Intelligence, let us first go back to Binet's theory of abnormal children and the need for special education classes, which in turn led to the need for psychometric assessment. In their 1907 publication *Abnormal Children*, Binet and Simon developed a theory of mental retardation, taking a stand different from the two most widespread stands at the time. The first stand was based on Jean Etienne Esquirol's distinction between the idiot and the dement. The idiot is wholly unable to acquire any new knowledge, and mental development thus essentially is impossible. The second stand is that the abnormal child suffers from mental retardation, with a level of functioning of a normal but much younger individual. Binet rejected the first stand because he believed in the perfectibility of the human mind. He rejected the latter stand because it was based on superficial and only partly accurate observations.

Binet believed that the implications and impact of an acquisition are linked to the age at which the acquisition is made. Thus, learning to read at age 6 does not have the same implications as learning to read at age 12. What characterizes the abnormal child is notable imbalance, for even though there might be an important delay in the acquisition of certain aptitudes, the development of other aptitudes (cognitive and somatic) may be normal. The abnormal child who learns to read at age 12, for example, has a wider vocabulary and more extrascholastic interests than does the normal 6-year-old. According to Binet and Simon, the abnormal child is not a normal child who has either stopped developing or who has slowed down in development, but rather a child with a different developmental pattern. This pattern is unbalanced, with some aspects identical to those of normal children, and others, different. It is this lack of balance between the different developmental aspects that constitutes the abnormality. Abnormality can be characterized by three major components: a global developmental delay, the inequality of this delay depending on the aspects measured, and the resulting lack of coordination in the functioning of the mind. It is precisely because abnormality is seen as a different developmental pattern, and not as mere retardation, that special education is possible and also is needed.

The rationale for the Metric Intelligence Scale devised by Binet and Simon, as well as the scale itself and the guidelines for its administration, was published in 1905. The scale was based on the principle that by sampling a large number of heterogeneous situations or examples of cognitive functioning, one will obtain a better picture of a person's general level of intelligence than by studying a smaller number of mental operations in depth. This notion of sampling justifies why several measures can be added. One must keep in mind that Binet's conception of intelligence as higher order processes was novel, and almost provocative, at the time. Before Binet, most experimental psychologists, following Wundt's example, thought that intelligence was best explored by studying lower order, very simple, processes. Binet not only decided to explore higher order cognitive functions but to do so with the same experimental rigor that had previously been applied to simpler processes.

Binet was also a pioneer in postulating the existence of a unified general intelligence, when most of his predecessors and contemporaries believed in separate mental functions. The Metric Intelligence Scale contained 30 tests, some of them expressly created for the scale and some adaptations of existing cognitive tests, namely those developed by the French physicists Alfred Blin and Robert Damaye (Minton, 1998). Binet defined tests as "quick experiments aimed at assessing children's faculties" (Binet & Simon, 1905, pp. 195–196). All tests had been piloted on samples of "normal" and "retarded" populations ages 2 to 12. The different tests measured everything from such basic tasks as movement coordination, or imitation, to complex processes such as comprehension, judgment, or abstract reasoning. Among the tests, Binet distinguished between tests of results, that is, those tests aiming to assess the level attained by the student (what are today referred to as *achievement tests*), and tests of analysis, that is, those tests aiming to understand underlying cognitive constructs (what are today referred to as *ability tests*). The tests were presented in order of increasing difficulty, and at different levels distinctions could be established between normal and retarded children on the one hand and between younger and older normal children on the other. The easiest tests distinguished severely and profoundly mentally retarded children (at the time labeled as *idiots*) from the rest; tests of intermediate difficulty distinguished between severely retarded and moderately retarded (then labeled as *imbeciles*); and higher level tests distinguished between mildly retarded (those corresponding to Goddard's category of *morons;* Minton, 1998) and normal children of the same age, as well as between younger and older children. As a member of the ministerial committee on education, Binet's main purpose was to identify the mildly retarded children to provide them with the special education that was thought to be able to increase their cognitive functioning.

In the first 1905 publication of the Metric Intelligence Scale, Binet and Simon emphasized that the scale should only be used as an indication of the child's cognitive level at the time of administration and that this performance level could be subject to change through an appropriate education. The 1905 scale was administered to a broad sample of children, and the tests then were rearranged by age level. A revised version of the scale was published in 1908 and offered the possibility of establishing a child's "mental age," a notion first introduced by Chaillé in 1887. If 65%–75% of the children from a given age group, 6 years, for example, succeeded on a test, the test was classified as corresponding to that age level. A child could thus succeed on tests at a "mental age" level that was lower, equal to, or higher than the level corresponding to the child's biological age. This mental age simply corresponds to the performance norm of a given age group and does not, as was thought in the American adaptation of the scale, give an indication of the stage of developmental progression reached by the child. Having a given mental age does not imply functioning as a child of that age; it only implies that the performance on the test corresponds to what the majority of children at a given age will achieve. Binet explicitly warned against the use of performance on an IQ test as a fixed measure of intelligence. It must be repeated that, by construction, many children of a given age would not succeed on a test intended for their age (Lippmann, 1922, cited in Jacoby & Glauberman, 1995).

To facilitate the selection of children eligible for special education, Binet introduced "pedagogical distinctions" among idiocy, imbecility, and debility. The categorization of an individual was not viewed as a mere judgment but rather as founded on a psychological examination that minimized the risk of an erroneous diagnosis. First, the schoolteacher needed to make a list of "possibly retarded" pupils, based not on personal impression but on weak performance in their studies. This first impression, however, needed to be corroborated by the administration of instructional-level achievement tests, chosen by the principal or regional inspector. A possible confusion between normal-but-ignorant and abnormal children is still possible, however. The last step must therefore be a psychological examination. Binet made it clear that the scale was just one assessment tool and that the observation of the "global person" and the test taker's reaction to the situation are as important as the quantitative test results per se. More than the end results, it is the paths by which they are reached that interested Binet. Binet also insisted on the importance of not knowing the prior diagnosis of the child being examined. Otherwise, one risked a kind of confirmation bias whereby one would confirm the diagnosis already made.

Binet's aim was to detect abnormality in children, not to segregate them. Binet was convinced that retarded children could and would profit from special education and also that they would be at a loss within the regular school system. His aim was to prevent further rejection of these children by supplying them with special education that would eventually enable them to return to the regular school system. Unfortunately, the American developers of his work believed in fixed IQ and substantially modified Binet's original ideas and intentions. As opposed to most of his contemporaries, Binet believed that "abnormality" could be cured, and his faith in education seemed to have practically no limits.

Once again, it is important to remember that Binet did not view intelligence as an entity fixed at birth but rather as incremental. It is precisely because of the elastic nature of intelligence and the possibility of developing it through education that children with specific needs, who were not totally benefiting from the regular school system, needed to be identified and to be given the special education that would help them develop their intellectual abilities. This, however, was not the belief of the "Galtonian" researchers who imported Binet's instrument to the United States and Great Britain. Lewis Terman, who in 1916 introduced a U.S. version of the Metric Intelligence Scale—the Stanford–Binet Intelligence Scale—stressed the importance of hereditary factors in explaining IQ performance. Terman considered this genetic influence to be so strong that it could not possibly be altered through education. Terman advocated placing children with low IQ scores in special classes, not in order that they get the special attention they needed to progress, but because there was no hope of their being able to integrate into and profit from normal schooling. The Metric Intelligence Scale proved to be powerful in distinguishing even "high-grade defectives," that is, those children closest to normal functioning. For Terman, there was no doubt that the identification of these children would

> ultimately result in curtailing the reproduction of feeble-mindedness and in the elimination of an enormous amount of crime, pauperism, and industrial inefficiency. It is hardly necessary to emphasize that the high-grade cases, of the type now so frequently overlooked, are precisely the ones whose guardianship it is most important for the State to assume. (Terman, 1916, cited in Jacoby & Glauberman, 1995, p. 545)

The importance of psychometrically sound assessment scales to measure the level of cognitive development was soon generalized beyond the population of abnormal children and constitutes one of Binet's most important legacies to the field. The high positive correlation between children's scores on the Binet–Simon Metric Intelligence Scale and the children's school performance, which is due in part to the scholastic nature of the test items, was seen as a proof that the scale was indeed measuring intelligence and contributed to its widespread success (Eysenck & Kamin, 1981).

IMPACT ON THE FIELD OF PSYCHOLOGY

In this section, we examine Binet's view on four specific learning-related issues: the nature of the learner, the nature of the learning process, optimal conditions of instruction, and the nature of important learning-instructional outcomes.

The Nature of the Learner

The nature of the learner is a question mainly addressed in Binet's *Modern Ideas on Children* (1909).[2] In the early 20th century, children were often considered to be miniature adults, "homonculi" (Binet, 1909, p. 7) who were only quantitatively rather than qualitatively different from adults in everything from physical attributes such as size to cognitive skills. Binet insisted on the importance of studying individual differences, not only between age groups but also between children of a given age, to better address the needs of different learners. A teacher should not teach in the abstract without taking into consideration differences in memory ability, preferred learning strategy, or even age (it was not uncommon practice in Binet's time to group children of various ages in the same classroom) and visual or auditory capacities. Binet and his team were the first, in the Paris school district, to impose annual tests of vision and audition for all children attending school. In a study of apprentice teachers that Binet conducted with Victor Henri (Binet, 1909), he showed that, on all the tests related to scholastic aptitudes (close to the knowledge taught in school), the apprentice teachers designated as bright by their instructor excelled. On other tasks, requiring practical or sensitive skills, the individuals defined as less bright, however, performed as well as or better than those belonging to the top group of the class. From this, Binet (1909) concluded the importance of (a) assessing a broad range of skills to increase all students' chances of showing their strengths and (b) teaching in ways that correspond to different children's patterns of abilities (pp. 10–11). Taking individual differences into account should not, however, mean that each child is taught individually with a method suited only for her or him. Rather, it means that teachers should strive to find a balance between individual strengths and the requirements of the collective learning environment. In practical terms, this could, for example, mean that, in larger schools, stu-

---

[2]Its title nonwithstanding, *Modern Ideas on Children* was written almost a century ago, thus, although the content is still relevant, the style is dated. Binet adressesed his readers as "fathers, teachers or sociologists," the latter two in the masculine form of the French word (Binet, 1909, p. 2).

dents of a given grade level be regrouped in different classrooms according to their pattern of abilities.

The Nature of the Learning Process

For Binet, repetition and training were the key to learning (Binet, 1909). According to Binet, whatever the domain, be it typewriting or learning to cross out specific letters on a sheet of paper, the precision and speed of execution would increase with repeated training until they reached a given level, at which performance is stabilized. This growth curve was similar across domains, and the role of education was to help children reach their highest level of performance. Because learning follows a curve, it was important to assess which point of the learning curve a given child has reached in order to adapt the level of teaching to the child's level. In Binet's words,

> Suppose that we are being given a lecture on geometry, and that the 100th theorem is being taught, even if we had the mind of a Pascal,[3] we would be unable to understand had we not been taught the previous 99 theorems. (Binet, 1909, pp. 147–148)

Binet pointed out that, although some difficulty is beneficial and would bring the child to grow, all too often it was the case in the classroom that children were taught things that were out of their reach. The ideas developed by Binet in *Modern Ideas on Children* (1909) and discussed in very broad terms were to be much more systematically explored by Lev Vygotsky and his work on the notion of "zone of proximal development" (Vygotsky, 1934/1962). Once a child's level of functioning had been determined, learning would increase through repeated exercises and a gradual increase of the level of difficulty. According to Binet, learning came with practice, and the student must not only be lectured to but also be given frequent opportunities to practice his or her knowledge. Such activities as manipulation, practical applications, visits to businesses, or walks in the forest should be promoted. "Above all, the student must be active," said Binet (1909, p. 156), and referred to American researchers and Herbert Spencer's[4] notion of "learning by doing" (1909, p. 159). Again without theorizing or explicitly naming it, Binet's conception was close to what was later to be defined as "constructivism."

Optimal Conditions of Instruction

Binet (1909) considered the key to good instruction to be in teacher training, and he stressed the importance of teaching future teachers to ob-

---

[3]Blaise Pascal, French philosopher and mathematician.
[4]In *Modern Ideas on Children* (1909), Binet referred his readers to Herbert Spencer's *On Education*, Gustave Le Bon's *Psychology of Education*, and Buyse's *American Methods of Education*. In general, Binet was very inspired by American educational research.

serve. By learning to observe, teachers would become aware of individual differences, and it would help them to adapt the level of teaching to the child's level of knowledge, as described earlier. According to Binet, the most frequent error in education was to forget that one must "proceed from the simple to the complex" (Binet, 1909, p. 148). Developing teachers' observational skills could be achieved by an increased focus on practical, case-based, exercises during preservice and by making pedagogical consultations by specialists readily available to all classroom instructors.

The Nature of Important Learning-Instructional Outcomes

Binet was convinced that, within a certain limit, children's cognitive functioning and abilities could improve when the children are placed in optimal conditions for learning. He was also of the opinion that cognitive functioning cannot be separated from emotions and that a multitude of factors must be taken into account when studying the complexities of human functioning. This broad interest in the child's development and well-being is exemplified by the studies Binet conducted on the relation between eating habits and intellectual achievement (Binet, 1899). In Wolf's (1973) translation, Binet stated that

> Intelligence is susceptible to development. With practice and training, and especially with appropriate methods (of teaching) we can augment a child's attention, his memory, his judgment—helping him literally to become more intelligent than he was before . . . right up to the moment when he arrives at his limit. (see Wolf, 1973, p. 207)

This is illustrated by the instructional methods Binet advocated for abnormal children. Once these abnormal children had been recognized and put into special education classes, what tools were used to favor their development? Binet did not consider abnormality to be a kind of retardation. He gave specific guidelines on the didactics to be used with abnormal children (Binet & Simon, 1907). Binet and Simon stressed the importance of capitalizing on the children's strengths, diminishing the number of pure analytical activities in favor of more practical exercises. More instruction should be carried out in the workshop instead of the classroom, and teachers were encouraged to spend time on "everyday activity exercises," such as putting on one's shoes or sending a letter. New disciplines, such as "Mental Orthopedics," were also introduced, with the aim of re-educating psychological functions and attaining increased developmental synchrony. One example is the "statue game," in which all the students must freeze and keep immobile. This exercise proved beneficial to increase children's concentration and focus, and it considerably calmed down the classroom atmosphere. Many of these "orthopedic" exercises are still used in special education classes today. The importance of individually adapted teaching was also underscored.

BINET'S LEGACY

In retrospect, Binet's most well-recognized contribution to the fields of psychology and education is, quite ironically, the Stanford–Binet Intelligence Scale, which owes its popularity largely to the work of Lewis Terman rather than to Alfred Binet himself. The intelligence scale became the tree hiding the forest, for at the same time, much of Binet's outstanding and often revolutionary research is largely ignored, a paradox that has been pointed out before (Piéron, 1958; Reuchlin, 1957–1958; Siegler, 1992). This work includes research in the fields of perception, language development, memory, conceptual development, and other aspects of cognition. Binet was also a pioneer in his methods of investigation, resolutely turning his back to philosophical speculations and insisting instead on the necessity of empirical investigations (Fraisse, 1958; Reuchlin, 1957–1958).

To paraphrase the title of Sarason's (1976) article, the fate of Binet and school psychology was unfortunate. As described, Binet's aim with the Metric Intelligence Scale was to develop an instrument that would contribute to the identification of those children who needed special help in order to make the most of their potential. But this second aspect of optimizing on potential was all too often forgotten, and Binet's scale was used to weed out rather than to select children for special programs. As pointed out by Sarason (1976) and Wolf (1973), whereas for Binet the assessment scale was just a means to adapt and enrich education, the role of school psychologists today is all too often limited to evaluation without the psychologists' making the essential link to education. The school psychologist has become a test administrator without a broader perspective or influence on what happens to the child after she or he has been "labeled." Binet's contribution, therefore, has been misdirected in a way that might well have Binet turning over in his grave.

ISOLATING THE FACTORS THAT RENDERED BINET'S WORK SO INFLUENTIAL

What are the factors that have made Binet so enormously influential even today? Why does his work continue to have an impact on psychology, whereas the work of so many others does not?

1. *Having the right idea.* Most ideas in psychology, even influential ideas, are wrong in fundamental respects. Piaget (1972), for example, had many good ideas, but revisionist work in the 1970s and 1980s showed many of these ideas simply to be wrong (see, e.g., chapters in Flavell & Markman, 1983). Piaget overestimated ages at which children acquire cognitive functions, overestimated the domain specificity of these acquisitions, overstated the distinctness of stages, failed adequately to deal with nonscientific aspects of thought, and so forth. Thus, Piaget was a brilliant theorist but wrong in

some fundamental respects. Other theorists, such as Sigmund Freud, proposed enormously influential theories but did not adequately test those theories. Later research has not been particularly supportive of the validity of Freud's (1949) theorizing, although the results are mixed (Westen, 1998). Other theorists, such as Erik Erickson (1988), provided hardly any empirical verification at all for their ideas. Mental tests, for all their inadequacies and flaws, have proved to be remarkably robust for the prediction of various kinds of performance, especially school performance (Jensen, 1998). They are far from perfect in predicting performance, but Binet never claimed they would be perfect. They do what he claimed they would do and more.

2. *Having the idea at the right time.* In psychology and in any other science, timing matters a lot. An idea that at one time may take off may, at another time, have little or no influence (Sternberg, 1999). The world was ready for Binet's idea. Within a short time, there would be a world war and an extraordinary need to predict performance of soldiers. Schools were ready; the military was ready; the world was ready. Readiness is in part a function of people wanting to hear some new ideas and in part a function of people being dissatisfied with what they were hearing before.

3. *Capturing the imagination of the scientific and lay public.* A lot of theories that are correct and even well-timed never get much attention. They may be technically competent and even published in a major journal, such as *Psychological Review*, and yet are immediately forgotten. The ideas that last somehow capture the imagination of both scientists and the lay public. Binet, Freud, B. F. Skinner, and a handful of other psychologists have been able to capture the public imagination with their ideas in a way that few other people have. Of course, the question then becomes one of what kinds of ideas capture the imagination of the public. In a sense, that is the "$64,000 question." If people knew the answer to this question, they would be doing whatever it takes to capture people's imaginations. But a few elements seem to be common:

- *Surprise.* The ideas or findings are surprising in some way. Freud revealed a whole alleged layer of unconscious processing that people did not know was there. Skinner (like John Watson before him) claimed to be able to control through the environment aspects of behavior that previously had seemed to be beyond human control. In the case of Binet, people were and continue to be surprised at the extraordinary success of intelligence tests at predicting so many different kinds of behavior. Indeed, sometimes the prediction is annoying. For example, some hoped that the tests would not be predictive for certain groups, for whom they turned out to be predictive after all. Again, this is not to say that the tests are perfect; it is to say that they continue to surprise.

- *Paradox.* Many of the ideas that capture the imagination seem to have paradox embedded within them. In the case of Freud, how can we feel like we have so much control when, according to Freud's theory, we have so little? Or, in the case of Howard Gardner's (1983, 1999) theory, how can intelligences be multiple when the word has always been used in a singular sense? Or in the case of the construct of emotional intelligence (Goleman, 1995; Salovey & Mayer, 1990), how can something be both emotional and intelligent at the same time? The paradox in Binet's contribution of intelligence tests is that tests that seem so academic and removed from everyday life can predict so many different kinds of behavior in everyday life and provide scores that are so predictive throughout the life span even of themselves. Scores in middle childhood are even pretty good predictors of scores in later adulthood. The prediction is far from perfect but nevertheless impressive.
- *Fulfillment of desires.* The most influential ideas provide a satisfaction of desires that goes beyond the scientific. Freud's theory was first class in this effect. Some could take comfort in the idea that a bad childhood "made them do it," whatever "it" was. Or they could explain their curious behavior or that of others in terms of defense mechanisms. Gardner's (1983) and Peter Salovey and John Mayer's (1990) theories have allowed people who formerly thought themselves to be unintelligent to think of themselves now as intelligent. In the case of Binet, people now had what appeared to be a scientific way to find out how "smart" they and others are. Today, this contribution may not seem new. At the time, however, it was quite new. One can argue as to whether tests based on Francis Galton's (1883) theory, emphasizing psychophysical processes, predict other forms of behavior. One cannot argue, however, that these tests reach the level of Binet's in their predictive efficacy.

4. *Finding champions and converts.* All of those whose contributions we have mentioned managed to find both champions and converts to their ideas. The ideas became a bit like cargo cults. In exchange for goods and services rendered, followers respected, admired, and in some cases even at times have seemed to worship those whose ideas have influenced them. In Binet's case, Lewis Terman was probably instrumental to success. Terman publicized Binet's ideas far more widely and successfully than did Binet himself. And the testing movement during World War I, led by Henry Goddard, Arthur Otis, and others, also went far in propagating Binet's ideas. Great ideas need not only to be "discovered;" they need to be promoted actively and in a fairly systematic fashion.

5. *Platform.* Well-known scientists have access to the ears of their colleagues. Well-known journalists have access to the ideas of their colleagues. In essence, they have a platform. Binet had the platform offered by the Sorbonne, much as Skinner and later Gardner have had the platform offered by Harvard. Had any of these individuals been at obscure places, their contributions still might have been influential, but the process of gaining attention would have been more difficult. Had Binet not held a professorship at a highly reputed university, the likelihood of his being commissioned by the French government to create a cognitive assessment tool would have been slim. Moreover, those who have contributed to the European and North American intellectual tradition were, for the most part, born into relatively favorable circumstances. Had they been born into parts of the world that do not offer the opportunities offered in these locations, they might never have had the education or socialization to lead them to these ideas in the first place.

6. *Persuasive communication skills.* Most of the influential people who have been discussed, including without doubt, Binet, were wonderful communicators who could communicate both to scientific and to lay audiences. They made their cases—logically, forcefully, persuasively. Others with equally high analytical intellectual skills have had less success in selling their ideas. None of the great ideas are simply proposed and accepted without regard to the way in which they are communicated. For example, Salovey and Mayer (1990) proposed the construct of emotional intelligence prior to Daniel Goleman (1995), but Goleman's skills as a journalist served him very well in spreading the word (and in gaining a major part of the credit for the idea). Binet was a wonderful writer, and it paid off. Almost any of his articles published in *L'Année Psychologique* can be read as a short story, without the dryness typical of most scientific publications today.

7. *Business angles.* The ideas of Binet, Freud, Piaget, Skinner, Mayer, and Salovey, as elaborated by and communicated through Goleman and others, resulted in major business enterprises. Testing companies have made a fortune off Binet's ideas. Clinical psychologists have done well by Freud. In the 1960s and 1970s, many instructional programs were based on Skinner's theory. And emotional intelligence today is a huge industry. Much of the propagation of ideas comes about when entrepreneurial individuals and organizations realize, for better or worse, the financial gains to be made from scientific ideas.

8. *Size and scope of ideas.* We have saved for last what may be the most important aspect of the work of Binet and other great thinkers: the size and scope of their ideas. Binet, like Freud and Skinner before him, thought big. He was dealing with big problems of substantial reach. Although at first glance it may seem that he researched a large amount of unrelated topics, a general theme can be perceived throughout Binet's life and work. Binet's ultimate goal was to establish what he called "an individual psychology" (Binet, 1898)

and to understand the complexities of the human mind, by reaching beyond general psychology and studying individual differences. Scientists often are taught to deal with fairly small and narrow problems in a fairly small and narrow way. For the most part, the payoffs of the field are for smaller contributions that make conveniently sized journal articles. Those who think big often are laughed at. But every once in a while, the big thinkers get the last laugh. Perhaps Binet is somewhere still, getting that last laugh.

REFERENCES

Avanzini, G. (1974). A. *Binet: Ecrits psychologiques et pédagogiques* [Writings on psychology and pedagogy]. Toulouse, France: Privat.

Binet, A. (1890). Recherches sur les mouvements de quelques jeunes enfants [Research on the movements of some young children]. *Revue Philosophique, 29*, 297–309.

Binet, A. (1898). La mesure en psychologie individuelle [The measure in individual psychology]. *Revue Philosophique, 46*, 113–123.

Binet, A. (1899). Note relative à l'influence du travail intellectuel sur la consommation du pain dans les écoles [A commentary on the influence of intellectual work on the consumption of bread in schools]. *L'Année Psychologique, 5*, 332–335.

Binet, A. (1901). Recherches sur la technique de la mensuration de la tête vivante [Research on the technique of measuring a living head]. *L'Année Psychologique, 7*, 314–368.

Binet, A. (1903). *L'étude expérimentale de l'intelligence* [Experimental study of intelligence]. Paris: Schleicher Frères.

Binet, A. (1909). *Les idées modernes sur les enfants* [Modern ideas on children]. Paris: Flammarion.

Binet, A., & Henri, V. (1898). *La fatigue intellectuelle* [Mental fatigue]. Paris: Schleicher Frères.

Binet, A., & Simon, T. (1905). Méthodes nouvelles pour le diagnostic du niveau intellectuel des anormaux [New methods for diagnosing intellectual performance in abnormal persons]. *L'Année Psychologique, 11*, 191–244.

Binet, A., & Simon, T. (1907). *Les enfants anormaux* [Abnormal children]. Paris: Privat.

Binet, A., & Simon, T. (1908). Le développement de l'intelligence chez les enfants [The development of intelligence in children]. *L'Année Psychologique, 15*, 1–94.

Chaillé, S. E. (1887). Infants: Their chronological process. *New Orleans Medical and Surgical Journal, 14*, 893–902.

Delay, J. (1958). La vie et l'oeuvre d'Alfred Binet [The life and work of Alfred Binet]. *Psychologie Française, 3*, 85–95.

Erickson, E. (1988). On the generational cycle: An address. In G. H. Pollock & J. Munder (Eds.), *The Oedipus papers: Classics in psychoanalysis* (Monograph No. 6, pp. 241–259). Madison, CT: International Universities Press.

Eysenck, H. J., & Kamin, L. (1981). *The intelligence controversy*. New York: Wiley.

Flavell, J. H., & Markman, E. M. (1983). *Cognitive development*. New York: Wiley.

Fraisse, P. (1958). L'oeuvre d'Alfred Binet en psychologie expérimentale [Alfred Binet's work in experimental psychology]. *Psychologie Française, 3,* 105–112.

Freud, S. (1949). *Abriss der Psycho-analyse* [An outline of psychoanalysis] (J. Strachey, Trans). New York: Norton.

Galton, F. (1883). *Inquiries into human faculty and its development.* London: Macmillan.

Gardner, H. (1983). *Frames of mind: The theory of multiple intelligences.* New York: Basic Books.

Gardner, H. (1999). *Intelligence reframed: Multiple intelligences for the 21st century.* New York: Basic Books.

Goleman, D. (1995). *Emotional intelligence.* New York: Bantam Books.

Gould, S. J. (1981). *The mismeasure of man.* New York: Norton.

Jacoby, R., & Glauberman, N. (Eds.). (1995). *The bell curve debate: History, documents, opinions.* New York: Random House.

Jensen. A. R. (1998). The g factor and the design of education. In R. J. Sternberg & W. Williams (Eds.), *Intelligence, instruction, and assessment: Theory into practice* (pp. 111–131). Mahwah, NJ: Erlbaum.

Minton, H. L. (1998). *Introduction to "New Methods for the Diagnosis of the Intellectual Level of Subnormals": Alfred Binet and Theodore Simon.* Toronto, Ontario, Canada: York University Press.

Piaget, J. (1972). *The child's conception of the world* (J. Tomlinson & A. Tomlinson, Trans.). Totowa, NJ: Littlefield, Adams.

Piéron, H. (1958). Quelques souvenirs personnels [A few personal memories]. *Psychologie Française, 3,* 89–95.

Reuchlin, M. (1957–1958). La mesure de l'intelligence, œuvre paradoxale d'Alfred Binet [The measurement of intelligence—Alfred Binet's paradoxical work]. *Bulletin de Psychologie, 11,* 306–320.

Robinson, D. N. (Ed.). (1977–1978). Preface to Binet's *Alterations of Personality* and *On Double Consciousness.* In *Significant contributions to the history of Psychology, 1750–1920. Series C. Medical Psychology. Volume V.* Washington, DC: University Publications of America.

Salovey, P., & Mayer, J. D. (1990). Emotional intelligence. *Imagination, Cognition and Personality, 9,* 185–211.

Sarason, S. B. (1976). The unfortunate fate of Alfred Binet and school psychology. *Teachers College Record, 77,* 579–592.

Siegler, R. S. (1992). The other Alfred Binet. *Developmental Psychology, 28,* 179–190.

Sternberg, R. J. (1999). Looking back and looking forward on intelligence: Toward a theory of successful intelligence. In M. Bennett (Ed.), *Developmental psychology: Achievements and prospects* (pp. 289–308). Philadelphia: Psychology Press/Taylor & Francis.

Terman, L. M. (1916). *The measurement of intelligence: An explanation of and a complete guide for the use of the Stanford revision and extension of the Binet-Simon intelligence scale.* Boston: Houghton Mifflin.

Vygotsky, L. S. (1962). *Thought and language.* Cambridge, MA: MIT Press. (Original work published 1934)

Westen, D. (1998). The scientific legacy of Sigmund Freud: Toward a psychodynamically informed psychological science. *Psychological Bulletin, 124,* 333–371.

Wolf, T. H. (1973). *Alfred Binet.* Chicago: University Press of Chicago.

Zazzo, R. (1958). Alfred Binet et la psychologie de l'enfant [Alfred Binet and child psychology]. *Psychologie Française, 3,* 113–121.

Zuza, F. (1948). *Alfred Binet et la pédagogie expérimentale* [Alfred Binet and experimental psychology]. Paris: J. Vrin Editeur.

6

LESSONS IN "GREATNESS" FROM KURT LEWIN'S LIFE AND WORKS

ELLEN BERSCHEID

Great works are great because they cause people to see the world differently than before. As original and creative constructions of the world, they challenge accepted views, often those deeply held and cherished by powerful people in entrenched religious, political, financial, and academic establishments. For a new vision of the world to have an impact, it first must capture people's attention, including the attention of the people it threatens and, thus, who have every incentive to ignore it. If a work is successful in securing widespread attention, including the attention of hostile forces, both the work and its creator must then survive the soul-withering fire they often ignite. A work that cannot emerge whole from the furnace of fair—or even unfair—criticism will have no impact, and its creator will be buried in the crowded tomb of the "Unknown Great Scientist."

Some people believe the academy is different from other establishments—that a new vision of the world will gain easier acceptance there because all academicians vow fealty to the gods of logic, reason, and objectivity and dedicate their lives to the search for truth, wherever the search leads and whatever the consequences. In actuality, of course, the academic establishment is as ruthless, and occasionally as unethical, as any other in dealing with those who threaten established beliefs and the positions of the power-ful. Although those who commit academic heresy have not been burned at the stake in recent times, they not infrequently have been tortured and some have been driven to suicide. A case in point is Paul Kammerer, whose expe-riences are chronicled by Arthur Koestler (1971) in *The Case of the Midwife Toad*. Kammerer, a biologist, refused to accept Charles Darwin's theory that evolution proceeded through haphazard, random mutations and, instead, subscribed to Jean-Baptiste Larmarck's theory that acquired characteristics sometimes could be transmitted to offspring. When Kammerer presented evidence to support his thesis, he almost immediately became the target of ridicule, sarcasm, and other humiliations, lies, and injustices, both crude and ingeniously subtle. Crushed and broken by his colleagues, the gifted Kammerer committed suicide in 1926. An excerpt of a review of Koestler's book by Richard Holmes in *The Times of London*, featured on the book's jacket, tells the larger story: "Koestler has demonstrated, most memorably, that extraor-dinary and fearful narrow-mindedness of scientific orthodoxy; the massive presence of bad old human prejudice and subjectivity deep in the fortress of 'objective scientific debate'."

Statesman Henry Kissinger also had occasion to remark on the vicious enmities that sometimes boil within the academy. After being blackballed by his colleagues when he tried to resume his professorship at Harvard Uni-versity after serving his country as President Richard Nixon's Secretary of State, Kissinger was widely quoted as saying, "Academic politics are so ruth-less because the stakes are so small." Kissinger was only half right: Academic politics *are* ruthless, but the stakes are sometimes enormous, both for the scholars immediately involved and for humanity.

Some scholars who aspire to greatness believe that once they have pro-duced a truly creative and useful contribution to knowledge, their job is done. To the contrary, if their work is original and groundbreaking, their task has only begun. To make a great contribution to knowledge, successfully com-pleting the task of assuring the impact of an idea is as important as the idea's originality. Successfully selling the idea is perhaps even more important than the idea's originality because there are few entirely original ideas. Most ideas have already been thought of and expressed by someone else, although that person and the idea may have been lost for a long period of time. As Beveridge (1950) observed in *The Art of Scientific Investigation*:

> Edward Jenner was not the first to inoculate people with cowpox to pro-tect them against smallpox, William Harvey was not the first to postu-late circulation of the blood, Darwin was by no means the first to suggest evolution, Columbus was not the first European to go to America, Pas-teur was not the first to propound the germ theory of disease, Lister was not the first to use carbolic acid as a wound antiseptic. But these men were the ones who fully developed these ideas and forced them on a

reluctant world, and most credit rightly goes to them for bringing the discoveries to fruition. (pp. 49–50)

Forcing a new idea "on a reluctant world" requires not only enormous stamina and endurance but also a willingness to suffer the disapproval of others, including respected colleagues, as the life of Kurt Lewin illustrates.

LEWIN'S VISION OF PSYCHOLOGY

Kurt Lewin (1890–1947) is generally regarded as the founder of experimental social psychology, and he also was a seminal figure in the development of child psychology and of industrial/organizational psychology. Perhaps the first and most important lesson to be learned from the achievements of Kurt Lewin is that to advance from Point A, where one is, to Point B, where one wants to go, it is necessary to map the locations of both Point A and Point B. Lewin expended considerable time and effort to learn where psychology was before developing his vision of where psychology should go.

According to Alfred Marrow (1969), his biographer, Lewin began work toward his doctorate in philosophy at the University of Berlin in 1910, a time when philosophy was "king" of all the disciplines (the natural sciences, the social sciences, the liberal arts, and the humanities were all organized under the faculty of philosophy). Led by work conducted at the laboratory of experimental psychology founded in 1878 by Wilhem Wundt at the University of Leipzig and supported by the growing German Society for Experimental Psychology, psychology had begun to emulate the natural sciences, especially physics, in its philosophy and methods, partially owing to the efforts of physicist Ernst Mach, who emphasized the commonalties of purpose of physics and psychology (see Boring, 1950, p. 395). It adopted, as did physics, Mach's philosophy of science, which "discouraged theorizing by demanding direct experimental evidence for all scientific concepts" (Kadanoff, 2001, p. 2553).

Although Lewin initially intended to specialize in philosophy of science, he changed his mind when he met Carl Stumpf, director of the University of Berlin's Psychological Institute. Impressed with Stumpf and the ongoing experiments of the associationists, Lewin joined the institute, where he received the finest formal training in psychology available in his day. However, "after three years of experimenting with nonsense syllables and reaction times split to one thousandths of a second, Lewin came to a stop" (Marrow, 1969, p. 12). Lewin now knew precisely where psychology was. Moreover, influenced by his service in the German army in World War I, he had returned to the institute with a vision of where psychology should go. He concluded that his research activities at the institute were not going to help him realize his vision.

Lewin's vision of psychology was very different from the views of his contemporaries:

> The psychologist finds himself in the midst of a rich and vast land full of strange happenings: there are men killing themselves; a child playing; a person who, having fallen in love and being caught in an unhappy situation, is not willing or not able to find a way out; . . . there is the reaching out for higher and more difficult goals; loyalty to a group; dreaming; planning; exploring the world; and so on without end. It is an immense continent full of fascination and power and full of stretches of land where no one ever has set foot.
>
> Psychology is out to conquer this continent, to find out where its treasures are hidden, to investigate its danger spots, to master its vast forces, to utilize its energies.
>
> How can one reach this goal? (Lewin, 1940, cited in Marrow, 1969, p. 3)

It is safe to say that when Lewin was measuring reaction times to the thousandth degree, few of his colleagues at the institute believed psychology was out to conquer the continent of behavior Lewin described. Their continents, and their aims, were undoubtedly much smaller than Lewin's, circumscribed by Wundt's vision of "physiological psychology" (as Wundt called his new science), by the ongoing work in their laboratory and the psychophysical methods in vogue, and by the reigning associationist doctrine.

Like many other great psychologists, Lewin did not allow others to define for him what behaviors psychologists could or should study. He also did not confine himself to second-hand observations of human behavior made by others. The wellspring of virtually all of Lewin's original ideas were his own observations of humans behaving in their natural habitats. What Lewin saw and experienced himself in his daily life outside the laboratory and the library provided the grist for his vision of psychology and for his subsequent theory and research.

MAPPING THE ROUTE TOWARD THE VISION

After locating where psychology was on the map of science and developing a vision of where it should go, Lewin was acutely aware that the road he was planning to traverse would be difficult, and he tried to identify in advance the potholes, detours, and obstacles he was likely to encounter along the way. Lewin's superb formal training in psychology allowed him to foresee that one of the most formidable obstacles he would encounter on his journey would be the philosophy of science then guiding psychology.

At the University of Berlin, Lewin had taken several philosophy of science courses from Ernst Cassirer, who was especially interested in the developmental stages of the natural sciences (see, e.g., Cassirer, 1923). According to Lewin (see Marrow, 1969), Cassier taught his students that, to advance knowledge, they probably would have to hurdle conceptual and methodological taboos—taboos rooted in philosophical assumptions about how science can best proceed. Lewin knew that he not only had to develop a conceptual framework and methodologies that would allow him to investigate behavioral phenomena believed to be outside the realm of science at the time, but he also had to directly confront differences between the philosophical assumptions underlying currently accepted concepts and methodologies and those he would propose.

Lewin (1931) confronted those philosophical differences in one of his most important and influential papers, which he distributed widely and presented at conferences in Europe and the United States before he published it under the title, "The Conflict Between Aristotelian and Galileian Modes of Thought in Contemporary Psychology." Thus, yet another lesson from Lewin's life and works is that aspiring scientific revolutionaries would do well to cultivate familiarity with the philosophical assumptions that constitute the foundation of the science they hope to radically change.

LEWIN'S "FIELD THEORY"

Lewin expressed the first "systems" view in psychology in his *field theory*, the core idea of which he expressed in his well-known equation $B = f(P, E)$: Behavior (B) is a function of the interaction between the person (P) and his or her environment (E). The term *environment* was intended to encompass both the physical and social environments in which the person is embedded. At the University of Berlin, Lewin, like many others, had been impressed with the development of field theory in physics and the revolutionary experiments of Michael Faraday and others. Physicists had discovered that their predictions of the behavior of interacting particles could be greatly improved not only by considering the properties (e.g., mass) of each individual particle but also by considering the properties of the "field" in which the particles were interacting (see Deutsch, 1954). They came to recognize that the field in which physical particles interact was not a causally innocuous "ether" they could continue to ignore; rather, the field in which particles were embedded possessed electromagnetic properties that interacted with the properties of the particles to influence their behavior.

Just as the properties of the field in which particles interact affect their behavior, so, too, Lewin theorized, is human behavior influenced by the properties of the field in which a person is behaving. The portion of the field in which people typically behave that was of special interest to Lewin was the individual's social environment, which provides the context for most human behavior (see Reis, Collins, & Berscheid, 2000). Lewin was especially interested in how people in groups influenced each other's behavior. The term *group dynamics*, in fact, was coined by Lewin, who established the Center for Group Dynamics at the Massachusetts Institute of Technology (moved after his death to the University of Michigan, where it remains a thriving enterprise). At the time Lewin proposed to study group dynamics, however, psychologists denied the existence and reality of groups, including "dyadic" groups, such as those composed of a husband and wife or parent and child. Only the individual was believed to be "real" and, thus, a proper subject for psychological study. The study of groups was taboo for psychologists (see Deutsch, 1954).

The view that only the individual was a proper subject of study by psychologists was proclaimed by the most powerful and respected members of the psychological establishment, including Floyd Allport (1924), the author of the first social psychology text to report empirical research. As Cartwright and Zander (1960) discussed, Allport (1924) declared that only individuals are real; groups are simply "sets of ideals, thoughts, and habits repeated in each individual mind and existing only in those minds" (p. 9), and "Psychology in all its branches is a science of the individual. To extend its principles to larger units is to destroy their meaning" (p. 4).

Like most scientists who have an impact on their field, Allport had his own carefully constructed and passionately pursued agenda. He, too, had a vision of social psychology. His vision—and his hope—was that the fledgling discipline of social psychology would be accepted by, and incorporated into, the science of psychology (see Barone, 1999; Berscheid, 2000). To achieve that goal—to win psychologists' acceptance of the young discipline—Allport used a tried-and-true method: Hewing closely to the norms and standards of the group one wishes to join usually is effective in winning the group's approval. The norms and standards of psychology were clear at that time: "Real" psychologists used the laboratory experiment, just as Wundt had done in his experiments in physiological psychology. They also used some sort of mechanical apparatus in their experiment, usually to produce an observable record, just as Wundt had done. Most importantly, real psychologists studied the psychological activity of the individual nervous system, just as Wundt had done. These standards of the reigning psychological establishment posed a problem for Allport.

The problem these standards must have posed for Allport was that social psychologists had not adhered to them. Many European psychologists had extensively theorized about and studied social influence, including Wundt himself. Some years after the publication of his influential volume describing a physiological psychology, *Grundzuge der physiologischen Psychologie* (1873–1874), viewed by many historians as "the most important book in the history of modern psychology" (Boring, 1950, p. 322), Wundt published the first volume of *Völkerpsychologie*, which he subsequently expanded into 10 volumes over the following two decades (Wundt, 1900–1920). In his later volumes, Wundt argued that group (or cultural) psychology was a necessary complement to a physiological psychology of the individual, the model of psychology that Wundt had promulgated in his first work and the model subsequently adopted by Allport and other American psychologists. Only a social psychology, Wundt maintained, could scientifically attack questions of higher mental processes (see Boring, 1950, p. 326).

Wundt's later works had little impact. Among the possible reasons for their lack of influence is the one discussed earlier: Because he died shortly after the last volume of *Volkerpsychologie* was published, Wundt was unable to sell his vision of a nonexperimental "social–group–cultural" psychology and to overcome opposition inspired by beliefs that already had become well established in psychology. Wundt's writings on physiological psychology had succeeded too well. The psychological establishment, founded on Wundt's first but incomplete vision of psychology, was reluctant to accept the idea of a nonexperimental psychology that would complement physiological psychology.

Allport solved his problem by simply ignoring the European theorists and by exhuming an obscure experiment from its grave in the dissertation archives at the University of Indiana, where it was submitted as part of the requirement for a master's degree by an otherwise unknown student by the name of Norman Triplett (see Barone, 1999). Allport dubbed Tripplett's study the "first" social psychology experiment and, today, virtually every social psychology text marks Triplett's experiment as a milestone in the history of social psychology. Barone (1999) persuasively argued that Allport crowned Triplett's study (which contrasted the speed with which people wound fishing reels when alone to their speed of winding in the presence of other fishing-reel winders) because it exemplified Allport's idea of what social psychology should be: It was an experiment, it had a "social" element (i.e., the influence of the presence of others on motor task performance), and, most importantly, it focused on the individual.

Allport's idea of what social psychology should be was not Lewin's idea of what it should be. Lewin saw the declarations made by Allport and others that only the individual exists, or is real, for what they were—preemptory attacks on the study of groups. In a paper published in 1947, "Frontiers in Group Dynamics," Lewin stated,

> Labeling something as "nonexisting" is equivalent to declaring it "out of bounds" for the scientist. Attributing "existence" to an item automatically makes it a duty of the scientist to consider this item as an object of research; it includes the necessity of considering its properties as "facts" which cannot be neglected in the total system of theories; finally, it implies that the terms with which one refers to the item are accepted as scientific "concepts" (rather than as "mere words"). . . .
>
> Like social taboos, a scientific taboo is kept up not so much by a rational argument as by a common attitude among scientists: any member of the scientific guild who does not strictly adhere to the taboo is looked

upon as queer; he is suspected of not adhering to the scientific standards of critical thinking. (see Lewin, 1951, p. 190)

Once again, Lewin's formal training from Cassirer proved helpful. Cassirer had instructed that scientific progress is frequently marked by changes in what is considered real or existing (Lewin, 1951, p. 189). But Lewin elaborated Cassirer's observation: Whereas in physics controversial debates periodically have taken place concerning whatever was believed at the time to be the smallest element of physical material (e.g., a debate about the existence of the atom, then about the existence of the electron, followed by whatever was currently proposed to be the smallest particle), Lewin noted that in the social sciences it has been the larger whole—not the smaller parts—whose existence has been doubted.

As Beveridge (1950) observed, the laurel leaves do not necessarily go to the person who has the original idea; rather, the wreath of victory goes to the person who can sell the idea, which almost always requires executing the idea and showing in concrete ways that it has important implications for understanding the world and for improving human welfare. The execution of a new idea is seldom easy, for it not only requires a new conceptual framework but also often requires the modification of old methodologies and the creation of new methodologies. Lewin realized that psychologists' denial of the existence of groups and group phenomena was based on arguments concerning the proper size of the unit of analysis for psychology. Arguments about the proper unit of analysis for a discipline, in turn, are heavily influenced by conceptual and methodological considerations—on what is believed to be "doable" in terms of systematic observation.

Thus, Lewin was aware that to take psychology where he wanted it to go—to understand a person's love or hatred for another, or an individual's level of aspiration, or how the groups to which a person belongs influence his or her behavior—he would have to demonstrate that these things could be successfully studied by accepted scientific methods. Of all scientific methods, the most highly revered is the experimental method. Hence Lewin (1951) concluded, "The taboo against believing in the existence of a social entity is probably most effectively broken by handling this entity experimentally" (p. 193). Others were coming to the same conclusion.

"MAY THE FORCE BE WITH YOU"

It is helpful to those who wish to change the world, in science or in any other sector, to have the winds of the zeitgeist—the invisible "spirit of the times"—blowing at their backs. The zeitgeist was beginning to blow at Lewin's back when he began his experimental research in group dynamics. Concern with group phenomena began to increase in the United States in the 1930s, prior to America's entry into World War II (see Cartwright & Zander, 1960). The rise of fascism in Europe contributed to the widespread interest in groups, and it also was at least partially responsible for Lewin's interest in racial and ethnic prejudices and aggression. While Lewin was giving a guest lecture at Stanford University, Adolf Hitler was elected chancellor of Germany, and Lewin, who was Jewish, realized that it would be dangerous for him to return to his native land. Friends helped him secure a post at the "child station" at the University of Iowa, but many of Lewin's family, friends, and colleagues were forced to remain in Germany and died in the Holocaust.

Lewin's demonstrations that such "mystical" concepts as "group atmosphere" could be experimentally manipulated and that group atmosphere made a significant difference in the behavior of group members were extremely influential. In one study, Lewin, Lippitt, and White (1939) randomly assigned children to groups that were led in an "authoritarian" style and compared their behavior with children assigned to "democratically" led groups. Different leadership styles produced dramatic differences in the children's behavior (e.g., an order of magnitude increase in hostility expressed in the authoritarian groups as opposed to the democratic groups). This experiment attracted a great deal of attention and helped break down resistance to the study of group influence.

Lewin's experimental study of social influence was different from the Triplett model presented by Allport. Triplett's fish-reel winders were studied as individuals. The social aspect of the experiment was minimal: No social interaction was permitted between the individual and the other persons also winding fishing reels. Thus, the other persons in the Triplett experiment were no more than a passive presence (just as the social "other," usually a stranger to the individual, would be in thousands of social psychology experiments that followed). In Lewin et al.'s (1939) experiment, in contrast, the group members were allowed to interact with each other in a free and natural manner and, over time, came to know each other. Another difference, of course, was that the behaviors focused on by Lewin and his associates had direct import for the practical problems society wished to understand.

The idea that an individual's behavior could be influenced not simply by the individual's internally held and presumably stable attitudes and beliefs but also by the situational influence exerted by others in the individual's social environment, as well as the idea that groups could develop "cultures" that outlived the lives of the individual members (just as an individual's body outlives the death of its cells by continually creating new ones), was shared by Muzafer Sherif. Sherif's (1936) demonstrations that the concept of *social norm* helped account for behavior, and his ingenious employment of the autokinetic effect in his experiments demonstrating the influence of group norms, also helped break down the taboo against the study of groups. Newcomb's (1943) longitudinal study of change in political orientation and attitudes as a function of group norms (i.e., over their 4-year course of study, initially conservative students at Bennington College became more liberal in their political attitudes) also weakened prejudice against the study of groups.

REVOLUTIONARIES NEED DISCIPLES

No one can change the world alone. Disciples are crucial. Lewin was fortunate to attract gifted people to work with him. In retrospect, it is not clear whether those who found themselves being trained in psychology by Lewin were significantly more talented than their cohorts who chose to be trained by others or whether each was inspired by Lewin to rise to the challenges Lewin presented them. What is clear is that many of Lewin's students, and the students of Lewin's students, became significant generators of their own great works. For example, one of Lewin's first students was Leon Festinger, who, along with two of Lewin's other students, helped develop the level-of-aspiration theory (Lewin, Dembo, Festinger, & Sears, 1944). Subsequently, Festinger (1950) formulated the theory of informal communication, which outlined the conditions under which people in a group will attempt to communicate with other group members; the theory of social comparison processes (Festinger, 1954), which was an extension of informal communication theory that focused on when people will seek out others to evaluate the correctness of their attitudes and beliefs and to calibrate their performance skills; and the theory of cognitive dissonance (Festinger, 1957). The literature spawned by all of these theories is massive and, in the case of social comparison processes, still growing.

Festinger's student (and Lewin's grand-student), Stanley Schachter, focused his doctoral dissertation research on a test of Festinger's theory of informal communication, and his classic experiment, "Deviation, Rejection, and Communication" (Schachter, 1951), was the result. Again, in this experiment people were permitted to interact freely, and their patterns of communication and sentiment toward the other group members were assessed over time. Schachter's subsequent work, *The Psychology of Affiliation* (1957), led to his theory of emotion (Schachter, 1964), and his seminal experiments in that arena sparked a renaissance in the study of emotion in psychology, which continues to the present day. Harold H. Kelley, another of Lewin's students, played an important role in theory and research on cognitive attribution processes (e.g., Kelley, 1967). Kelley also is the coauthor of interdependence theory (Kelley & Thibaut, 1978; Thibaut & Kelley, 1959) and coauthor of *Close Relationships* (Kelley et al., 1983) and other works widely regarded as seminal in the development of relationship science (see Berscheid, 1999; Berscheid & Reis, 1998). It would be impossible to trace the impact of the work of all of Lewin's students, Lewin's grand-students, great grand-students, and on down through generations of psychologists, for Lewin's impact continues to be felt in the 21st century.

THE LIFE OF A SCIENTIST MATTERS

Lewin took his professional work in psychology seriously. One can, however, question the quality of his personal life. Exiled from his native land, separated from his family and friends, thrust by circumstance into the heartland of an unfamiliar country whose language he never fully mastered, he worked like a man possessed—possessed by the specters of the demons ravaging his country and killing his loved ones. He worked unstintingly to raise funds to help Jews get out of Germany (for a period of time the Nazis allowed Jews to buy their freedom); to write his theoretical papers; to give lectures on his field theory and studies at other universities and at meetings of scholarly societies (one of which he founded); to conduct his experiments; to train his graduate students; to conduct research with Margaret Mead as part of the war effort; and to teach courses at Iowa and, later, at the Massachusetts Institute of Technology. All of these activities left Lewin bone-weary much of the time. Lewin was sometimes so exhausted that he would have to lie down on the lecture table and teach facing the ceiling (see Marrow, 1969).

Lewin's work had enormous impact. But how many of those who aspire to greatness in psychology would be willing to lead the life he led? One answer is that only a person driven to understand human behavior would do so—perhaps only one who has seen the horrific side of human behavior first hand, especially the terrors of war and the devastation and heartache that prejudice, hatred, and greed leave in their wake. One does not lead the life Lewin led to earn tenure, to obtain a larger office or salary, or to be invited to speak at the next prestigious conference. Only those who believe deeply that their theory and research have the potential to matter to humankind—who believe themselves capable of changing the human condition for the better—are likely to make the many sacrifices necessary to achieve their goal. Thus, yet another lesson to be learned from Lewin's life and work is that psychologists who do not take themselves and their work seriously are not prime candidates for creating a great work that makes a strong impact on the world.

CODA

Many psychology students and professionals do not take themselves and their work seriously in the sense that Lewin did. Many, perhaps most, are "careerists" who as undergraduates found the discipline interesting and decided on psychology as a desirable vocation. They do not necessarily desire to change the world but, rather, simply aspire to an interesting, well-paying, and secure job. If that job is an academic one, however, scholarship and research are required. That research usually is performed within the mainstream of current thought and, sometimes, in perfunctory fashion. The lion's share of "normal scientific activity" is derivative of other scientists' theory and research—often the theory and research of those who are, or will be, regarded as great scientists. Normal science activity, it should be noted, is itself essential to the advancement of knowledge. Although it has become a cliché for great scientists so honored within their lifetimes to acknowledge that they stand on the shoulders of "giants," the truth of the matter is that they also stand on the shoulders of an army of "pygmies" who followed their lead and who did the painstaking research needed to develop and support the great scientist's vision.

Not everyone aspires to be a great scientist, but those who do might conclude from Lewin's life and work that necessary to success are self-confidence, intellectual curiosity, independence of thought and action, and the ability to articulate a different vision of the world simply and persuasively. Self-confidence in one's capabilities to change the world can develop in a wide variety of ways, but it often seems to emerge from knowing the discipline well, which begins with excellent formal training. In addition to the self-confidence that knowledge of the discipline imbues, knowing the state of the discipline is important for another reason: Impact is measured by change. Change cannot be effected without first understanding the thing that is to be changed. Lewin's odyssey also suggests that the aspirant's formal training should include philosophy of science because radical changes in the constructs and methods that form the spine of the discipline are supported by philosophical assumptions which, when challenged, become a source of strong resistance.

Intellectual curiosity is essential to the development of a vision of new directions a discipline might profitably take. Lewin's life illustrates that a radically new vision of the world is not likely to emerge from talking to one's colleagues in the laboratory or by reading others' writings in the library to "get some new ideas" because their opinions are likely to mirror conventional wisdom. As a behavioral scientist, Lewin maintained an avid curiosity about why people behave the way they do in matters important to them and to others, and he continually observed people behaving in vivo and in situ. People who are not observant, who do not question what they see, and who are not alert to discrepancies between what they see and what their training has told them they ought to be seeing are not likely to develop a world vision different from those around them.

Intellectual curiosity and independence go hand in hand. Lewin did not allow others to tell him what ought to be studied or how it should be studied. In his independence of thought, Lewin was like most other great scientists. Nasar (1998), biographer of Nobel prize winner John Nash, wrote, "Even as a student, his indifference to others' skepticism, doubt, and ridicule was awesome" (p. 12). C. P. Snow (1966) wrote of another Nobel prize winner, Albert Einstein, that he "was beyond the normal limits of independence" (p. 95). Having made his signal contributions to physics at a young age,

Einstein spent the remainder of his life trying to develop a theory of the "unified field," a quest his colleagues tried to persuade him was a wild goose chase that was wasting the most powerful intellect of their age and depriving them of his leadership. Nevertheless, "in the private world of theoretical physics, with . . . quiet but total intransigence, he would not budge against the combined forces of the colleagues he loved, Bohr, Born, Dirac, Heisenberg, the major intellects in his own profession" (Snow, 1966, p. 110). Einstein, Lewin, and other great scientists are driven by their visions—not by their colleagues and not by the prospect of personal honor and other extrinsic rewards.

The ability to express a new vision of the world simply, regardless of the underlying complexity of the idea and regardless of how much it defies conventional belief, also appears to be essential to those who wish their work to have an impact. Disciples are unlikely to be attracted if the vision is poorly articulated or expressed in a way that seems discouragingly complex (even though great complexity often underlies ideas that seem simple on the surface, as many of Lewin's writings elaborating his basic idea illustrate). Lewin's core idea, expressed in the equation $B = f(P, E)$, was simple and easy for others to understand—so simple that it now seems ridiculously obvious, especially as the importance of context in the prediction and understanding of human behavior has become recognized in virtually all areas of psychology. The importance of simple and brief articulation also is illustrated by Einstein's initial publication of his theory of relativity; his journal article not only was brief, according to Snow (1966, p. 101), but also contained no references, quoted no authority, and contained very little mathematics:

> There is [however] a good deal of verbal commentary. The conclusions, the bizarre conclusions, emerge as though with the greatest of ease: The reasoning is unbreakable. It looks as though he had reached the conclusions by pure thought, unaided, without listening to the opinions of others. (Snow, 1966, p. 21)

Another example of forceful brevity comes from the work of Hans Selye (e.g., Selye, 1976), generally regarded as the father of psychosomatic medicine. Selye (1936) presented his seminal finding—that the physiological effects of a stressor are not specific to the nature of the stressor but are similar across stressors—in a 74-line journal note.

To self-confidence, intellectual curiosity, independence, and the ability to clearly articulate the vision should be added mental and physical health. Only a mentally and physically healthy person is likely to be able to travel the arduous road to acceptance of a radically new idea—to make the many personal and professional sacrifices necessary to bring the vision to reality. Perhaps the most important lesson to be learned from examining the anatomy of impact is that impact rarely comes cheap, which explains why it so seldom comes at all.

REFERENCES

Allport, F. H. (1924). *Social psychology*. Boston, MA: Houghton-Mifflin.

Barone, D. F. P. (1999). *The problem of interaction in empirical social psychology*. Unpublished manuscript, Illinois State University, Normal.

Berscheid, E. (1999). The greening of relationship science. *American Psychologist, 54*, 260–266.

Berscheid, E. (2000). Back to the future and forward to the past. In S. S. Hendrick & C. Hendrick (Eds.), *Close relationships: A sourcebook* (pp. ix–xxi). Thousand Oaks, CA: Sage.

Berscheid, E., & Reis, H. T. (1998). Attraction and close relationships. In D. T. Gilbert, S. T. Fiske, & G. Lindzey (Eds.), *The handbook of social psychology* (4th ed., pp. 193–281). New York: McGraw Hill.

Beveridge, W. I. B. (1950). *The art of scientific investigation*. New York: Norton.

Boring, E. G. (1950). *A history of experimental psychology*. New York: Appleton-Century-Crofts.

Cartwright, D., & Zander, A. (1960). Origins of group dynamics. In D. Cartwright & A. Zander (Eds.), *Group dynamics: Research and theory* (2nd ed., pp. 3–32). Evanston, IL: Row, Peterson.

Cassirer, E. (1923). *Substance and function*. Chicago: Open Court.

Deutsch, M. (1954). Field theory in social psychology. In G. Lindzey (Ed.), *Handbook of social psychology* (pp. 181–222). Reading, MA: Addison-Wesley.

Festinger, L. (1950). Informal social communication. *Psychological Review, 57*, 271–282.

Festinger, L. (1954). A theory of social comparison processes. *Human Relations, 7*, 117–140.

Festinger, L. (1957). *A theory of cognitive dissonance*. Evanston, IL: Row, Peterson.

Kadanoff, L. P. (2001). Boltzmann's science: Irony and achievement. *Science, 291*, 2553–2554.

Kelley, H. H. (1967). Attribution theory in social psychology. In D. Levine (Ed.), *Nebraska symposium on motivation* (Vol. 15, pp. 192–240). Lincoln: University of Nebraska Press.

Kelley, H. H., Berscheid, E., Christensen, A., Harvey, J., Huston, T. L., Levinger, G., et al. (1983). *Close relationships*. San Francisco, CA: Freeman.

Kelley, H. H., & Thibaut, J. W. (1978). *Interpersonal relations: A theory of interdependence*. New York: Wiley.

Koestler, A. (1971). *The case of the midwife toad*. New York: Random House.

Lewin, K. (1931). The conflict between Aristotelian and Galileian modes of thought in contemporary psychology. *Journal of Genetic Psychology, 5*, 141–177.

Lewin, K. (1951). *Field theory in social science: Selected theoretical papers* (D. Cartwright, Ed.). New York: Harper.

Lewin, K., Dembo, T., Festinger, L., & Sears, P. (1944). Level of aspiration. In J. M. Hunt (Ed.), *Personality and the behavior disorders* (pp. 333–378). New York: Ronald.

Lewin, K., Lippitt, R., & White, R. (1939). Patterns of aggressive behavior in experimentally created "social climates." *Journal of Social Psychology, 10,* 271–299.

Marrow, A. J. (1969). *The practical theorist: The life and work of Kurt Lewin.* New York: Basic Books.

Nasar, S. (1998). *A beautiful mind.* New York: Simon & Schuster.

Newcomb, T. M. (1943). *Personality and social change: Attitude formation in a student community.* New York: Dryden.

Reis, H. T., Collins, W. A., & Berscheid, E. (2000). The relationship context of human behavior and development. *Psychological Bulletin, 126,* 844–872.

Schachter, S. (1951). Deviation, rejection, and communication. *Journal of Abnormal and Social Psychology, 46,* 190–207.

Schachter, S. (1957). *The psychology of affiliation.* Stanford, CA: Stanford University Press.

Schachter, S. (1964). The interaction of cognitive and physiological determinants of emotional state. In L. Berkowitz (Ed.), *Advances in experimental social psychology* (Vol. 1, pp. 49–80). New York: Academic Press.

Selye, H. (1936, July 4). A syndrome produced by diverse nocuous agents. *Nature, 138,* 32.

Selye, H. (1976). *The stress of life.* New York: McGraw-Hill.

Sherif, M. (1936). *The psychology of social norms.* New York: Harper.

Snow, C. P. (1966). *Variety of men.* New York: Scribner's.

Thibaut, J. W., & Kelley, H. H. (1959). *The social psychology of groups.* New York: Wiley.

Wundt, W. (1873–1874). *Grundzuge der physiologischen Psychologie* [Principles of physiological psychology]. Leipzig, Germany: Engelmann.

Wundt, W. (1900–1920). *Völkerpsychologie* [Cultural psychology] (Vols. 1–10). Leipzig, Germany: Engelmann.

7

THE DRAMATURGICAL APPROACH TO SOCIAL PSYCHOLOGY: THE INFLUENCE OF ERVING GOFFMAN

THEODORE R. SARBIN

When invited to write a chapter on a work that has had lasting impact, without a moment's hesitation I thought of the writings of Erving Goffman, especially his first major work, *The Presentation of Self in Everyday Life* (1959; hereinafter *Presentation*). Although nominally a sociologist, Goffman's *oeuvre* was indifferent to disciplinary boundaries—all his perceptive analyses centered on understanding the varieties of conduct at the heart of human interaction.

I begin this appreciative essay, first, with some descriptive comments about the basic theme of *Presentation*. Second, I review briefly a sampling of the conceptual categories in the book that have helped illuminate many dark corners of the phenomena of social interaction. Third, I incorporate some comments to support the claim that the book has had an impact on theory and method in social psychology and offer some observations on the reasons for the book's impact. Finally, I conclude with a brief coda.

I am grateful to Ralph Carney, Gerald Ginsburg, John Kitsuse, and Karl Scheibe for their critical readings of this chapter.

THE THEME OF *PRESENTATION*

The central message of *Presentation* is that human beings are actors, both in the sense of being agents and in the sense of pretending to be what they are not. As agents, human beings are responsible for their actions. They learn early in life that their actions are under the scrutiny of judgmental others so that any violation of the rules of propriety is potentially a threat to one's self. Living in a precarious social world, every turn and juncture presents people with the possibility of shame or embarrassment, of damaging a fragile self. To avoid or to minimize embarrassment, individuals must be ready to use strategies of impression management; that is, they must be ready to *create* performances, to become actors in the theatrical sense. As in theater, the actors strive to present a convincing image of self to dialogue partners and other audiences. Goffman's men and women are less individuals trying to enact conventional roles as in trying to *be* someone or something.

Conventional psychologists of the first half of the 20th century were obsessed with discovering the covert variables of human thought and action. They were insensitive to the everyday observation that human beings are role takers, thereby failing to take advantage of the analytic power of constructions that recognized that a person could legitimately enact a particular role and also could pretend or dissimulate that he or she was legitimately entitled to perform that role. A man could legitimately be a physician and act according to society's role expectations; another man, not a physician, could act *as if* he were.

Presentation was the first of Goffman's 11 books. The framework is out-and-out dramaturgical. Goffman acknowledged the usefulness of technical, political, structural, and cultural perspectives and the "dramaturgical approach may constitute a fifth perspective" (Goffman, 1959, p. 240). Although not the first to write a social psychology from the perspective immortalized by Shakespeare that "all the world's a stage," Goffman can be credited with being its most visible 20th-century proponent. Unlike the authors of standard social psychology texts, in *Presentation* Goffman eschewed the laboratory experiment, the survey, and census figures as data sources. The data for his conceptual analyses were his detailed observations of the expressive behavior of everyday people in interaction with other everyday people, in uncontrived settings. Besides his acute firsthand observations, he made use of illustrative newspaper stories, anecdotes reported by journalists and novelists, guidebooks on proper etiquette, not to mention relevant conceptual distinctions made by social theorists such as Robert Park, Margaret Mead, Charles Cooley, William James, Georg Simmel, Emile Durkheim, Kenneth Burke, Jean-Paul Sartre, and others.

Whatever theoretical conclusions readers may draw from *Presentation*, they would necessarily be limited to propositions about what happens when people are in one another's presence. Goffman's gaze was directed to persons-in-interaction, not to encapsulated individuals. As a social psychological set of constructions, the focus is on episodic interpersonal encounters. For Goffman, life is lived through small interpersonal episodes that are fluid and transient. Men and women are flexible players who improvise gestural and rhetorical tactics to make warrantable their role enactments and their moral claims. The interactants attribute meaning not only to the contents of verbal speech of their dialogue partners but also to the coughs, shrugs, pauses, postural adjustments, grimaces, nods, winks, and so on. The meanings assigned to the intentional communicative acts provide the subtexts for little dramas that threaten or protect the fragile self. At the same time, the interactants assign meanings to cues unintentionally given off by others.

CONCEPTUAL CATEGORIES

It is not possible in this brief essay to touch on all the categories employed by Goffman that give body to his claims about the ubiquity of dramaturgical practices in everyday settings. To provide the reader with the flavor of these categories, I identify a sampling of these categories that, incidentally, are usually overlooked in traditional theorizing or in preparing experiments. Throughout the text, Goffman coined a special but not recondite vocabulary to describe the contexts in which actors present themselves. Being committed to a dramaturgical perspective, he drew many of the concepts from stagecraft. For example, he made use of the *front stage* and *back stage* terms from traditional theater and such modifications as *front regions* and *back regions*. Some impression management goals involve concealment and secretiveness. "Barriers to perception" (Goffman, 1959, p. 106) facilitate the attainment of such goals. The front region is where the actor performs before the audience; the back region is where "the impression fostered by the performance is knowingly contradicted" (p. 112). Goffman illustrated with a quotation from Simone de Beauvoir that describes women's back stage activities when male dialogue partners are not present. The woman "is getting her costume together, preparing her make-up, laying out her tactics; she is lingering in dressing-gown and slippers in the wings before making her entrance on the stage" (p. 113).

Goffman cited examples of social establishments where members of the audience are not allowed entry into certain regions. Whether in an automobile repair shop, a department store, a courtroom, or a hospital, the performers put on their masks for front stage appearances and remove them back stage. A critical time to observe impression management is when the performers move from front to back stage or from back to front. Goffman (1959) noted that "at these moments one can detect a wonderful putting on and taking off of character" (p. 112). Such observations raise questions about the claim in many personality theories of the presence of a core or "authentic" self.

Some expressive acts of the performer are given and some are given off. *Given acts* are the deliberate verbal and gestural behaviors that the actor performs to create a particular impression of self. *Given off acts* are expressions that are unintended or unwitting, mainly nonverbal. The acts are important cues to dialogue partners and other audience members for creating impressions. People are sometimes capable of finely tuned impression management skills and can simulate acts that appear to be given off. The talent to simulate emotional expressions challenges the claims of some students of emotional life who assume that most facial and bodily emotional displays are not under the actor's control but are hard-wired through evolutionary design.

A chapter devoted to *performance teams* makes clear that in most real-life situations actors are parts of teams, such as doctor and nurse, collaborating coworkers on a production line, teachers in a school, and so on. Although the concept of team suggests cooperative conduct, there is also the implication of conspiracy, collusion, and complicity. To advance their complicit goals, members of a team may create and harbor secrets. There are inside secrets, dark secrets, and strategic secrets. *Inside secrets* are practices shared simply in virtue of being a member of a collaborative work group. *Dark secrets* must be kept under cover because, if revealed, they would cancel out the impression that the team is trying to present. *Strategic secrets* are bits of knowledge that may be part of a plan to outwit an antagonist at some future time. Goffman (1959) pointed out that such secrets are rarely perfectly concealed because the "congruence among functions, information possessed, and accessible regions is seldom complete" (p. 145). The failure to keep secrets is attributed in part to people enacting discrepant roles, an example of which is the informer. Such a person gains entry into backstage practices and maneuvers and reveals the secrets to persons in the front regions.

Every reader of *Presentation* as a performer or member of a performance team can recall engaging in communicative acts that are incongruent with the impression he or she intends to maintain during an interactional episode. Goffman identified four types of such communications out of character: treatment of the absent, staging talk, team collusion, and realigning actions.

Treatment of the absent is the practice in which customers, for example, are ridiculed, criticized, lampooned, and cursed back stage although acting decorously and respectfully when in front stage. The self that is presented to back stage coworkers is not the self that is presented to the customer. Goffman suggested that such back stage communicative acts provide an opportunity for morale building among the workforce. The front stage activities are designed to satisfy the mutual goals of the salespeople and their customers.

Staging talk occurs out of the presence of the audience. Discussion among the actors turns to problems of staging the performance. For example, performers might engage in discourse about the reception given one's recent performance, it is "mulled over in what are sometimes called 'post mortems,' wounds are licked and morale is strengthened for the next performance" (Goffman, 1959, p. 176).

Team collusion is an especially subtle strategy. It typically occurs with the audience present, but the members of the audience are not aware that the definition of the situation is different from what it appears to be. Team members collusively perform communicative acts without disabling the impressions they have been communicating to the audience.

> Persons who are admitted to this secret communication are placed in a collusive relationship to one another vis-à-vis the remainder of the participants. By acknowledging to one another that they are keeping relevant secrets from the others present, they acknowledge to one another that the show of candor they maintain, a show of being only the characters they officially project, is merely a show. By means of such byplay, performers can affirm a backstage solidarity even while engaged in a performance, expressing with impunity unacceptable things about the audience as well as things about themselves that the audience would find unacceptable. (Goffman, 1959, p. 177)

Realigning reactions are those performances in which the performer goes beyond the safe means of telling about their dissatisfaction but without threatening the quality of the performance or the relationship of the team members' connections with the audience.

Goffman, in characteristic fashion, offered numerous examples of such communications out of character. They tend to satisfy the requirements of back stage performers for relaxation and morale building. At the same time, these examples point to the requirements for collusive communications with the audience being present, without disrupting the quality of the performance or the proper relationship with the audience. But there are breakdowns in communication. Performances are sometimes spoiled or derailed. It is such conditions that "techniques of impression management function to avoid" (Goffman, 1959, p. 208).

IMPACT ON THE FIELD

The claim that *Presentation* has had substantial and sustained impact can be readily documented. In a retrospective review in *Contemporary Psychology* (1987) 28 years after its initial publication, Karl Scheibe described *Presentation* as having earned the status of a modern classic. At that time, more than 600,000 copies had been sold, and the book was still selling at the rate of 1,500 copies a month. It had been translated into 12 languages. The *Social Sciences Citation Index* (which began publication in 1973) noted the book was consistently cited at least 100 times a year. From 1975 to 2000, *Presentation* was cited well over 4,000 times. For the year 2000 alone, 176 citations were reported. It is safe to say that the recognition of the seminal value of Goffman's constructions has not diminished. For example, Goffman was cited in connection with the proposition that "embarrassment is vital to the social order" (Keltner & Anderson, 2000). A current textbook on personality devotes substantial space to Goffman's interactionist and dramaturgical constructions (Hogan & Smither, 2001).

Why did Goffman's work have such impact on theory and practice in social psychology? To answer this question, one needs, first, to review the background for Goffman's work. *Presentation* was published in 1959. Goffman wrote in the preface that the book was an elaboration of a monograph published in 1955 that, in turn, was based on his doctoral dissertation, the report of ethnographic field work on communication conduct carried out in the Shetland Islands (1953). The doctoral dissertation was supervised by Everett C. Hughes, the University of Chicago professor of sociology, an expert on the social psychology of occupations. Hughes was an exponent of the position that one should be sensitive to the nuances of interaction in the workplace. Goffman was also influenced by William Lloyd Warner, a professor of anthropology, who emphasized the importance of microanalysis of interaction.

The social science departments at the University of Chicago had a long history of studying behavior in situ. Classical examples of this genre are *The Ghetto* (1928) by Louis Wirth, *The Jack Roller* by Clifford Shaw (1930), and *The Gold Coast and the Slum* by Henry Zorbaugh (1929), among others. Goffman's analysis of social interaction in and out of work settings was an extension of the Chicago tradition and brought to the fore the agentic, intentional nature of human action. People were not solely driven by tissue needs, complexes, and personality traits but by the exigencies of social situations. Unlike analyses stemming from psychodynamic doctrines in which action was a function of assumed mental structures, Goffman advanced the notion that people purposefully made choices in their performances to maintain what he called *the definition of the situation*. Goffman's unique contribution was the development of categories of microanalysis that facilitated the recognition of subtle interactions, verbal and nonverbal. A large body of research has emerged from Goffman's theses on impression management (see, e.g., Schlenker, 1980, 1985). The research findings are consistent with Goffman's claims that people will employ strategic acts, tactical maneuvers, and protective behaviors to maintain a definition of the situation in the service of maintaining one's self. A close reading of the text reveals that actions to maintain one's self-presentation are at the same time in the service of maintaining civility and social order. *Presentation* helped to initiate studies in the rapidly expanding field of discourse analysis.

Effect on the Reader

I can identify at least three reasons why *Presentation* has been widely read, cited, and quoted. The first is the effect on the reader of Goffman's unique writing style: matter-of-fact, nonjudgmental descriptions of the theatrical performances of ordinary people in quotidian situations. The reader discovers himself or herself in the detailed descriptions of people using their dramaturgical and rhetorical skills in the interest of presenting a self. The many examples of strategies employed to avoid embarrassment, to save face, or to enhance the self serve as cues to readers that call up autobiographical rememberings of their own use of dramaturgical strategies. In general, people avoid admitting to others (and even to self) that they use pretense and role playing in their commerce with others. This avoidance is related to the value that official morality places on being authentic in the presentation of self. Recognizing oneself in reading the descriptions of the dramatic performances of ordinary people provides a warrant of validity for Goffman's claims.

The claim that the person is primarily a performer trying to impress audiences might be interpreted as a form of cynicism. From the dramaturgical perspective, there is no controverting the claim that social life is in great measure a matter of putting on a show. Goffman is clear in his arguments that being a socialized human inevitably implies that situations will arise in which it is necessary to engage in deception, sham, and pretense.

A thoroughgoing cynic would be a person who interprets all human action as arising from unacceptable motives. Although Goffman's writing style frequently reflected an attachment to irony, he was not a cynic. He did not evaluate the use of dramaturgical acts as immoral. On the contrary, he treated the person's use of artifice as an unavoidable consequence of maintaining social equilibrium, of facilitating an acceptable definition of the situation. Instead of attributing cynicism to Goffman, the argument can be made that he regarded as a form of altruism the use of artifice to maintain civility and social order. How Goffman handled the moral issue of inauthenticity connected with pretense and other strategies must be inferred from his apparently nonjudgmental descriptions. However, in a concluding statement, he explicitly comes to grips with the moral issue:

> In their capacity as performers, individuals will be concerned with maintaining the impression that they are living up to the many standards by which they and their products are judged. Because these standards are so numerous and so pervasive, the individuals who are performers dwell more than we might think in a moral world. But, *qua* performers, individuals are concerned not with the moral issue of realizing these standards, but with the amoral issue of engineering a convincing impression that these standards are being realized. Our activity, then, is largely concerned with moral matters, but as performers we do not have a moral concern with them. As performers we are merchants of morality. . . . To

use a different imagery, the very obligation and profitability of appearing always in a steady moral light, of being a socialized character, forces one to be the sort of person who is practiced in the ways of the stage. (Goffman, 1959, p. 251)

As "merchants of morality," Goffman's characters are not entirely free—they are imprisoned by the rules, norms, and expectations that define a given dramatic encounter. Goffman would make the claim that social systems, even minisystems, *require* performers to make use of impression management techniques. The observations about differences in front stage and back stage performances lead to the inference that authenticity is a chimera. Goffman would argue that the spontaneity that goes with freedom has unpredictable risks, if the spontaneous actions disrupt the ongoing drama, what he repeatedly calls the definition of the situation.

Demands of the Zeitgeist

The second reason for the impact of *Presentation* can be related to the demands of the zeitgeist. After World War II, psychologists were exploring ways of departing from their historically pre-emptive interest in the study of mental life, a vestigial remnant of Cartesian epistemology. Gilbert Ryle's *Concept of Mind* (1949) had delivered the *coup de grace* to theories that assigned causal properties to "mind." Behaviorist reinforcement theory had been introduced as a replacement to the claim that "mental processes" were the source of variation in response to experimenter-controlled stimuli. The prevailing paradigm had been mechanistic: Experimenters sought causality by assessing "responses" to socially generated stimuli after the pattern of the laboratory scientist measuring muscle twitches in response to tactile stimuli. People were regarded as passive processors of stimuli. As laboratory specimens, they were not regarded as agents whose actions were guided by purposes and intentions. In the prevailing ideology, "responses" were mechanically "emitted" under the control either of internal mental processes or of reinforcement contingencies.

Reinforcement theory was feebly inadequate to explain such phenomena as choice behavior in conflict situations, particularly behavior that was counterintuitive. Dissatisfied with the trivial outcomes of standard research designs based on stimulus–response models, social psychologists turned to models in which the human being was an agent with intentions and purposes. A conative perspective—performances of everyday people in concrete situations—became the focus, departing from exclusive attention to stimulus–response connections and from the search for causal variables in the mental apparatus or in reinforcement contingencies. The shift was from "happenings" in the mind to the "doings" of persons. The pivotal question became "What does the person *do* in a problematic situation?"

Goffman wrote *Presentation* during the period when the social sciences, including social psychology, were becoming disillusioned with the yield from veiled mechanistic theories. The notion of reinforcement, a fixture of mechanistic learning theories, could not illuminate the conduct of men and women trying to solve identity and existential problems arising in the course of living a life. The zeitgeist encouraged the use of metaphors drawn from humanistic sources such as drama and rhetoric as a replacement for such mechanistic metaphors as energy, force, valence, reinforcement, and so on.

The zeitgeist promoted the introduction of fresh metaphors for understanding psychological phenomena, among them dissonance and role. *Dissonance* referred to the condition in which a person had to deal with two or more incompatible beliefs or actions. It was the antecedent condition in the cognitive dissonance model developed by Leon Festinger (1957), a model that had its origins in the field-theoretical perspective of Kurt Lewin. Although Festinger and his associates wrote about incompatible cognitions as stimulus conditions, they were ultimately interested in actions taken, choices made, explanations given, and so on. Through manipulating variables in the laboratory, dissonance researchers demonstrated that people are agents.

Role was borrowed from the drama and was consistent with the worldview that people are actors. Role concepts were central to a number of emerging conative models, among them the frameworks advanced by Theodore Newcomb (1951) and Theodore Sarbin (1954) in social psychology and Norman Cameron (1947) in abnormal psychology. These conative frameworks flowed in great measure from the seminal constructions of George Herbert Mead (1934) in which role-theoretical concepts were central. *Presentation* was a refined development of the conative perspective that made use of Mead's observations on role taking. Goffman's contribution stemmed from the recognition that attention had to be directed to the subtle, fleeting, finely nuanced microactions of people as performers in quasi-theatrical settings.

Goffman conducted his studies not by manipulating variables in the laboratory but by observing people in their daily interactions with coworkers, family members, guests, customers, and other face-to-face participants. His interest was in the interaction order: how persons, as performers in face-to-face situations, modulated their actions to present a self that would be instrumental in resolving potential or actual strains in the social system.

Context

A third reason for the impact of *Presentation* is the emphasis on context. Any reader of *Presentation* recognizes that the interpersonal situations that give rise to the necessity for dramaturgical acts provide a contextual base of ever-increasing complexity. Although Goffman does not allude to Pepper's (1943) thesis on contextualism as a worldview, the content of *Presentation* is continuous with a contextualist epistemology.

The root metaphor of contextualism is the historical act. To enter into the complexity of any historical act, the observer must try to take into account the prevailing historical conditions, the geographical setting, the moral climate, the stage props, the nature of the built and natural environment, and so on. To take into account the context of any particular interactional episode, Goffman made use of narrative reporting, the method practiced by historians and other practitioners of the humanities who are guided by the proposition that narrative is the most felicitous way of representing the fullness of context for any historical act. In a sense, the need to incorporate the context justified Goffman's rejection of the standard methods of doing social psychology that artificially impoverish context: hypothesis-testing experiments, social surveys, quantification, and other technologies associated with the mechanistic tradition.

CODA

In numerous places in *Presentation*, Goffman wrote of dramaturgical actions being in the service of maintaining a definition of the situation. The contexts usually provide clues as to the referents for "situation." Today, as a result of the recent developments in narrative psychology, the definition of the situation would be translated in narrative terms. When confronted with an ambiguous situation, the person silently asks the questions: What story have I entered? What is the plot? What roles are the other actors performing? The "story," unlike the ambiguous "situation," has a beginning, a middle, an ending, and a moral point. From cues given and given off by other performers, the actor silently formulates answers to such questions suggesting what reciprocal or complementary role to adopt and what dramaturgical strategies to enact to stay within the bounds of a particular story line. Translating situations into narratives does no violence to Goffman's theses. In fact, narratives are implicit in the descriptions that are summarized as the definition of the situation. As I mentioned before, his rhetorical style is narrational. His descriptions allow the inference that stories lived, stories read, and stories told guided the dramaturgical performances of the exemplars who populate his text.

Throughout the text, Goffman wrote about the rich variety of acts that people perform in the interest of presenting a self. It remains problematic what he meant by self. His purpose was to report on the complexities of the interaction order, not to write a unified theory of the self. In most of his examples, the self is no more than the image that the individual wants to portray at a given juncture in an interpersonal episode, that is to say, a social self, the contents of which are context dependent. In other examples, the self is something like a personal possession. Because his framework is that of actions in the presence of others, it is safe to say that his main concerns were with the social self and his recognition that people will do almost anything to present a self in an acceptable moral light. Without applying moral criteria, in an objective fashion he painted portraits of interactants masking their "true feelings," telling lies, and expressing half-truths. Absent an explicit moral judgment on acts that are not sincere, some critics have assumed that Goffman was an advocate for insincerity. Critical readers, in disapproving the dramaturgical conduct of Goffman's exemplars, can reject Goffman for his interest in the theater as a model for social action. Some of his critics (see, e.g., Gouldner, 1970) have trivialized Goffman's claims by interpreting the use of artifice as serving sinister machiavellian motives. Behind this criticism is the claim that dramaturgy erodes the virtue of sincerity. Implied is the superiority of the virtue of authenticity.

By regarding dramaturgical strategies as instances of Sartrean "bad faith," critics fault Goffman for not recognizing that moral life is a matter of living up to an "authentic" self. The latter essentialist conception of self is posited in most personality theories and in existentialist writings.

Those who disapprove of Goffman's self as context-dependent argue for the moral superiority of being authentic. Polonius's counsel, "To thine own self be true," reflects the moral posture. But what is the true self? Which of the many presentations in the course of a day reflects the true self? Those who claim that "being true to oneself" is morally superior need to be reminded that history records the malevolent deeds of figures such as Attila, Nero, Joseph Stalin, Adolf Hitler, and more recently Timothy McVeigh, who were all guided by an ethic of authenticity.

The scores of social acts described in *Presentation* reveal a concern with saving people from embarrassment and with promoting the flow of sociality. Practices that are tactful, diplomatic, and kind help maintain the flow of collaborative narratives. Rather than pejoratively labeling Goffman's dramaturgical strategies of self-presentation as reflecting a lack of sincerity, it would be more to the point to construe such actions as expressions of civility. Without civility, social life would be brutish, and probably unbearable.

REFERENCES

Cameron, N. (1947). *The psychology of behavior disorders*. Boston: Houghton-Mifflin.

Festinger, L. (1957). *A theory of cognitive dissonance*. Evanston, IL: Row Peterson.

Goffman, E. (1959). *The presentation of self in everyday life*. New York: Doubleday.

Gouldner, A. (1970). *The coming crisis of Western sociology*. New York: Basic Books.

Hogan, R., & Smither, R. (2001). *Personality: Theory and applications*. Boulder, CO: Westview Press.

Keltner, D., & Anderson, C. (2000). Saving face for Darwin: The functions and uses of embarrassment. *Current Directions in Psychological Science, 9*, 187–192.

Mead, G. H. (1934). *Mind, self, and society*. Chicago: University of Chicago Press.

Newcomb, T. M. (1951). *Social psychology*. New York: Holt, Rinehart & Winston.

Pepper, S. (1943). *World hypotheses*. Berkeley: University of California Press.

Ryle, G. (1949). *The concept of mind*. London: Hutchinson.

Sarbin , T. R. (1954). Role theory. In G. Lindzey & E. Aronson (Eds.), *Handbook of social psychology* (Vol. I, pp. 223–258). Reading, MA: Addison-Wesley.

Scheibe, K. E. (1987). Goffman redux. *Contemporary Psychology, 32*, 501–502.

Schlenker, B. R. (1980). *Impression management*. New York: Wiley.

Schlenker, B. R. (1985). *The self and social life*. New York: Wiley.

Shaw, C. R. (1930). *The Jack Roller*. Chicago: University of Chicago Press.

Social Sciences Citation Index. (1973–present). Philadelphia: Institute for Scientific Information.

Wirth, L. (1928). *The ghetto*. Chicago: University of Chicago Press.

Zorbaugh, H. W. (1929). *The gold coast and the slum*. Chicago: University of Chicago Press.

8

A SCIENCE OF PERSONS: EXPLORING THE IMPACT OF R. D. LAING'S *THE DIVIDED SELF* ON PSYCHOLOGY

FREDERICK J. WERTZ AND MICHAEL ALCEE

As the decade of the 1950s drew to a close and the gathering momentum of humanistic and cognitive currents was aiming to change the course of psychology, Ronald D. Laing published his first book, *The Divided Self* (1960). Although this book's potential impact on psychology is great and although it has been enthusiastically embraced by many, *The Divided Self* has had very limited influence on our science and profession. This chapter analyzes the reception of this work, which challenged and attempted to change deeply held assumptions and well-established practices in the field of psychology. We begin with a synopsis of the book, highlighting its specific contributions to clinical psychology as well as its implications for general psychology. The text's actual impact on psychology and its relation to popular cultural trends are then assessed. Our analysis of the book's impact requires, beyond a consideration of the book's merits, attention to dialectical relations among the author's career, historical trends in psychology, and societal context. This study brings to light some of the difficulties encountered by innovative work that draws on traditions outside of mainstream psychology. We also glean some lessons for psychology, which could benefit from a more open and better-informed dialogue with works that diverge from the dominant, mainstream approach.

PSYCHOLOGY FROM THE STANDPOINT OF *THE DIVIDED SELF*

Although the topic of Laing's (1960) book is schizophrenia, the focus is even more narrow and the ambition more broad. Laing presented a psychological study of one way that some people become "schizophrenic." He does not indicate what other ways involve, let alone suggest any universal description or etiology. Because Laing's greater aim was to propose and demonstrate a special way of researching the lives of people, his approach was not limited to "one way of becoming schizophrenic," to other forms of schizophrenia, or even to the broad field of psychopathology. It could be applied to all subject matter in psychology, for it provides the unique scientific foundation that in Laing's view psychology is lacking.

By 1960, the existential–phenomenological approach used by Laing had a long and distinguished history in psychology, but it had only recently been introduced in the United States through difficult works that use philosophically derived language. Laing claimed that this approach makes possible the achievement of a most difficult goal, that of *understanding* "schizophrenics." Although volumes of studies have provided us with knowledge of their neurophysiology and brain anatomy, of their hereditary and social etiological factors, and of their demographics, these works have provided only information about the organism, decontextualized factors, and impersonal figures. One could master all this knowledge without being able to understand one single schizophrenic person. Understanding requires different methods, different concepts, and, moreover, a different kind of relationship with the people being studied.

For Laing, a *person* is an original center of experience and of action in the world. We *understand* a person when we are able to grasp particular expressions, such as nonverbal conduct and speech, in the context of that individual's *being-in-the-world*. This means grasping how the person experiences and comports himself or herself with other people, how a given moment of a person's life follows from his or her past and aims to bring about an intended future. In schizophrenic persons, we must come to know the place of "hallucinations" and "delusions" in the overall context of the person's being-in-the-world.

Laing asserted that we must empathically enter into the other person's life and grasp the meanings of situations for him or her. This work requires a special social–emotional attitude which, mincing no words, Laing called *love*. Love is the basic requirement of all research that aims to understand people, especially when it involves a person-to-person relationship. People more readily disclose their meaningful experiences when they feel genuinely cared for, respected, and valued by an inquirer. When people are leery and apt to conceal or deceive, an inquirer's trustworthiness is essential. The extreme social uneasiness of people with schizophrenia allows Laing's study to demonstrate attitudes that are important for all psychology.

The knowledge in *The Divided Self* is acquired by an empirical *phenomenological* method. After setting all theories and knowledge methodically aside, Laing shared patients' lived experiences and reflectively described what is essential to these individuals' psychology. Although it is often naively presumed that *case studies* can provide only idiographic knowledge, Laing found many commonalities, enabling him to describe one general path to schizophrenia. Common essential themes and intricate, temporally unfolding organizations of experience and conduct were evident in numerous patients, including other therapists' with different orientations.

Understanding Schizophrenia

Ontological Security and Insecurity

Laing found that some individuals diagnosed with schizophrenia are struggling with fundamental life challenges concerning their being consistently real and embodied in relation to other people. Those with *ontological security* are neither problem-free nor necessarily happy, perhaps even afflicted with severe psychopathologies, but this is not the starting point of the path to schizophrenia described by Laing. Others feel more unreal than real, less at one with their bodies, less continuous through time, and more vulnerable to dissolution in relating to others. Some of these ontologically insecure people become primarily concerned with protecting themselves from dissolution as they encounter a world that for them is overwhelming and liable to destroy their being (as a person, which means their being a center of worldly experience and an author of their own action). Such people are no longer concerned with *gratifying* themselves but with *preserving* themselves.

Becoming a "Schizoid" Person

Some ontologically insecure people attempt to preserve themselves by bifurcating their lives. On the one hand, they live in unembodied, private ways that they regard as their "true" self. On the other hand, they use their embodied life, including behavior relating to others, as a cover of protection that they regard as "false." This "schizoid" mode of existence is a midpoint on the path some traverse toward schizophrenia. However, the schizoid person is "sane" and may achieve a satisfying, creative, and successful life. Because such people do not share their true experiences with others, they are not well understood; others see only the false (embodied) self. Such a person might be considered "a loner," "a private sort," or "an enigma." However, such people may be very reflectively aware of the split they are cultivating and may take pride in knowing well how they truly feel. They value the safety and freedom gained by keeping their inner experiences from the judgments, manipulations, and meddling of others. Every psychological way of life is fraught with numerous possibilities, is dynamic, and does not stand still. Whatever benefits and advantages are afforded by the schizoid way of existence, it may lead to schizophrenia.

Becoming Schizophrenic

The most conceptually difficult part of Laing's account concerns the movement from a schizoid lifestyle to a schizophrenic one. Schizophrenia admits of numerous individual and typical variations that culminate in phenomena of many different forms and varieties. Also, the transition from the schizoid to the schizophrenic may be very fluid and is by no means a one-way or all-or-none transition; there are a vast array of gradations and reversals. One possibility of the schizoid way of life is the complete severance of the inner, disembodied, true self and the outer, false one. One's outer behavior may become more and more a role, a fake, a contrivance that has no genuine meaning to the actor. More and more detached from the bodily, perceptual, and social world, one's inner, unembodied self may become increasingly "liberated" thought and fantasy in a realm of omnipotent self-determination. The embodied self may cease any functional relation to the social world as the person identifies more completely with the unembodied self, for the organization of behavior requires some purpose rooted in the life of the actor. Behavior, perception, and relations with others then become increasingly futile and meaningless. The freedom, safety, and transparency undertaken in this project of disconnection turn out to be only apparent as the person increasingly departs from the one and only real world and travels down a "vortex on nonbeing." Rather than preserving oneself, one destroys oneself as a person, as a center of meaningful experience of and action in the world.

Being Schizophrenic

The transition from a schizoid to a schizophrenic existence may occur abruptly or gradually, relatively partially or completely. The schizophrenic person may also revert back to a functional schizoid lifestyle to flee the perils of schizophrenia. In schizophrenia, the radical split between inner and outer, between true and false selves, may be abolished. A schizophrenic person may attempt to abandon the false self because of its futility or absurdity, as do some catatonic people. The schizophrenic person may throw caution to the wind and express outright the "true" private self, which by now may be fantastic, volitized, or incomprehensible. One may proclaim oneself to be Christ or the Devil; to have special magical powers; or to be a sibling, mother, or father. One may proclaim that one is "a lost baby," "not a human being," or simply "nothing." One may protect this fragile, vulnerable self—so fragmentary and permeated with nothingness—by contriving ever more false and absurd comportment to keep threatening others at bay or by deliberately being obtuse and elusive. As the schizophrenic person ceases to uphold the appearance of normality to others, ontological insecurity can reach glaring and transparent intensity, for instance, in the form of persecutory hallucinations and delusions that are now openly expressed. This transition into schizophrenia may involve honesty inasmuch as previously private beliefs are expressed. However, because personal meaning has been cut off and removed from existence-with-others so thoroughly, the person's "inner truth" may be so equivocal that it cannot be expressed at all and may not even exist except as a pure "potential."

Becoming Ontologically Secure

It is possible that a person remains schizophrenic. It is also possible that a person "recovers" from schizophrenia by readopting a schizoid lifestyle. However, Laing's case material also shows that it is possible for a schizophrenic person to develop primary ontological security. One of Laing's disorganized patients, while watching Federico Fellini's film *La Strada*, realized that, although the central character's station in life was far worse than her own, this character never conspired in her own destruction and was able, despite everything, to feel worthwhile as a person and to take simple joy in the world. This sudden insight transformed the patient. She stopped "destroying herself" and began to see her own value and possibilities for pleasure in the world. Another patient felt more valued by her psychoanalytic therapist than by anyone she had known, including herself. She began to enjoy situations and to express herself genuinely, basking in the sun of this therapist's nonpossessive affirmation. The possibility of beginning an authentic life—including joy, a significant sense of self, temporal continuity, and meaningful relations with other people—is present in schizophrenia. This does not mean a life without suffering, for in a sense real suffering is accepted for the first time.

Image of the Person in *The Divided Self*

Laing's view of the person as a center of experience and an agent of action contrasts with the view of the person as an organism offered by reifying psychological theory. Laing's phenomenological method presents psychological processes not as determined by physical or any other external forces, nor as fixed or final; instead, every psychological process holds numerous possibilities for becoming and in an important way determines itself through its own unfolding course. Descriptive evidence shows that the person is self-determining. This is not to say that a person is unaffected by or impervious to his or her surroundings. On the contrary, psychological processes are essentially open to the world and therein to the influence of other people. Profoundly subject to his or her surroundings, the person is nevertheless an original center of that experience and an author of action in that situation. Genuine psychological knowledge features this centrality and does not reduce the person to a "thing" determined by impersonal forces or laws of hereditary, environmental, or even cognitive variables.

The Divided Self includes a focus on the social and familial contexts that, essential in understanding schizophrenia, were to become central in Laing's subsequent research. Because being-in-the-world is not a construct that refers to isolated psychological processes but to *existence*, the "understanding" achieved in this book already acknowledges the "social intelligibility" of schizophrenia. By delineating an interpretation of psychological phenomena in the context of the person's being-in-the-world, *The Divided Self* lays the groundwork for a more systematic investigation of psychological processes in social, familial, societal, cultural–historical, and even spiritual contexts. Consistently remaining within a holistic, Continental scientific framework that replaces etiology and theory with understanding and intelligibility, Laing extended and developed his radically contextual, relational, political view of the person in his later works (Laing, 1961, 1967; Laing & Cooper, 1964; Laing & Esterson, 1964).

Psychology as a Science of Persons

In *The Divided Self*, psychology's most distinctive scientific aim is to understand people. Valid understanding requires a special attitude that is loving, open, and nonmanipulative. Laing's psychology demands a meticulous description and rigorous, laborious, reflective interpretation of meaning in the natural contexts of human life. Abstract psychological constructs in themselves do not provide genuine understanding; at best they provide the starting point of a label–sign for something that requires concrete description, laborious analysis, and multicontextual interpretation if we are to understand "what it is" (the *essence*) to which the categorization, measurement, hypothesis testing, and theoretical explanation refer. Although focused on understanding and rendering intelligible individual persons, the insights gained by the researcher identify essential meanings that may be common among many individuals. As additional investigations of individuals proceed, the researcher discovers these generalities, or common psychological processes. Generalities are then illustrated by descriptions of individual people's lives, making a full circle. However, even such descriptive/interpretive knowledge always remains epistemologically subordinated to a fresh, open contact with people in application and practice. In this way Laing's psychology demands a high degree of scientific skepticism, that is, subordination of theories, constructs, abstract ideas, and even research findings, to ever more open and contextually varied empirical observation. Laing's psychology is maximally unpresumptuous, unwilling to take anything for granted, and welcoming of self-criticism. Above all, this psychology embodies a respect for the people confronting psychologists in clinical and research situations. Honoring their concrete expressions is the top scientific priority, the basis for developing new modes of conceptualization, research, and healing practice.

THE DIVIDED SELF IN PSYCHOLOGY AND THE WIDER CULTURE

Reviews

Reviews of *The Divided Self* came in two waves, the first after its original 1960 publication in England and the second in 1970 after the wider distribution of the second edition in the United States. The best-known original review, Brierley's (1961), was quite positive. Brierley considered the book most interesting, highlighted its contribution to our sympathetic understanding of schizophrenia, and applauded its wealth of clinical material. Although Brierley appreciated Laing's independence from psychoanalysis, her reservations centered around the interest in translating his findings into psychoanalytic terms and the fear that the work could lead to a discarding of psychoanalysis. The ambivalence of the psychoanalytic community toward *The Divided Self* came out more explicitly in Schafer's (1970) mixed review. With considerable defensiveness and hostility, Schafer expressed great doubt about Laing's abandonment of psychoanalysis. The eventual dismissal of Laing's work by many psychoanalysts appears to be more a protection of the institution of psychoanalysis than a refutation of any of the methods or insights offered in Laing's book.

Laing's empirical findings and "respectful" contributions to psychoanalysis were applauded without any reservation in the existential Van Kaam's (1962) early review, although he was disappointed that the book did not provide the much-needed introduction to existential psychology and a comprehensive theory of schizophrenia. Wortman (1973) applauded the publication and availability of Laing's books in the United States and recognized the varying opinions: "They have been analyzed, reviewed, shrugged off, and praised to the sky" (p. 301). Wortman himself held in high esteem the clarity, accessibility, and rightness of Laing's "radical new approach to the understanding of psychotics" (p. 312), appreciated Laing's inclusion of the political in his treatment of the topic, and hoped that Laing's treatment methods would be successful on a large scale.

The reception of Laing's early scientific and scholarly works—*Self and Others*; *Sanity, Madness, and the Family*; *Interpersonal Perception*; and *Reason and Violence* (see Coltart, 1965; Gage, 1968; Jourard, 1963; Lomas, 1965; Mischler, 1964)—was far more positive than that of Laing's later books, which were more personal, poetic, speculative, mystical, and socially critical (see Berscheid, 1977; Moldawsky, 1977; Rosenblith, 1978; Rychlak, 1983). Defenders of psychoanalysis have attacked Laing's scholarly works, for example, as Lowenfeld (1963) did in his review of *Self and Others*, objecting to Laing's philosophical language. Defenders of the psychiatric establishment have attacked Laing's socially critical works, which targeted that profession with sharp challenges (see Boyers & Orrill, 1971).

Textbooks

One indicator of the impact of Laing's book is the degree to which it is cited in undergraduate psychology textbooks. We reviewed those for introductory psychology, abnormal psychology, and personality. McKelvie (1984) reviewed introductory textbooks in response to a concern about an alleged left-wing political bias that could affect the psychology's funding and used citations of Laing and Szasz, "the two major antipsychiatrists," as indices of the bias. McKelvie found that only 10 of 23 texts cited any of Laing's works and that only 1 advocated his views; textbooks were not "contaminated with left-wing ideology" (p. 375).

Our review of 21 current introductory texts finds even fewer references to Laing. Only 1 (Zimbardo & Gerrig, 1999) cited *The Divided Self*, and 2 (Sdorow, 1998; Sternberg, 2001) cited other works by Laing. Of 17 abnormal psychology texts reviewed, only 3 cited *The Divided Self* (Comer, 2001; Halgin & Whitbourne, 2000; Nolen-Hoeksema, 2001), and 4 cited other Laing works. The absence of citations is consistent with the absence of Laing's approach in relation both to schizophrenia and to psychology generally. The few texts that presented Laing's ideas recast his phenomenological description of one path to schizophrenia into a universal theory or etiology of schizophrenia, yielding standard-type hypotheses purportedly in need of a test. Laing's ideas were grossly oversimplified and often inaccurately presented. For instance, Comer (2001), who included the most elaborate treatment of Laing's ideas, claimed that Laing argued that schizophrenia is a growthful, constructive process in which people try to cure themselves of the confusion and unhappiness caused by their social environment. Comer went on to quote Mark Vonnegut's article, "Why I Want to Bite R. D. Laing," saying, "One of R. D. Laing's worst sins is how blithely and misleadingly he glides over the suffering involved" (Vonnegut, 1974, p. 91). Laing is presented by Comer along with a picture of Pink Floyd's album *The Wall*, showing how antisocietal art mirrored Laing's theory. Popular press and culture pervade the treatment of Laing's ideas.

Although only 2 of 20 personality texts have included references to Laing (Feshbach, Weiner, & Bohart, 1996; Monte, 1999), here the only nonsuperficial and extensive treatment of *The Divided Self* was found. Monte's (1999) text, now in its sixth edition, has included an entire chapter on Laing's work with extensive exposition, citing 14 of Laing's writings since 1977. Monte highlighted the considerable value of *The Divided Self* and made a valiant effort to trace Laing's thought, in its changes and complexity, without many of the common misconceptions. However, in the end Monte assimilated Laing's work to the traditional hypothetico–deductive approach rather than adequately distinguishing the phenomenological nature of Laing's method and findings within its own meta-scientific context for evaluation.

Contemporary Journals

We also reviewed a sample of abstracts from professional journals in clinical psychology using *PsycSCAN: Clinical Psychology* (American Psychological Association, 2001). From July to October of 2000, there were 45 original articles (and 8 commentaries and replies) on schizophrenia. None appeared even remotely like or related to *The Divided Self* in aim, method, or findings. They addressed issues concerning diagnosis (4 articles), cognitive processes (11), neurology (16), genetics (3), drug effects (8), and short-term psychotherapy outcomes (3). If any research on schizophrenia is using Laing's approach or methods, it is not represented in the field's "subscriber preferred" journals. One would be hard pressed to find anything like a "science of persons" in the mainstream clinical literature on any topic.

Extended Scholarly Treatments

From the above professional literature, Laing's impact appears to be null and void. However, a host of books over the past 25 years have indicated that Laing has not been ignored. The 1990s in particular has brought a resurgence of interest in Laing and a sharp improvement in the scholarship devoted to his work. These books have focused on Laing as a person— including celebrity and political profiles—as well as on his scientific/scholarly contributions. These works have presented Laing, and *The Divided Self*, as being of much greater importance than have textbooks and mainstream journals. These works have suggested that Laing and his work have been misunderstood, especially by critics, with Laing himself in part to blame.

One of the earliest books on Laing, that of the eminent historian of psychology Richard Evans (1976), is the 10th in a series based on dialogues with "the world's most outstanding contributors to psychology" (p. xiii)— individuals of no less stature than Carl Jung, Erich Fromm, Erik Erikson, B. F. Skinner, Gordon Allport, Jean Piaget, Carl Rogers, and Konrad Lorenz. Evans, an intellectually sophisticated, fair, and clear-minded critic, has consistently defended Laing against the pervasive mischaracterizations of his personality, his beliefs, and his work. Evans (1976) noted that "Laing's difficulties communicating effectively with his colleagues in the behavioral sciences may stem from the unfortunate media image of him, particularly after the publication of *The Politics of Experience* (1967)" (p. 240). Collier (1977) saw *The Politics of Experience* as a turning point when Laing's rigorous and scientific efforts became overshadowed by his media image. Laing was depicted as a cult figure bent on destroying the psychiatric establishment with such rash ideas as that schizophrenia is only a label, that it is a healthy growth, and that people with schizophrenia are best left alone. "The fact that none of these conceptions of Laing or his ideas was particularly accurate appeared to be beside the point—he was good copy, and the often ambiguous content of his late work may have left them open to interpretations that seemed to reinforce the media image" (Evans, 1976, p. 240). *The Divided Self* received wide attention in the United States only after the media image had been proliferated. Laing's works after 1967—poetic, speculative, mystical, socially biting, less scholarly, and trashed in professional journals—were received by many Americans along with *The Divided Self* and Laing's early works as a single package.

Laing's Popular Appeal

Laing's popularity, media image, and relation to the wider culture affected the reception of *The Divided Self* in psychology. Peter Mezan's (1981) gave some of the flavor of Laing's image on the American scene as well as that of the zeitgeist:

> Under the mind's eye, under the magical sign of the caduceus, stands a gaunt, pixie-like man in the garb of a prophet—acid in his right hand, revolution at his left, his head haloed with the clear light of an Oriental paradise, his eyes intimating madness—crushing beneath his avenging foot the serpent of the Western rationalist tradition. (p. xxii)

Hardly an image likely to appeal to mainstream psychology! But others were fascinated by this Laing portrayed in the popular press less as a pioneer of a new form of science than as a leading instigator of the 1960s counterculture.

> Sprung upon an unwittingly ready world in 1960, with the publication of a lucid, deceptively innocent book called *The Divided Self*, the name R. D. Laing sank into the minds of my generation like a crystal into a solution, precipitating a growth unaccountably huger and weirder than any of the events that begot it, and it is growing every day. All the time's most plaintive urges and most temperamental ideas cluster around this elusive Scottish psychoanalyst as around a hero of a chivalric romance. Radicals honor him as a philosopher of revolution. Universities teach his books in courses in literature, psychology, and philosophy. Mental patients quote him reflexively to their psychiatrists, who often crimson reflexively at the mention of him. Runaways, street freaks, and disillusioned GIs pack his books in their shoulder bags as manuals for making sense of a berserk world, and intellectuals, who have taken Laing's ideas about sanity and madness as part of their conjectural furniture, totter between doubt and regard for a man whose ideas people seem to take as seriously as they do real life. . . .
>   For the fact of the matter is that a lot of people have the sense that this man has read and touched their most secret minds, and no one is

more curious about it than R. D. Laing himself, who hadn't quite foreseen that so many people would be so interested. "I get quite a lot of letters," Laing said to a group of psychoanalysts who wanted to know what he made of it all. "People tell me how they read *The Politics of Experience* ten times and still carry it around with them. They say it completely changed their lives, that it made them see everything differently, that it was the first time they discovered someone else thinking the way they were thinking. I really don't know what to make of that.... Several people even wrote to me saying that *they* had written *The Divided Self!* They wrote it!" (Mezan, 1981, pp. xxiii–xxiv)

Laing's "American tour" in 1972, on his return from India (where he had undergone a religious conversion), is likened it to the Beatles' invasion in the 1960s (Mezan, 1981). "A lonely hearts ad in the New York *Village Voice* read 'Two chicks who dig Coltrane, The Grateful Dead, and R. D. Laing seek compatible mates,' while bumper stickers proclaimed being 'totally mad about R. D. Laing'" (Mullan, 1999, p. 139). Laing's media image featured not only glorification of madness and condemnations of psychiatric practices but also numerous elements of the counterculture movement, including Eastern spirituality, political revolution, and even drugs. This strange mushrooming of events shocked Laing and wrought havoc on his personal life, but our point is that *The Divided Self* was read by many psychologists in this powerfully consuming context.

Laing's American tour, undertaken to avert financial disaster, did little to improve his reception in scientific and professional circles. His lectures and public appearances contained brilliant moments and dialogues, but they were unconventional (see Clay, 1996).

> While in Chicago, Laing was invited by some doctors to examine a young girl diagnosed as schizophrenic. The girl was locked in a padded cell in a special hospital and sat there naked. She usually spent her whole day rocking to and fro. The doctors asked Laing for his opinion. What would he do about her? Unexpectedly, Laing stripped naked himself and entered her cell. There he sat with her, rocking in time to her rhythm. After about twenty minutes, she started speaking, something she had not done for several months. (Burston, 1996, pp. 170–171)

In an "encounter" with Carl Rogers, Laing rudely attacked the humanist's denial of human evil and the banality of his ideas. Then Laing demonstrated his latest therapeutic technique by "rebirthing" 200 people, many of whom came for that purpose. "This bizarre spectacle turned the event into a total disgrace" (Burston, 1996, p. 130). One must transport oneself back into the psychedelic, irreverent, and liberating zeitgeist of the early 1970s to understand and feel sympathy for Laing's adventure in public relations!

Laing's public appearances played a role in alienating him from the scientific and professional communities. In a documentary reviewed by Fisher and Fisher (1978), Laing himself lamented that he had become "isolated from the psychiatric establishment in England and perhaps gone too far out on a limb"; he planned to review all his old cases and rethink his basic ideas and concepts (p. 93). Although Laing continued to write popular books and to live the life of the most famous psychiatrist since Sigmund Freud, he never reconnected with the psychiatric establishment or returned to the scientific program of his early research.

A Scholarly Appraisal

Other scholars have been doing this review and rethinking. Since Laing's death in 1987 and continuing into the new century, a growing body of sophisticated scholarship has been reassessing Laing's complex and substantive legacy. Collier (1977) had recognized important scientific contributions in Laing's work, including its philosophical foundations, methodological innovations, complementarity with psychoanalysis, and social criticism. More recent works have carefully distilled Laing's contributions to psychology and to the larger history of Western thought, setting them apart from his media image and personal life.

In a series of articles in the *British Journal of Psychiatry* reconsidering books of major impact on the field and public opinion, David (1994) argued that *Sanity, Madness, and the Family* may be judged more favorably in hindsight when its contribution to less formal and more eclectic care for the severely disturbed is recognized. He defended that work as "ahead of its time," cited later support for its thesis, and delineated its impact on practice. David noted that an earlier reappraisal of *The Divided Self* (Smith, 1982) added to the growing weight of opinion, even in the 1980s, that it is a major contribution to psychiatry. David added, "it is after all [still] on the Royal College of Psychiatrists 'Current Psychotherapy Reading List'" (p. 219). Mullan (1999) argued that Laing's ideas do indeed have "true validity and relevance" and were written "in hope that he is listened to with more understanding and sympathy" (p. 5).

Clay (1996) not only sorted through the complicated intertwinings of Laing's personal life and scholarship but also offered an edifying exposition of unrecognized contributions of *The Divided Self* to psychology. New light is shed on connections with the ideas of William James, the backgrounds of the cases, the research methods, the use of language, and Laing's special relationship to the reader. Clay emphasized Laing's utilization of existential and phenomenological thought, his friendliness to Freud and psychoanalysis, the power of his prose, his ability to speak the secrets of many, and the originality of his integration of psychiatry and Continental philosophy. Clay gave scholarly weight to the appraisal of an early review in the *New York Times Book Review* (Berman, 1970) that the work is a possible contribution of the first order to psychological medicine. Clay cited psychoanalysts who were favorably impressed by the book, including David Winnecott and John Bowlby, the latter who admitted privately to Daniel Burston that Laing had a very strong influence on him and that he considered *Sanity, Madness, and the Family* to be the single greatest book on the family in the 20th century (although he complained that Laing never published his research on normal families; see Burston, 2000, p. 76). Clay (1996) cited Laing's anticipation of important contemporary critiques and theories in psychoanalysis.

Michael Thompson (1996, 1997, 1998, 1999) had extensively studied Laing's relationship with psychoanalysis, including the reasons for his limited impact. Thompson (1999) traced Laing's apparent movement away from the psychoanalytic establishment, but his more probing analysis revealed an ingenious synthesis of the finest 20th-century Continental philosophy and psychoanalysis. Thompson found a deep commonality between Laing and Freud that distinguishes their virtues from the vulgar misrepresentations of both. Thompson viewed Laing as a psychoanalyst in its best tradition and made the important point that Laing's phenomenological method and skepticism are of greater import in his work than the ideological content of existential philosophy. Thompson (1999) viewed contemporary psychoanalysis as verging on extinction and found Laing's work to be at one with the most vital forefront of contemporary psychoanalysis that holds its only hope for an authentic future. "Perhaps the day will come when Laing's contribution will finally receive the attention it deserves" (p. 77). Thompson is working toward that day.

The current reevaluation may be best exemplified by Burston's (1996, 2000) excellent books. Burston's (1996) thesis is that Laing's contribution to human science is on the same order as that of Freud and Jung when Laing's intellectual work is differentiated from his personal life and placed in the context of the history of ideas. This placement brings out profound implications for the future of psychological theory and research. Burston's searching and meticulous analysis of Laing's personal life and intellectual works distills the core of Laing's contributions to psychology. He critically evaluates them and systematically relates them to the major contemporary models in psychology. Laing's work is also distinguished from that of Szasz, the "antipsychiatry" movement, American humanistic psychology, and psychoanalysis. Laing's originality and value for psychological theory and research is found in his appropriation of Continental schools of science.

Burston's positive appraisal of *The Divided Self* was shared by those who reflected on Laing's work shortly after his death.

> [There was] a strong measure of convergence among the many tributes and reminiscences that flooded the British and American press at the time of Laing's death [in 1989]. Despite differences in emphasis they all praise *The Divided Self* and lament the decline of [Laing's] creative power that seemed to follow his increasing infatuation and fame. (Burston, 1996, p. 145)

Burston's 2000 book extends insight into Laing's substantive contributions by placing his work even more squarely in the existential–phenomenological tradition. Burston combs through *The Divided Self* and Laing's other works to address such areas in contemporary psychology as psychotherapy, the theory of psychopathology, the relation of neurology and psychology, psychological research methods, the definition of psychological normality, and the conceptualization of mental health. In each of these areas, important original contributions of Laing's work are brought out. Burston views apparent contradictions among Laing's works as good, creative tensions and affirms Laing's abstention from building a grand system or theory. He concludes, "perhaps one day when the limitations of biological psychology are palpable once more, we can build again on a finer foundation, inspired by [Laing's] shifting, kaleidoscopic vision" (Burston, 2000, p. 146). Such "building" is under way, as evidenced by the recent special issue of the journal *Janus Head*, which contains 12 articles exploring the substantive legacy of Laing's work (see Burston, 2001). This journal issue, since it has been available on the World Wide Web (www.janushead.org), has attracted on the average 10,000 visits ("hits") per month (D. Burston, personal communication, June 2001), suggesting that Laing's work is of considerable interest beyond the discipline of psychology.

REFLECTIONS ON THE LIMITED IMPACT

The Divided Self's lack of impact on psychology tells us as much about the limitations of psychology as it does about the shortcomings of Laing's book and career. The lacking impact is best conceptualized as a dialectic involving the contributor, the discipline, and society.

The Book and Author's Career

The difficulty of Laing's writing has been exacerbated by many readers' lack of education in the Continental metascientific tradition that informs Laing's work. Terms outside of psychological parlance, such as *ontological*, may have alienated readers. Laing's work is not itself a good introduction to phenomenological psychology (Van Kaam, 1962), and the scientific status, goals, and value of Laing's descriptive methodology were not grasped by readers. Laing's conceptualizations, deliberately rejecting efficient causality, are not assimilable to traditional etiology with such familiar concepts as genetics, neurology, and environment. *The Divided Self* is not fully explicit about innovative therapeutic practices, which may be a *sin qua non* for high impact. Taken as a specialized work on schizophrenia in clinical psychology, which is isolated from the academic psychology as a whole, *The Divided Self* was too compartmentalized to be considered as an option for psychology's basic approach as a science.

Impact, especially of a new general approach to psychology, requires that a single work occur in a series that introduces, broadly elaborates, develops, extends, and applies that new approach. Although the initial 7 years of Laing's career did begin to produce such a series, including brilliant extensions of phenomenological method into social psychology, Laing then produced writing without comparable scholarly quality over the next 22 years. Rather than devoting himself to a proper introduction, continuing scientific research, and developing his approach in dialogue with misunderstandings and criticisms, Laing addressed popular culture. Laing's popularity with the counterculture, his celebrity/crank image, and his radical politics did little to further his scientific credibility or motivate scientists and professionals to seriously study his early works. It would seem that extrascientific activities, such as spiritual experiences, speculation, drug experimentation, and poetic expression, as well as social action, must remain related to, or at least not supplant, scientific activities if a contributor's career development is to effectively increase impact on a scientific discipline. We also see the importance of cultivating a mutually respectful dialog with scientific and professional colleagues and, beyond this, situating one's work in a legitimately established institution or creating new ones that allow spreading collaboration. Innovations require building and proliferating educational and training opportunities in which contemporaries and subsequent generations can learn and carry forward new ways. Laing declined prestigious university positions (e.g., at Princeton University) and opportunities to teach in programs inclined to build on his work (e.g., at Duquesne University). He deserted the psychoanalytic establishment. Although he did found the Philadelphia Association as a model for therapeutic practice, its mission did not include training and productivity in scientific research, and in time Laing withdrew from this project.

The History of Dominant Trends in Psychology

In the 40 years since the publication of *The Divided Self*, some things in psychology have changed, while others have not. Laing's work arose after a long period dominated by behaviorism. In 1960, both cognitive and humanistic challenges to behaviorism had been articulated and were growing. In the past 40 years, cognitive psychology has overthrown radical behaviorism and has been joined by a vigorously flourishing neuroscience as the dominant trend. What has been conserved—what has not changed—is the natural science approach to psychology. One could argue that the success of cognitive psychology, in contrast to that of humanistic psychology, is based in the discipline's conservative adherence to the natural science model still embodied in cognitive psychology. In clinical psychology of schizophrenia, this trend is evident in the *PsycSCAN* we reviewed, not only in cognitive and neurological studies but also in the emphasis on diagnosis, psychopharmacology, genetics, and experimentally designed therapy research.

Laing's holistic, qualitative "science of persons," which deliberately operates within the *Geisteswissenschaften* (Human Science) tradition rooted in Continental thought, has remained marginalized along with that entire approach. Humanistic psychology, which enthusiastically embraced Laing's work (Burston, 2000), is heterogeneous in its own right, including Carl Rogers's emphasis on quantitative methods and Abraham Maslow's grand theory, as well as nontraditional qualitative methods emphasizing *Verstehende* (understanding) and using human science paradigms. Only those aspects of humanistic psychology that could be assimilated to the natural science approach have had an impact on the science of psychology. To the extent that humanistic psychology could generate quantitatively testable hypotheses, it has been incorporated. To the extent that it has involved a radically different philosophy of science and research methods, it has remained outside of the textbooks and mainstream journals, at the margins of the discipline (Wertz, 1998), just as has *The Divided Self*. Laing's impact has been limited by the incompatibility of his work with the dominant philosophy of science in psychology. Psychologists could see value only in Laing's empathic abilities and the vividness of his case conceptualizations, as the most sympathetic early reviews of his work did, but removed from Laing's alternative scientific framework, these do not carry much scientific weight or impact. This core scientific conservativism is evident when we turn to Laing's contributions to psychoanalysis, clinical psychology, and social criticism.

Psychoanalysis

Laing's criticism of psychoanalysis has made his work difficult for analysts to accept (Thompson, 1999). Psychoanalysts, even into the 1970s, held dear theories that Laing criticized and discarded. However, analysts have recently begun to discuss commonalities and convergences with central elements of Laing's therapeutic practice, research methods, and philosophy of science. Guntrip's (1971) assertion that "people are more important than ideas" and his formulations of the schizoid and schizophrenia conditions provided striking early convergences with *The Divided Self*. Laing's criticisms of psychoanalytic theory anticipated those of object relations, self, intersubjective, and interpersonal schools of psychoanalysis. Laing's emphases on the self, agency, the social–relational nature of human experience, empathic modes of knowing and healing, qualitative and hermeneutic research methods, the growth potential of psychopathology, and emancipatory cultural criticism have all become vital and central themes in contemporary psychoanalysis (see Kohut, 1977; Mitchell, 1988; Schafer, 1976; Stolorow & Atwood, 1992). These changes have taken place with a growing awareness of the pluralistic nature of psychoanalytic theory as well as of its roots in the

Continental tradition of metascience. However, this alternative form of science is what has made psychoanalysis so resistant to integration within mainstream psychology all along. These contemporary developments in psychoanalysis are as absent from the mainstream psychological literature as is Laing. Only the psychoanalytic work that has generated operationalizable constructs and testable hypotheses has been accorded scientific credibility. Psychoanalysis as a school is itself in crisis—rare in *PsycSCAN* journals and less represented in textbooks with each new edition—and threatened with extinction.

Clinical Psychology

Clinical psychology emphasizes practice, particularly psychotherapy, but has increasingly attempted to establish its value by natural science type research. *The Divided Self* does not focus explicitly on effective therapy. Laing's other works do not address therapy in detail even though he practiced, supervised, and directed clinical work. Impactful contributions to clinical psychology, for example, those of Sigmund Freud, Carl Rogers, B. F. Skinner, and Aaron T. Beck, give rise to new methods of treatment. Now more than ever, the only acceptable approach to establishing the legitimacy of treatments is the experimentally designed outcome study that mimics medical research on the effects of drugs. Freud and Rogers are quickly fading from clinical psychology (having always seemed "too soft" to many); they are falling by the wayside of a clinical psychology whose rigor ever more rigidly models the natural sciences.

Social Criticism

Psychology is not opposed to participating in social reform, but it requires that directives be based on empirical research within the natural science approach. Psychology quickly distances itself from social criticism and reform that is not based on such research. Most psychologists feel that these limits on missions of reform are proper and necessary for an aspiring science. Accordingly, movements that have denounced psychology's natural science orientation have been most harshly dismissed. Laing's social criticism not only lacked any basis in orthodox empirical research but also challenged psychology's very commitment to this form of research, rendering his views outside the realm of acceptability.

Society, History, and Human Values

The dialectic of the individual contributor and the scientific discipline is nested in a larger dialectic of psychology and society. The value and esteem accorded to natural science and technology—with its emphasis on objectification, prediction, and control—is evident in economic and educational institutions of our society shared by psychology. There is a strong belief that natural-science-style knowledge and practice is the only legitimate ap-

proach to remedy human suffering, and big-money interests such as the lob-
bying health care industry, including drug companies, stand to gain from this
belief and societal investment. A psychology that defines itself by means of
less-dominant, let alone countercurrents that value understanding and care
for the individual person, risks cultural marginalization, including a lack of
funding and a loss of status. Barlow (1996) explained why criticisms of the
way science is conducted and interesting philosophically based alternatives
to mainstream psychology, despite potential contributions to research on
psychotherapies, will not be successful. Support and funding require that research and evidence of efficacy conform to the paradigm established by medical
science.

> Arguments about philosophy, although popular in academic circles, are
> unlikely to affect Congress or health care policymakers at every level of
> government. . . . [W]hether it is NIH [the National Institutes of Health],
> the National Institute of Occupational Safety and Health, the National
> Institute of Education, or the Food and Drug Administration, these rules
> of evidence have been well worked out. . . . It is unlikely that they would
> make an exception for psychotherapy. Although methods of evaluating
> psychotherapy are flawed and subject to considerable improvement . . .
> anti-science arguments have not been, and will not be, influential.
> (Barlow, 1996, pp. 1052–1053)

Well-institutionalized societal structures will not allow the discipline
of psychology to define and practice "science" in a manner different from
physical science. A psychology not modeled on natural science is relegated
to an ivory tower status, removed to the margins alongside philosophy, literary studies, religion, and the arts. It is unclear to what extent psychology can
change the fundamental values of our culture, on which its current success
rests. Social criticism and reform from the humanities and arts have been a
cultural presence but do not seem to have changed the course of history or
mitigated the dominance of the scientific and technological status quo. If
psychology joined forces with such trends in other disciplines, its impact
would be minimal, and the success it has achieved would almost certainly be
lost as a consequence.

Perhaps alternative scientific approaches require linkages with grassroots
cultural movements in the hope that broad-based societal reform would offer
them a legitimate place. Laing's move from scientific to countercultural practice, apart from his financial motivations, may reflect his awareness of the
extent to which the real power lies outside psychology and in our broader
cultural–historical life. Laing's unconventional career direction becomes more
understandable in light of our reflections. What has become of the
countercultural forces of the 1960s? Are there any contemporary movements
that might support a "science of persons"? Feminism, multiculturalism, and
their underlying democratic politics place high value on individual persons

as centers of experience and agency. Accordingly, they have challenged the hegemony of the natural science approach to knowledge and have suggested alternative ways of knowing, but their ultimate disciplinary and larger historical impact remains uncertain.

LESSONS FOR STUDENTS AND THE FIELD OF PSYCHOLOGY

What lessons can we glean from this chapter? What can we tell aspiring students who would like their work to "have impact"? We do not suggest that a student must either conform to received views or put aside a revolutionary approach until the zeitgeist is ready to accept it. Laing's case does suggest some lessons that might aid a student in increasing the chances of a divergent approach making impact.

1. To the extent that one's contribution involves something new and different, it needs an introduction that can be readily understood by readers without the required background. This introduction must include the larger scholarly tradition of which the work is a part.
2. Innovative language must engage rather than alienate a critical mass of readers.
3. A new approach and conceptual advances should have practical consequences that follow closely from scientific innovations, and the benefits to humanity should be demonstrated.
4. A given contribution should be followed by a progression of works within a larger research program that develops and extends a new approach while addressing misunderstandings and criticisms of readers.
5. A contributor's career development and personal conduct must support and be consistent with one's scientific and professional program of research and practice.
6. Extrascientific activities such as spiritual experiences, drug experimentation and poetic revelations as well as projects of societal change should relate and contribute to, or at least not interfere with, scientific activities.
7. One must cultivate a mutually respectful dialog with scientific and professional colleagues.
8. One must install one's work in legitimately established institutions or create new ones that engage collaboration and joining in. To the extent that one is innovative, one must utilize or build and proliferate educational and training opportunities in which contemporaries and subsequent generations of scholars can learn and carry forward the innovations.

This study also shows that impact is not a one-way street; it involves not only the activities of the potential contributor but also the character and politics of the receiving discipline. Psychology's rejection of *The Divided Self* reveals a continuing narrowness in a discipline, which leaves little room for the voice of experience and for much in the rich intellectual heritage of Western and global thought. Impact has been limited by a definition of "science" that excludes or downgrades potentially valuable contributions. Psychology can cultivate greater respect for diversity and plurality.

Education in psychology can better utilize knowledge of the full spectrum of Western and global intellectual traditions to properly situate new and innovative works that draw on them. Psychology can be open and willing to learn, can be less defensive in the face of criticism, even radical criticism that brings to light unacknowledged assumptions limiting knowledge and practice. Textbooks and educators do a disservice to students by their internal homogeneity as well as their oversimplification, distortion, disparagement, and trivialization of what does not fit the dominant paradigm. When dismissive pseudo-knowledge replaces respectful scholarship and criticism, potentially valuable works are prevented from properly informing students. Textbooks can better prepare students to fairly evaluate different approaches to psychology, which requires careful study of original works in light of the history of ideas.

Psychology can be more aware of and self-critical about its values and their relation to those of society. Psychology can take a special leadership role in our democratic society by using methods that foster a close and faithful understanding of the voices of individuals' experience. A psychology that honors people as centers of experience and action in its theories, research, and practices, can adequately advocate for people amid dehumanizing social trends.

CONCLUSION

The case of Laing is interesting because, although he has had only limited impact on mainstream psychology, he has had considerable impact on popular culture and on sophisticated scholarship in psychology. Our study shows that a psychologist's involvement in popular culture and in cultural change is a double-edged sword. It holds potential financial success and fame but may detract from the work's scientific and disciplinary status. With some imagination, one can think in principle that a psychologist's involvement in cultural revolution could contribute to a change of societal values so pervasive that the foundations of psychology become infused with a new view of what science is and what psychology should be. However, Laing's work fell short of this, and we are hard-pressed to cite any case in which this has actually occurred. The "revolution" to which Laing contributed has affected society to some extent, for instance, policies regarding patients' rights, but has not profoundly changed society's demands on science. Nevertheless, in the case of the marginalized approach of Laing, an enigmatic popularity has attracted attention on a scale sufficient to include the work of serious scholars who are furthering Laing's approach and promoting change in the nature of science even as the disciplinary and cultural mainstream opposes it. The scholars who continue to pour over Laing's works are keeping alive the dynamic potential of Laing's impact on the discipline of psychology and are empowering the long and important tradition in which Laing's work is a seminal part and in which *The Divided Self* is a true classic.

REFERENCES

American Psychological Association. (2001). *PsycSCAN: Clinical Psychology, 22*(1).

Barlow, D. H. (1996). Health care policy, psychotherapy research, and the future of psychotherapy. *American Psychologist, 51*, 1050–1058.

Berman, M. (1970, February 22). Review of *The Divided Self. New York Times Book Review*, p. 1.

Berscheid, E. (1977). Review of *Do You Love Me? An Entertainment in Conversation and Verse. Contemporary Psychology, 22*, 229.

Boyers, R., & Orrill, R. (1971). *R. D. Laing and anti-psychiatry*. New York: Perennial Library.

Bricrley, M. (1961). Review of *The Divided Self. International Journal of Psychoanalysis, 42*, 288–291.

Burston, D. (1996). *The wing of madness: The life and work of R. D. Laing*. Cambridge, MA: Harvard University Press.

Burston, D. (2000). *The crucible of experience: R. D. Laing and the crisis of psychotherapy*. Cambridge, MA: Harvard University Press.

Burston, D. (Ed.). (2001). Special Issue: The Legacy of R. D. Laing. *Janus Head, 4*(1).

Clay, J. (1996). *R. D. Laing: A divided self*. London: Hodder & Stoughton.

Collier, A. (1977). *R. D. Laing: The philosophy and politics of psychotherapy*. New York: Pantheon.

Coltart, N. E. C. (1965). Review of *Reason and violence. International Journal of Psychoanalysis, 46*, 394–395

Comer, R. J. (2001). *Abnormal psychology* (4th ed.). New York: Worth.

David, A. S. (1994). Review of *Sanity, Madness, and the Family*. In S. Crown & H. L. Freeman (Eds.), *The book of psychiatric books* (pp. 215–220). Northvale, NJ: Jason Aronson.

Evans, R. I. (1976). *R. D. Laing: The man and his ideas*. New York: Dutton.

Feshbach, S., Weiner, B., & Bohart, A. (1996). *Personality* (4th ed.). Lexington, MA: Heath.

Fisher, S., & Fisher, R. I. (1978). Review of the film *R. D. Laing on R. D. Laing (1976)*. *Contemporary Psychology, 23*, 92–93.

Gage, N. L. (1968). Review of *Interpersonal Perception: A Theory and a Method of Research*. *Contemporary Psychology, 13*, 78–79.

Guntrip, H. (1971). *Psychoanalytic theory, therapy, and the self*. New York: Basic Books.

Halgin, R. P., & Whitbourne, S. K. (2000). *Abnormal psychology* (3rd ed.). Boston, MA: McGraw-Hill.

Jourard, S. M. (1963). Review of *The Self and Others: Further studies in sanity and madness*. *Contemporary Psychology, 8*, 330–331.

Kohut, H. (1977). *The restoration of self*. New York: International Universities Press.

Laing, R. D. (1960). *The divided self*. London: Tavistock.

Laing, R. D. (1961). *Self and others*. London: Tavistock.

Laing, R. D. (1967). *Politics of experience*. New York: Pantheon.

Laing, R. D., & Cooper, D. G. (1964). *Reason and violence: A decade of Sartre's philosophy—1950–1969*. London: Tavistock.

Laing, R. D., & Esterson, A. (1964). *Sanity, madness, and the family*. London: Tavistock.

Lomas, P. (1965). Review of *Sanity, madness, and the family: Vol. 1*. *International Journal of Psychoanalysis, 46*, 390–392.

Lowenfeld, H. (1963). Review of *The Self and Others*. *International Journal of Psychoanalysis, 44*, 116–118.

McKelvie, S. J. (1984). Left-wing rhetoric in introductory psychology textbook: The case of mental illness. *Psychological Reports, 54*, 375–380.

Mezan, P. (1981). R. D. Laing: Portrait of a twentieth-century skeptic. In R. I. Evans (Ed.), *Dialogues with R. D. Laing* (pp. xxii–lxxv). New York: Praeger.

Mischler, E. (1964, Winter). Review of *Sanity, Madness, and the Family*. *Community Mental Health Journal*, pp. 355–356.

Mitchell, S. (1988). *Relational concepts in psychoanalysis: An integration*. Cambridge, MA: Harvard University Press.

Moldawsky, S. (1977). Review of *The facts of life: An essay in feelings, facts, and fantasy*. *Contemporary Psychology, 22*, 227–228

Monte, C. F. (1999). *Beneath the mask: An introduction to theories of personality* (6th ed.). Fort Worth, TX: Harcourt Brace.

Mullan, B. (1999). *R. D. Laing: A personal view*. London: Duckworth.

Nolen-Hoeksema, S. (2001). *Abnormal psychology* (2nd ed.). New York: McGraw-Hill.

Rosenblith, J. F. (1978). Review of *Conversations with Adam and Natasha*. *Contemporary Psychology, 23*, 534.

Rychlak, J. F. (1983). Review of *The Voice of Experience*. *Contemporary Psychology, 28*, 697.

Schafer, R. (1970). Review of *The Divided Self* and *Self and Others* (2nd rev. ed.). *Contemporary Psychology, 15*, 542–543.

Schafer, R. (1976). *A new language for psychoanalysis*. New Haven, CT: Yale University Press.

Sdorow, L. M. (1998). *Psychology* (4th ed.). Boston: McGraw-Hill.

Smith, L. M. (1982). Books reconsidered—R. D. Laing: *The Divided Self*. *British Journal of Psychiatry, 140,* 637–642.

Sternberg, R. J. (2001). *Psychology: In search of the human mind* (3rd ed.). Fort Worth, TX: Harcourt College.

Stolorow, R., & Atwood, G. (1992). *Contexts of being: The intersubjective foundations of psychological life*. Hillsdale, NJ: Analytic Press.

Thompson, M. G. (1996). Deception, mystification, trauma: Laing and Freud. *Psychoanalytic Review, 83,* 827–847.

Thompson, M. G. (1997). The fidelity to experience in R. D. Laing's treatment philosophy. *Contemporary Psychoanalysis, 33,* 595–614.

Thompson, M. G. (1998). Existential psychoanalysis: A Laingian perspective. In P. Marcus & A. Rosenberg (Eds.), *Psychoanalytic versions of the human condition: Philosophies of life and their impact on practice* (pp. 332–361). New York: New York University Press.

Thompson, M. G. (1999). The heart of the matter: R. D. Laing's enigmatic relationship with psychoanalysis. *Humanistic Psychologist, 27,* 51–79

Van Kaam, A. (1962). Review of *The Divided Self*. *Review of Existential Psychology and Psychiatry, 2,* 65–68.

Vonnegut, M. (1974). Why I want to bite R. D. Laing, *Harper's, 248,* 91.

Wertz, F. J. (1998). The role of the humanistic movement in the history of psychology. *Journal of Humanistic Psychology, 38,* 42–70.

Wortman, A. G. (1973). Review of *The Divided Self* and *Self and Others*. *Psychoanalytic Review, 60,* 301.

Zimbardo, P. G., & Gerrig, R. J. (1999). *Psychology and life* (15th ed.). New York: Longman.

9

CONTENT AND CONTEXT: THE IMPACT OF CAMPBELL AND STANLEY

WILLIAM R. SHADISH, GLENN PHILLIPS, AND M. H. CLARK

The year was 1957. The United States, a world power arising out of the ashes of World War II, was entering an age of economic prosperity. Especially in the United States, the many successes of science had created optimism about a new age of technological and social well-being. But at the same time, Sputnik had just been launched by the Soviet Union. The Cold War was in its second decade and still growing. The civil rights era was just beginning in the United States, where social and economic disparities were about to generate a war on poverty.

Amidst this social context, Donald T. Campbell, having recently been told he was unlikely to be tenured at the University of Chicago because of his sparse publication record (Campbell, 1981), was in his third academic position, an associate professorship in psychology at Northwestern University. At Northwestern, Campbell continued to pursue several related programs of research that he hoped would eventually garner him both academic tenure and the respect of his colleagues.[1]

---

[1]In this chapter, we focus more on Campbell than on his coauthor, Julian Stanley. In part, this focus is well-justified intellectually, for most of the key ideas in Campbell and Stanley (1963a, 1963b) were first published by Campbell (1957), and Campbell continued to elaborate these ideas throughout his

Among these was a program in experimental and quasi-experimental design for field research—exactly the kind of research the times seemed to require to evaluate the effects of social interventions. At that time, randomized experiments had recently come into prominence in the social sciences, often taught as if random assignment were the only methodological control that needed to be taught. In counterpoint, Campbell wanted to show that randomization did not account for many important threats to validity, threats that nonrandomized experiments sometimes *could* account for (Campbell, 1986). He first published these ideas in a 1957 *Psychological Bulletin* article entitled "Factors Relevant to the Validity of Experiments in Social Settings." In that article, he coined the term *internal validity* to cover those threats to valid causal inference that randomization controlled and the term *external validity* to cover those it did not control. He also identified a class of nonrandomized experiments that he first called *compromise designs* but later called *quasi-experiments*. This 1957 article was the first published work in a program that Campbell pursued for 40 years until his death in 1996 and that garnered him more scientific recognition than any of his other accomplishments.

A few years later, Campbell was asked to contribute a chapter on this topic to the *Handbook of Research on Teaching*. He asked his colleague at the University of Wisconsin, Julian Stanley, to coauthor the chapter with him, citing a need for Stanley's superior statistical expertise (Campbell, 1981). According to Stanley, that chapter (Campbell & Stanley, 1963b) "proved so popular and costly to us (we gave away 500 reprints) that Don Campbell and I arranged for Rand McNally to offprint it as a small book" (personal communication, Stanley, May 2001). That book appeared with a 1963 copyright (Campbell & Stanley, 1963a), but it was also reprinted in 1966. So, it is cited as Campbell and Stanley (1963a), Campbell and Stanley (1963b), and Campbell and Stanley (1963/1966). We refer to all three of these works as "Campbell and Stanley" in this chapter.

This work had enormous impact in psychology, in the social sciences, and even in fields such as epidemiology and medicine. This impact is partly reflected in citation counts (see Figure 9.1) that reached a peak of 285 in 1979, and it was still being cited 131 times in 1999, 36 years after its initial publication. The decline after 1979 was due substantially to the publication of Cook and Campbell (1979), a major elaboration of Campbell and Stanley that is also highly cited, reaching a peak of 237 citations in 1999, and still climbing. Together, these closely related works have been cited more than

---

career in a way not reflected in Stanley's subsequent career interests in gifted and talented children. In part, our focus on Campbell reflects a historical accident, that the first author of the present chapter was a postdoctoral student of Campbell and his colleagues, collaborated with them throughout his career, and so is more familiar with the particulars of Campbell's life and career than with Stanley's. Yet it is clear from Campbell's biographical writings that Stanley's contributions to Campbell and Stanley were crucial. We regret our inability to do Stanley's contributions to Campbell and Stanley the full justice that they undoubtedly deserve.

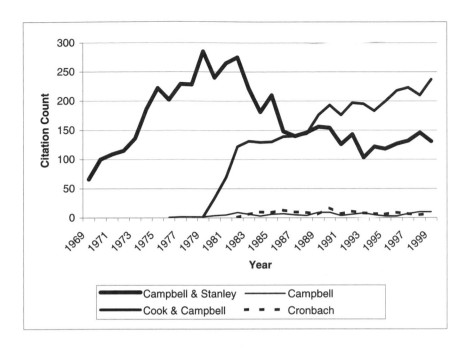

Figure 9.1. Number of citations of Campbell and Stanley (1963a, 1963b, 1966), Campbell (1975), Cook and Campbell (1979), and Cronbach (1982).

8,600 times, with an annual citation count nearing 400 per year—a figure that is likely to increase with the recent publication of a third book that expands Campbell and Stanley even further (Shadish, Cook, & Campbell, 2002).

Yet citation counts fail to reflect the full impact of Campbell and Stanley. Campbell was the heart of a group of colleagues and students who expanded his work and its impact, many of whom are scholarly and organizational leaders in methodology and related areas such as program evaluation. Many books were written as Festschrifts to Campbell (e.g., Bickman, 2000a, 2000b; Brewer & Collins, 1981). Years after his death in 1996, new books on design list Campbell as coauthor (e.g., Campbell & Kenny, 1999; Campbell & Russo, 1999; Shadish et al., 2002). A section of his vita listed the books dedicated to him, most of which were about methods (Campbell, 1981). The Policy Studies Organization named its annual prize for lifetime contributions to methodology after Campbell. Many of the terms that Campbell and Stanley invented, especially *internal validity*, *external validity*, and *quasi-experiment*, are so much a part of scientific language that they are used without any citation to Campbell and Stanley. Such tributes reflect the kind of greatness described by Friedrich Nietzsche (1980) when he said "one thing will live, the monogram of their most authentic essence, a work, a deed, a rare inspiration, a creation: it will live because posterity cannot do without it" (p. 16).

In this chapter, we base our analysis of Campbell and Stanley's impact partly on a survey of eminent scholars who were mostly on hand when Campbell and Stanley appeared, spanning a broad array of disciplines. First, we asked them

- Why did Campbell and Stanley have the impact that it did? Why was it so successful in terms of influencing the field? What distinguishes this piece as great?

We also asked them to compare Campbell and Stanley with two works of lesser impact (Campbell, 1975; Cronbach, 1982) that are cited fewer than 10 times a year (see Figure 9.1):

- Why did Campbell and Stanley have greater influence than Cronbach (1982)?
- Why did Campbell and Stanley have greater influence than Campbell (1975)?

Of the 30 scholars we contacted, 15 responded. These included Mark Appelbaum, Robert Boruch, Marilynn Brewer, Thomas Cook, Lee Cronbach, David Kenny, Mark Lipsey, Fred Mosteller, Robert Rosenthal, Howard Sandler, Robert Stake, Julian Stanley, Daniel Stufflebeam, Carol Weiss, and Paul Wortman. Much of the prose in this chapter is quoted[2] from their responses, but to preserve confidentiality we do not attribute quotes by name except when a respondent specifically asked us to. We acknowledge our debt to these scholars for the contribution they made to the material that follows.

WHY CAMPBELL AND STANLEY HAD GREAT IMPACT

The results of our survey suggest that, not only do great works have great *content*, but they also require a catalytic social and academic *context*.

Great Content

Campbell and Stanley was simple, brief, well written, and creative. It also had general applicability across many fields, imposed order on a disorganized field, included a meta-theoretical component, was pedagogically and practically useful, and generated much like-minded work by other scholars.

Simplicity

Simple prose enhances understanding of ideas. Campbell and Stanley presented its key ideas simply, so that, according to one respondent,

---

[2]We do not necessarily agree with all that is said in these quotes nor vouch for the accuracy of facts cited in them. Some of their prose is a bit hyperbolic or might be subject to disagreement by reasonable colleagues. We cite them verbatim nonetheless because we believe the perceptions that these quotes reflect is crucial to understanding the impact of Campbell and Stanley.

one could see if one's study was valid by answering a few seemingly simple questions. Campbell came to view this checklist idea as illusory, but people love a simple set of steps to answer what are in fact very difficult questions.

Another respondent wrote that Campbell and Stanley

> contained not a single equation, and the logic and theme is plain and often plainly put. This is great science put simply. Cronbach invented a notational system for describing evaluations that is neither esthetically appealing nor easy to learn. It involved using both lower case and upper case UTOS [Units, Treatment, Observations, Settings], sometimes punctuated and sometimes decorated with asterisks and prefixes, each decoration implying something different about the evaluation design. Not as user friendly as Campbell and Stanley's X's and O's. The writing in the Cronbach book is more dense. It takes time to absorb.

Brevity

According to the survey, a brief work is more likely to be read. Campbell and Stanley was "a piece short enough that people could read it and summarize it," stated one respondent. Its key ideas were presented concisely, such as the "brief and memorable list of such threats" to validity. So, Campbell and Stanley "was just the right size to be supplemental reading for many courses," which increased the exposure of the book to a generation of students.

Good Writing

Well-written works are easy to read, and Campbell and Stanley "was extremely well written." This survey respondent added,

> I once told Don Campbell that his piece read to me (a music major in college) like a good piece of classical music. The main themes of design types and criteria of sound research were elaborated to provide the specific designs. In addition, the minor themes relating to methodological issues were woven throughout the piece, like counterpoint in music. Students found the piece to be lucid, practical, and easy to remember.

Campbell and Stanley "crystallized in relatively brief form and clear writing a message on the nature and functions of sound experimental designs."

Creativity

This simple, brief, and clear writing presented creative ideas. One respondent commented,

> The more lasting impact of the article has come from the elegant epistemology provided by the first section of the paper on the definition and rationale for true experimental designs, the definition of internal validity, and list of sources of threats to internal and external validity. It is this part of the paper that has become the "Bible" of research methods courses in the social sciences for more than 30 years.

These ideas were creative in many respects. First, they "provided a new vocabulary for design that covered concepts with an important range of applicability that opened up new possibilities"; for example "the notions of internal and external validity gave researchers a way of talking about the world that had previously been unavailable to them." Second, "the very idea that you could approximate experimental research with quasi-experimental research is a radical idea." Third, "the idea that you needed different statistical tools for different designs was relatively new." Fourth was "that scientific rigor (i.e., internal validity) is not the only goal of research. The goal of external validity also has an important role. Precise laboratory research on highly selected participants may be less interesting than 'sloppy' research in the field."

Generality

The generality and scope of Campbell and Stanley ensured its relevance to the interests of many people. In the words of one respondent, "It provided the scientific rigor in methods and thinking necessary to make an entire approach to psychology respectable." It was much broader than our two comparison works, for "Campbell (1975) was about comparative political studies, and Cronbach (1982) was about educational and social program evaluations, whereas Campbell and Stanley was about *all* experiments." Campbell's (1975) article on case studies was especially narrow by comparison. It was "only 16 pages long and deals with a specific issue. Campbell and Stanley is much longer and far more general and overarching." Further, Campbell's (1975) "main argument was too contingent, that case studies work if the following conditions are met, but they are rarely met."

Synthesis: Imposing Order

Campbell and Stanley synthesized and imposed order on the design literature: "They classified the designs, named them, and identified their weaknesses and strengths, giving a sense of structure to a messy assortment of designs. Then they provided principles for choosing among designs by highlighting threats to validity." By doing so, they showed "that there was a continuum of research designs from the experimental to the nonexperimental. Before the book, all nonexperimental research was lumped together and viewed negatively: Research designs were a dichotomy of good and bad."

Meta-Theoretical Content

Campbell's work on experimental design was part of a highly interrelated program of research that included evolutionary epistemology, a social vision of an experimenting society, and a social psychology of human bias (Shadish, Cook, & Leviton, 1991). All these themes were displayed in Campbell and Stanley, so that "the paper is both methodological and meta-methodological." Campbell and Stanley "combined Don's sophisticated grasp of the philosophy of social science research with a straightforward, well-explained checklist of threats to the internal and external validity of experiments."

Pedagogical Usefulness

Campbell and Stanley was pedagogically useful, so it was used to teach generations of students. According to the survey respondents,

> Campbell and Stanley not only provided an exhaustive listing and description of types of research designs, and of threats to validity, but they packaged these descriptions in a pedagogically powerful context that sensitized researchers to subtle and nonsubtle limitations on drawing justifiable causal inference from variations in research designs.
>
> [The] lists such as the threats to validity are useful to professors and give students a signal of what will be tested.
>
> [The book had] simple visual depiction of designs with Os and Xs.
>
> The charts on design types and threats to validity are transparent and interpretable by people who have no particular training in statistics or scientific method [and were] exceedingly good summaries of dozens of pages of prose.

Practical Usefulness

Campbell and Stanley addressed "designs that were *in use*. They did not perform a hypothetical exercise." As one respondent noted, Campbell and Stanley's

> concept of threats to validity was a serious contribution. It gave some legitimacy to quasi-experiments. It did not just tar them with the brush of unacceptability that was common in psychology at that time. It showed what they were good at and where they were weak. It proposed ways around the weaknesses, such as the patched-up design and multiple strategies. It showed a respect for real constraints on research. It recognized the need for quasi-experimental designs when researchers went out into the real messy world. Researchers who had to cope with less than ideal conditions welcomed the perspective.

By contrast, Campbell's (1975) article was "interesting but just not as useful," and it contained "no simple message about what to do when." A respondent who had previously described Cronbach's theory extensively in a textbook said, "we excluded the chapter that we previously used on Cronbach's Units, Treatment, Observations, Settings (UTOS) model. It turns out that our readers hadn't used or found this approach of interest or use."

Generativity

Campbell and Stanley, commented one survey respondent, "has been heuristic in stimulating further development of experimental design." Researchers used their typology of designs to characterize and criticize the internal and external validity of research (Shadish & Reis, 1984), and they wrote books on topics such as interrupted time series (McCleary & Hay, 1980) and regression discontinuity (Trochim, 1984) to elaborate coverage in Campbell and Stanley. Still other books on methodology are structured around Campbell and Stanley's ideas (Bickman, 2000a, 2000b; Judd & Kenny, 1981; Mohr, 1995).

Social and Scientific Context

To have great impact, a work also must exist in a context that is receptive, in which the content fits intellectually, is compatible with existing paradigms, fits in the social context, comes at the right time, faces no real competition, and has tribal leadership.

Intellectual Context

Great works arise in a context of prior and contemporary intellectual work that provides an intellectual genre in which they can fit, an important set of problems, and an existing base of readers who might notice and comprehend their message. The following remarks by one respondent highlight this point:

> At the time that Campbell and Stanley was published, social psychology was a new, emerging discipline. It had two competing traditions: the European influence of Kurt Lewin that emphasized applied, field research such as "action research" and the more traditional, laboratory approach pioneered by one of Lewin's most famous students, Leon Festinger. Festinger had tried the field approach to testing his theory of cognitive dissonance in "When Prophecy Fails" (co-authored with his students Stanley Schachter and Henry Riecken; Schachter succeeded Festinger as a rigorous laboratory experimenter dealing with applied problems, while Riecken became an action/evaluation researcher). The field study was not rigorous and ethically suspect. The laboratory approach took off and dominated American social psychology; field research was left for others with less scientific rigor. Then in the early 60s, at the height of the dissonance/laboratory frenzy, along comes Campbell and Stanley. It provides the scientific rigor needed to make field research respectable. It didn't replace the lab study, but extended it. The Lewinian field approach to social psychology was rescued by Campbell and Stanley. That was a *major* event that is reflected in the coverage and emphasis on internal validity in most methods books, especially those written by social psychologists. It also accounts for why Cronbach's tome had little impact; it was not arguing about a fundamental change in methods, but emphasis—external over internal validity. His argument seemed retrograde with respect to the most fundamental and important contribution of Campbell and Stanley. But Cronbach was not a social psychologist and probably was unaware of the sociology of science that he was inadvertently trying to undo.

Paradigm Compatibility

Campbell and Stanley fit well with how scientists thought about experiments. According to survey respondents, it "worked within the widely accepted framework of experimentation writ large," and its "conceptualization of external validity as an interaction fit into the ANOVA [analysis of variance] framework that dominated the thinking of many psychologists at that time." By contrast, both Campbell (1975) and Cronbach (1982) fit poorly into existing paradigms. Both advocated qualitative methods, but "neither psychologists nor educators are sympathetic to qualitative work," and Cronbach "sometimes pushed his positions to extremes that backfired, for example, that journalistic methods are prototypic for explanation."

Social Context

The context of the 1960s called for field methods to test the effects of social interventions. Campbell and Stanley fit this need well. As one respondent noted,

> In 1963 the field of education was on the brink of the accountability-oriented programs of the War on Poverty. These programs included the first federally supported research and development centers, which were launched in 1964, and the government's substantial investment in educational research training, starting about 1964. Especially influential was the Elementary and Secondary Education Act Title I program launched in 1965, which would require virtually all school districts in the country to begin evaluating and become accountable for their use of federal War on Poverty funds. Conceptually, Campbell and Stanley provided educational research teachers, researchers, and evaluators with useful tools for judging designs for educational research and evaluation, and for planning such studies.

After Suchman's (1967) pioneering book cited Campbell and Stanley as a model for how to do evaluation research (e.g., Weiss, 1972), Campbell and Stanley became the most influential early paradigm for doing such work (Shadish et al., 1991).

Timing

The influence of timing on impact is crucial. A respondent explained,

> Fame is a matter of timing, timing, timing. When Campbell and Stanley came out, it was about five years post-Sputnik; hard-headed "good" science was to answer our problems. It was the beginning of the Great Society programs. Meaningful social research was to be valued. The problems of society (e.g., poverty, racism) were *going* to be solved. But almost every quantitative methods course in graduate school in psychology was being taught out of Winer or Edwards, which were both almost totally limited to laboratory randomized experiments. Skinnerian psychology,

although in slow decline, was still the model. We operated with a logical positivist philosophy of science. Studies were valid because our measurement was valid, we randomized, we controlled, we controlled, and we controlled a bit more. Nowhere, however, did we worry about the "social" validity of studies. So in the context in which Campbell and Stanley fit: (1) science was salvation; (2) socially meaningful research (read here: non-laboratory studies) was in demand and we could be part of the solution of the terrible problems of our society; (3) virtually all of our texts dealt with a kind of science that was not the science that was suddenly in demand (read here: that was cool). Along came Campbell and Stanley— very well written, very complete, at some levels both simple and directive, very well reasoned, and broadly applicable.

Lack of Competition

In addition, Campbell and Stanley was "without real competition," for "there was nothing else like it." According to one respondent,

> The experimental design books of the 1950s and 1960s (and 1970s and 1980s and 1990s) were ANOVA texts (Winer, Lindquist, Kirk, Keppel, etc.), but by the 1960s, a practical guide to field research was badly needed. Campbell and Stanley provided a new way of thinking about educational research that freed the researcher to be more creative in both design and thought" in field experimentation. No other work did so.

Tribal Leadership

Campbell (1979) once wrote that Edward Tolman's failure in debates in the 1950s with Kenneth Spence about cognitive versus behavioral psychology was a failure of tribal leadership—Tolman did not motivate colleagues and students to pursue his ideas. In contrast, wrote one respondent,

> Campbell and Stanley each recruited and trained a cadre of very bright, outstanding students, including Les McLean, Dave Wiley, Gene Glass, Andrew Porter, Bob Boruch, and others. They effectively spread the word about and taught others to apply the contents of Campbell and Stanley.

According to another respondent, just as Spence's students dominated learning theory in the 1950s, Campbell and Stanley's students

> dominated research methods from the late 60s on—Crano, Brewer, Kenny, Kidder, and others wrote the texts that every graduate student in education, psychology, and other social sciences read in their first year of graduate school. It became the "received view" of methodology. Campbell generated tremendous loyalty in his students who, in turn, essentially took over the field by force of numbers. Campbell's personal charisma contributed, especially as it led his students to work within the Campbellian way of thinking. Their productivity quickly filled the ecological niche in the world of methodology in ways that are still obvious today.

NEGATIVE IMPACTS

Some respondents pointed out that Campbell and Stanley's impacts were partly negative in legitimizing poor experiments, an overemphasis on experiments, and a particularly narrow view of validity.

Legitimizing Poor Experiments

One respondent stated that Campbell and Stanley's system for categorizing and criticizing nonrandomized designs

> provided a nomenclature that "gave cover" to the sloppy educational researcher; for example, somehow a Campbell and Stanley Design 2 became just as respectable as a Lindquist Type IV design. In my view, the text had more than one audience—it had the thoughtful researcher as well as the sloppy researcher.

Indeed, Campbell once expressed regret that their focus on quasi-experimental designs may have discouraged researchers from using randomized designs when the latter were feasible.

Overemphasis on Experimentation

One respondent wrote that, especially in program evaluation during

> the early days of War on Poverty programs, there was great emphasis on employing evaluation designs that effectively addressed threats to internal validity. Education evaluators were essentially directed to evaluate the school-based projects using a true experimental design or a strong quasi-experimental design. Millions of dollars were wasted in these efforts, partly because the requirements of experimental design were often antithetical to the needs and realities of urban schools. Experimental design based reports at the annual American Educational Research Association meetings of the late 1960s and early 1970s were largely disappointing, even useless. They presented little more than explications of the designs employed and brief reference to "no significant difference" findings. Schools needed formatively oriented needs assessments to target projects and process evaluations to guide and document project implementation. But experimental designs called for clear outcome criteria at the outset of a project and invariant treatments throughout the evaluation. The requirement of random assignment of students to federally supported interventions or control conditions was typically not acceptable, workable, or legal. Because Title I projects were targeted to increasing and improving educational services for the most disadvantaged students in our society, schools couldn't legally randomly assign children entitled to receive Title I to experimental or control conditions. They also didn't have sufficiently clear and strong educational treatments to confidently

assign, deliver, and control; and available, standardized student achievement instruments were not valid for measuring achievement at the bottom of the distribution. The failures of experimental design in such settings led to the development of alternative and often more applicable and productive approaches to evaluation.

By the early 1970s, evaluators had relegated field experiments to a small part of their repertoire (Shadish et al., 1991).

Overemphasis on One Notion of Validity

Campbell and Stanley did not invent the concept of validity; for example, test theorists discussed validity in the 1940s. But Campbell and Stanley's particular notion of validity, especially internal validity, dominated some areas of scientific discourse. One respondent remarked,

> But as all great inventions, such as money, automobiles, or Coca Cola, Campbell and Stanley had a downside. For educational research, it was a terrible downside. It unbalanced attention between the content and method of studies. The choice of research question, which didn't have a rubric, was seen as much less needing deep thought than the choice of which data to gather, guided by Campbell and Stanley. Young researchers were intimidated by this chapter and their professors over-valued it as a standard for doing research. The effect on the training of minor researchers and users of research was not seriously studied. Of course, validity is as important as any idea in research, theory, and practice. But the authors, academic statesmen though they were, did not recognize the threat to the abiding state of research brought about by their work. Voltaire said the best is the enemy of the good. In many instances, I believe, research became poorer because of the attention to the threats to validity. The attention furthered the separation between personal study, action research, critical review, and formal research. Eventually, however, quantitative designs became austere, and in reaction the use of qualitative methods became more common, disciplined, and respected. Questions of validity are as important in qualitative work, of course, as an empathic Don Campbell pointed out. But with a more a constructivist and less realist epistemology, the meaning of validity changed. Not one truth, but many, each needing to worry about credibility, but not in the way called for in the chapter.

DISCUSSION

Great works can have many characteristics, but must they have *all* of the ones we have listed in this chapter? We doubt it. The most highly cited work of all time presents a laboratory method for measuring protein (Lowry, Rosebrough, Farr, & Randall, 1951; see also Garfield, 1979). It was brief, simple, creative, and practically useful to many biomedical researchers who needed to measure protein. But it was narrow in scope, competing methods existed, and tribal leadership was not a factor. So we should not generalize from the characteristics of one great work—those characteristics may only be correlated with impact rather than cause it. We would need to assess many high-impact works to see what characteristics they share consistently.

We should also assess works that had these characteristics but did not have great impact. A telling example is one of Campbell's least highly cited works, the 1957 *Psychological Bulletin* article that presaged Campbell and Stanley. These two works share the same creative ideas, ability to synthesize and impose order, and intellectual history. Three pertinent differences may clarify the discrepant impact of these two works. First, Campbell (1957) may have been too short to convey the ideas fully or to provide pedagogical aids. Second, the journal in which Campbell (1957) appeared may have been too little read or read by an audience less likely to use it (academic psychologists rather than applied educational researchers). Third, Campbell and Stanley entered a social context in the 1960s with a huge demand for program evaluation, a demand that did not exist 6 years earlier, in the 1957 publication. Perhaps Simonton's (1989) chance configuration model is partly right—that great impact requires a set of impact-facilitating events and characteristics to come together at one time and place. Simonton's empirical data suggest that scientists best increase their chances of having such impact by publishing more works over many years, for with each new publication the chances are increased that the right configuration will occur.

But it is hoped that scientists can do better than just publish more. They can learn to be brief and simple, write well, and make their work pedagogically useful. They can choose problems and write solutions that reflect practical usefulness, paradigmatic consistency, and generality. They can improve their tribal leadership, although there are limits to how much one can control personality variables such as charisma. Other characteristics are harder but not impossible to control. Embedding a work in one's own metatheory takes intellectual maturity and breadth requiring decades of effort. Writing works that are creative, generative, synthetic, and that impose order can be learned (e.g., McGuire, 1997; Sternberg, 2001), although perhaps only partly. Some characteristics may be indirectly controlled through problem selection—social and intellectual context, timing, and lack of competition. However, our experience is that few scientists even try to influence these characteristics by thinking about their own metatheories, by learning to be more creative, or by choosing problems with high impact potential. Sometimes this disinterest in impact reflects ignorance of these issues, bad research habits, or an unwillingness to learn new ways of working. But often this disinterest is because scientists have other good reasons for their choices, such as love of knowledge for its own sake, personal curiosity about a problem, devotion to solving a social problem of little interest to others (e.g., the problems of people with chronic mental illness), or fundability. Having impact is just one of many noble goals in science.

The difficulty of intentionally producing high-impact works is illustrated by one of our favorite cartoons about science. It pictures Louis Pasteur, who discovered the germ theory of disease. The caption reads, "Louis Pasteur, after discovering that microbes transmitted disease, experimented with ways of killing them." In the drawing, Pasteur is about to hit a petri dish of germs with a hammer. The absurdity of hammering germs to death highlights how hard it is, even for scientists of great achievement, to intentionally and repeatedly produce great works. Similarly, looking at Digital Equipment Corporation founder Ken Olsen, who dismissed the personal computer revolution as a passing fad, Microsoft chairman Bill Gates commented, "Success is a lousy teacher. It seduces smart people into thinking they can't lose" (quoted in Gerst, 1995, p. G3). In trying to understand and produce great works, a little humility goes a long way. We can learn about impact by studying works like Campbell and Stanley. With effort, we can even increase the odds that our own works will have such impact. But in the end, we do well to remember how very often our reach will exceed our grasp.

REFERENCES

Bickman, L. (2000a). (Ed.). *Research design: Donald Campbell's legacy* (Vol. 2). Thousand Oaks, CA: Sage.

Bickman, L. (2000b). (Ed.). *Validity and social experimentation: Donald Campbell's legacy* (Vol. 1). Thousand Oaks, CA: Sage.

Brewer, M. B., & Collins, B. E. (Eds.). (1981). *Scientific inquiry and the social sciences: A volume in honor of Donald T. Campbell.* San Francisco, CA: Jossey-Bass.

Campbell, D. T. (1957). Factors relevant to the validity of experiments in social settings. *Psychological Bulletin, 54,* 297–312.

Campbell, D. T. (1975). "Degrees of freedom" and the case study. *Comparative Political Studies, 8,* 178–193.

Campbell, D. T. (1979). A tribal model of the social system vehicle carrying scientific knowledge. *Knowledge, 2,* 181–202.

Campbell, D. T. (1981). Comment: Another perspective on a scholarly career. In M. B. Brewer & B. E. Collins (Eds.), *Scientific inquiry and the social sciences: A volume in honor of Donald T. Campbell* (pp. 454–501). San Francisco, CA: Jossey-Bass.

Campbell, D. T. (1986). Relabeling internal and external validity for applied social scientists. In W. M. K. Trochim (Ed.), *Advances in quasi-experimental design and analysis* (pp. 67–77). San Francisco, CA: Jossey-Bass.

Campbell, D. T., & Kenny, D. A. (1999). *A primer on regression artifacts*. New York: Guilford Press.

Campbell, D. T., & Russo, M. J. (1999). *Social experimentation*. Thousand Oaks, CA: Sage.

Campbell, D. T., & Stanley, J. C. (1963a). *Experimental and quasi-experimental designs for research*. Chicago: Rand McNally.

Campbell, D. T., & Stanley, J. C. (1963b). Experimental and quasi-experimental designs for research on teaching. In N. L. Gage (Ed.), *Handbook of research on teaching* (pp. 171–246). Chicago: Rand McNally.

Campbell, D. T., & Stanley, J. C. (1966). *Experimental and quasi-experimental designs for research on teaching*. Chicago: Rand McNally. (Reprinted from *Handbook of research on teaching*, pp. 171–246, by N. L. Gage, Ed., 1963, Chicago: Rand McNally).

Cook, T. D., & Campbell, D. T. (1979). *Quasi-experimentation: Design and analysis issues for field settings*. Chicago: Rand McNally.

Cronbach, L. J. (1982). *Designing evaluations of educational and social programs*. San Francisco, CA: Jossey-Bass.

Garfield, E. (1979). Is citation analysis a legitimate evaluation tool? *Scientometrics, 1*, 359–375.

Gerst, M. (1995, December 3). Gates vows to usher in a new age. *The Memphis Commercial Appeal*, p. G3.

Judd, C. M., & Kenny, D. A. (1981). *Estimating the effects of social interventions*. Cambridge, England: Cambridge University Press.

Lowry, O. H., Rosebrough, N. J., Farr, A. L., & Randall, R. J. (1951). Protein measurement with the folin phenol reagent. *Journal of Biological Chemistry, 193*, 265–275.

McCleary, R. D., & Hay, R. A. (1980). *Applied time series analysis for the social sciences*. Newbury Park, CA: Sage.

McGuire, W. J. (1997). Creative hypothesis generating in psychology: Some useful heuristics. *Annual Review of Psychology, 48*, 1–30.

Mohr, L. B. (1995). *Impact analysis for program evaluation* (2nd ed.). Thousand Oaks, CA: Sage.

Nietzsche, F. (1980). *On the advantage and disadvantage of history for life*. Cambridge, MA: Hackett.

Shadish, W. R., Cook, T. D., & Campbell, D. T. (2002). *Experimental and quasi-experimental designs for generalized causal inference*. Boston, MA: Houghton-Mifflin.

Shadish, W. R., Cook, T. D., & Leviton, L. C. (1991). *Foundations of program evaluation: Theories of practice*. Newbury Park, CA: Sage.

Shadish, W. R., & Reis, J. (1984). A review of studies of the effectiveness of programs to improve pregnancy outcome. *Evaluation Review, 8*, 747–776.

Simonton, D. K. (1989). Chance-configuration theory of scientific creativity. In B. G. Gholson, W. R. Shadish, R. A. Neimeyer, & A. C. Houts (Eds.), *Psychology of science: Contributions to metascience* (pp. 170–213). Cambridge, England: Cambridge University Press.

Sternberg, R. J. (2001). What is the common thread of creativity? Its dialectical relation to intelligence and wisdom. *American Psychologist, 56,* 360–362.

Suchman, E. A. (1967). *Evaluative research: Principles and practice in public service and social action programs.* New York: Russell Sage Foundation.

Trochim, W. M. K. (1984). *Research design for program evaluation: The regression-discontinuity approach.* Newbury Park, CA: Sage.

Weiss, C. H. (1972). *Evaluation research: Methods for assessing program effectiveness.* Englewood Cliffs, NJ: Prentice-Hall.

10

UNDERSTANDING DISCIPLINARY SIGNIFICANCE: ALLEN E. BERGIN'S 1980 ARTICLE ON RELIGIOUS VALUES

BRENT D. SLIFE AND MATTHEW WHOOLERY

This chapter may be different from the other chapters of this book in focus and structure. First, the focus of this chapter is disciplinary significance rather than greatness. Although the analysis of greatness has obvious importance, few could ever hope to aspire to the works of psychology's greats, such as Sigmund Freud and William James. The student of psychology is more likely to write an article of significance than to write one of greatness. This focus also permits more contemporary works to be analyzed and allows access to crucial information (e.g., author interview) that a more historical work of greatness would preclude.

Second, the structure of this chapter is narrative rather than analytical. The chapter basically portrays two narratives about significance. The first describes how we (the authors) came to understand the complexities of disciplinary significance. The lessons of this narrative include issues of citation quantity and reception quality, pivotal elements in the recognition and understanding of significance. These lessons enabled us to establish criteria for the selection of a particular article of significance—Allen E. Bergin's (1980a) "Psychotherapy and Religious Values," published in the *Journal of Consulting and Clinical Psychology* (hereinafter referred to as "Bergin 1980"). The second narrative, then, is a story of the formulation, characteristics, and reception of this article. As we show in the final section, the lessons of this narrative entail 10 practical guidelines for those who wish to write significant works.

UNDERSTANDING DISCIPLINARY SIGNIFICANCE

We found the understanding of disciplinary significance surprisingly complicated. Unlike great works—which are often already recognized as such—recently significant articles have not undergone the "test of time," and so they are not as easily recognized. Great works are frequently marked by their role and survival through the various developments of history. Recently significant articles, in contrast, rarely carry such marks. This is not to say that they are not acknowledged as significant in some manner, but this acknowledgment is more subtle and complex.

Quantity of Citations

As an important case in point, consider how the simple quantity of citations does not necessarily denote a significant work. Although such quantitative measures are typically considered "relatively objective" (Sternberg, 1996, p. 70), they are not only contextless but also potentially misleading as an index of an article's reception in a discipline. For instance, an article could be widely cited as the antithesis of quality or insightfulness. Also, as Douglas (1992), himself the author of a highly cited article, described, many citations are simply incorrect, because the citation does not support its placement in the text—"as if the author had not read even so much as the [citation's] abstract" (p. 407).

Another problem with a mere count of citations is that the most highly cited articles are routinely articles about methods and statistics (Douglas, 1992; Sternberg, 1992). Apparently, psychology's "methodolatry"—its singular fascination with all types of methods—leads to this peculiarity (Danziger, 1990; Slife, 1998). In this sense, a high level of citations does not necessarily mean a high level of significance; citation numbers may indicate that everyone in psychology uses methods and statistics (and needs highly cited references to get their article through an editorial process). The high citation of method articles could also indicate a problem. When a discipline's most cited articles involve methods and statistics rather than ideas and theories, it could indicate greater concern with style than substance (Slife & Williams, 1995).

With this context of citations, our criteria for article selection included not only a relatively recent contribution (with an author who was alive and active) but also a theoretical contribution that significantly advanced, if not revolutionized, the ideas of the discipline. This implied for us both the *quan-*

tity and *quality* of citations. As problematic as the mere quantity of citations is, it would be difficult to consider a work truly significant if it were not highly cited. Although there are undoubtedly published works that are highly significant but not highly cited, we hoped to find an article that was acclaimed as well as incisive. As Douglas (1992) put it, citations are a "'blue-collar' index of impact, made primarily by people in the trenches rather than by the generals" (p. 405). However, we could not rely completely on numerical count because of its crudeness and potentially misleading nature. Therefore, we also needed some indication of the quality of an article's reception in the discipline.

Quality of Reception

A good reception, we reasoned, would minimally imply three qualities, particularly for a theoretical contribution: *positive recognition, dialectical opposition,* and *research stimulation*. First, some members of the discipline, preferably important members, should explicitly recognize an article's significance. This is not to assert that leading members of a discipline are the sole deciders of significance. Indeed, leading members may be entrenched in a paradigm that is giving way to "young turks," as Kuhn (1970) described. It is only to say that we preferred the article of our analysis to have some clear acclaim rather than deciding the import of the article on our own.

At the same time, we would not expect the response to a theoretical article to be total acclamation. A significant theoretical piece should "stir the pot" more than "keep the status quo." Our second criterion of quality, then, was a dialectical or oppositional response. That is, we expected a significant article to be controversial and thus have its detractors as well as its adherents. Particularly if the article had a revolutionary or paradigm-violating tone, it should not be received with total acclaim. It should have a number of leading thinkers in the discipline (presumably those with an investment in the prevailing paradigm) clearly and expressively challenging its conclusions. As the British science fiction character Doctor Who once put it, "You can always judge a man by the quality of his enemies" (British Broadcasting Company, 2001). We believe a similar dialectic is also part of the judgment of an article's significance.

With both positive and dialectical responses, how could such an article not be heuristic as well? How could these responses not lead to programs of research and new lines of application? Would not the innovations and controversies generated need to be explored and resolved? Here, we would envision not only the usual empirical research, whether quantitative or qualitative, but also well-reasoned theoretical contributions, looking at the assumptions and implications of the article in question. Ideally, an article of significance would be responsible for new lines of thinking or applications, or at least the reinvigoration or substantive modification of old lines. Either way, a significant article should lead to further disciplinary discussion and exploration.

MEETING THE CRITERIA OF SIGNIFICANCE

With these qualities as our criteria, we selected, as mentioned earlier, Bergin's 1980 article, "Psychotherapy and Religious Values." This selection was relatively surprising to us, because Bergin is a (retired) colleague at Brigham Young University, our own professional home. We realized immediately that our selection could appear to be "home-grown" and thus our analysis discounted. We admit that the convenience of interacting with the author occurred to us. However, this played no part in our selection, especially in view of recent advances in academic communication (e.g., e-mail). As readers will see, Bergin 1980 not only meets all the criteria we initially set forth but also surpasses them.

First, Bergin continues to be quite active in his scholarly pursuits (e.g., Richards & Bergin, 2000). In fact, in the past few years he has won two prestigious awards for excellence, including the "1998 Distinguished Career Award" from the Society for Psychotherapy Research and the "1998 Oskar Pfister Award" from the American Psychiatric Association for outstanding contributions to understanding the interplay between religion and social issues. Second, Bergin 1980 is clearly a theoretical contribution. Not only is it distinctly *non*methodological, in the sense described earlier, but it is also *non*empirical. Although Bergin discussed numerous empirical studies, he did not report an original empirical study in this article. Rather, he advanced knowledge through critically examining the ideas and assumptions of the discipline as well as by proposing an alternative for empirical test.

We quote excerpts from the article's abstract here so that readers have some sense of the article's main contents:

> The alienation of therapeutic psychology from religious values is described and contrasted with a growing professional and public interest in religious experience and commitment. Six theses . . . are presented and documented [that] include a contrast between dominant mental health ideologies, defined as clinical pragmatism and humanistic idealism, and theistic realism, which is a proposed alternative viewpoint. . . . It is argued that until the theistic belief systems of a large percentage of the population are sincerely considered and conceptually integrated into our work, we are unlikely to be fully effective professionals. (Bergin, 1980a, p. 95)

The content of this abstract may be striking. Few people would assume that an article about religious values is relevant to psychology and psychotherapy. Moreover, at the time of the article's publication, most psycholo-

TABLE 10.1
Number of Citations for Bergin (1980–August 2000)

Years	Citations
1980–1985	55
1986–1990	70
1991–1995	46
1996–Aug. 2000	44
Total	215

gists were quite satisfied to operate in an objective and a secular fashion, ignoring the issue of religious values altogether. However, part of the significance of Bergin 1980 is not only that it made religious values a topic of psychological study, but also that it facilitated, if not stimulated, an entire program of research on religion and mental health. As we attempt to show, this article has met both criteria of significance: a high quantity of disciplinary citations and a high quality of disciplinary reception, including a high impact on related research.

Quantity of Citations

To interpret the quantity of citations of Bergin 1980 (see Table 10.1), some sense of the context or norms of citation numbers is required. Many psychologists are shocked at how few citations even top-rated articles receive. This reaction could indicate psychology's lack of general influence or, more likely, that few psychologists know what to expect regarding citation quantities. As it happens, citations are generally rarer than many professionals realize. After all, the article being cited has to be read (to some degree) by a fellow professional (a phenomenon that is increasingly rare) and *then* deemed sufficiently important to be mentioned in that professional's work (another relative rarity). We submit that this two-part filter makes the citation process particularly arduous, especially given increasing specialization and decreasing time to read. To be cited at all is no mean feat.

As a pertinent illustration, the 10th most cited article (Cronbach, 1955) in one of the premier journals of psychology, the *Psychological Bulletin*, was only cited on approximately 400 occasions (Sternberg, 1992). This number might seem impressive, depending again on one's expectations, but this number is the accumulation of citations over nearly a 40-year span of time. This means that one of the top 10 articles of psychology—in a journal psychologists would expect to have generic and citable interest for the discipline—only garnered 100 citations *per decade* or approximately *10 per year*! Put in this context, the two-decade total of over 200 citations for Bergin 1980 is comparable (see Table 10.1).

As Table 10.1 indicates, Bergin 1980 appears to have considerable "staying" power—not diminishing much in citations after almost two decades. At this rate, Bergin 1980 could be comparable with Cronbach (1955), potentially another member of the top 10. Admittedly, this comparison is crude, but it is only intended as a way of putting the citation numbers in context. It shows how respectable, if not stellar, the citations numbers for Bergin 1980 are. As further support for this conclusion, we note that Bergin received over 1,000 reprint requests for this article (Bergin, 1985b). Again, most scholars lack norms for this obviously high number. Still, it is safe to say that few scholars have even come close to receiving this many reprint requests. For example, after hearing about the number of Bergin 1980 reprint requests, leading psychotherapy researcher Sol Garfield made clear that he had never experienced such a flood of requests (A. E. Bergin, personal communication, March 19, 2001).

Quality of Reception

What about the quality of disciplinary reception to Bergin 1980? Although perhaps unlikely, the 1,000 reprint requests could have evidenced an intense negative response toward Bergin's article. Many scholars could have been citing this article for its vices rather than its virtues. Recall that we postulated three main characteristics of reception quality that should indicate an article's significance: positive recognition by leading scholars in the discipline, dialectical opposition by leading scholars in the field, and some evidence of a resulting program of research. How did Bergin 1980 fare in relation to these three criteria of reception?

Regarding positive recognition, Bergin has kept and published many of the letters he received with the requests for reprints (Bergin, 1985b). Even a brief scan of these letters reveals the number of disciplinary leaders who applauded and lauded Bergin 1980, although they did not always agree with the article. The high praise of Ellen Berscheid (at the time a professor of psychology at the University of Minnesota) is representative: "I congratulate you for saying what I believe has needed to be said for a long time . . . I very much hope that this paper will, in retrospect, be considered one of the most important to have been published in the area in the new decade." Obviously, if our analysis is correct, Berscheid's hope has been fulfilled.

Consider the quality of the following commenters (with their affiliations at the time) as well as the quality of the brief excerpts from their letters:

> I commend you on your excellent article (Karl Menninger, The Menninger Foundation).
>
> On the whole, I am very much in agreement although we may differ on some aspects (Hans Strupp, distinguish professor of psychology, Vanderbilt University).
>
> It is through writings such as yours that religious values will receive greater consideration in psychotherapy (Albert Bandura, professor of psychology, Stanford University/past president of the American Psychological Association).

I don't disagree as much as you might think . . . I do believe there is some kind of transcendent organizing influence in the universe which operates in man as well (Carl Rogers, Center for the Studies of the Person/past president of the American Psychological Association).

Even someone with a relatively superficial understanding of psychology would instantly recognize the stature of these commenters. Berscheid, Menninger, Strupp, Bandura, and Rogers are widely acknowledged not only as leaders in the fields of psychology and psychiatry but also as *the* leaders at the time of these comments. The enthusiasm of the comments, often in spite of disagreements with Bergin 1980, surely fulfills the first (if not second) criterion of reception quality—the positive recognition of disciplinary leaders. As Bergin reported (personal communication, March 19, 2001), one leading psychiatrist, David Larson (formerly with the National Institute of Mental Health and currently president of the National Institute for Health Care Research), confessed to being so positively moved by Bergin 1980 that he had "tears in his eyes" after reading it. Surely, few journal articles in recent psychology have spurred such an emotional and stellar response.

What about the dialectical and oppositional elements of this response? Here again, Bergin 1980 has met with a singular set of rejoinders and negative responses, signaling its controversial and perhaps even revolutionary nature for the discipline (which we explore later). Perhaps the most prominent of these rejoinders was the response of Albert Ellis (1980), a leading scholar and therapist in the field. Ellis identified himself as a "probabilistic atheist" and contended that "human disturbance is largely (though not entirely) associated with and springs from absolutistic thinking—from dogmatism, inflexibility, and devout shoulds, oughts, and musts—and that extreme religiosity . . . called true believerism, is essentially emotional disturbance" (p. 635). Bergin replied to Ellis and others in the same journal issue (Bergin, 1980b).

This "dialogue" between Bergin and Ellis played for almost two decades, with several conference encounters (e.g., Bergin, 1985a, 1996; Ellis, 1985, 1996) as well as reprints of this dialogue in psychological readers (e.g., Miller, 1992; Slife & Rubinstein, 1992). Other noted scholars have also published primarily negative responses (e.g., Walls, 1980) but, again, a sense of perspective is needed to understand this dialectic. Although published responses are routine in some journals (e.g., the *American Psychologist*), published responses are extremely rare for most other publications, particularly continuing responses (over two decades) from leading psychotherapists and researchers the caliber of Ellis. Clearly, such responses meet our dialectical criterion.

Research Stimulation

The only criterion of quality that remains is research stimulation: Did Bergin 1980 positively stimulate further disciplinary discussion and exploration? Again, this article seems not only to have met this heuristic criterion but also to have surpassed it. It is true that the research on psychotherapy values precedes Bergin 1980, going back at least as far as Rosenthal's (1955) classic studies some 46 years ago. Still, there is no doubt about the heavy and stimulating influence of Bergin's 1980 contribution. The first author of the present chapter can attest to this influence because he had to review this rather voluminous research for two projects (Slife, Smith, & Burchfield, in press; Smith & Slife, in press). Bergin 1980 clearly figures prominently in all the modern phases of this research. In fact, researchers routinely cite this article first (chronologically), as if it is the primary historical stimulant for the modern phases of this research program (e.g., Chaddock & McMinn, 1999; Larson, Swyers, & McCullough, 1998; Shafranske, 1996; Shafranske & Malony, 1990; Watson, Morris, & Hood, 1989; Worthington, 1988).

The influence of Bergin 1980 is not limited to research on psychotherapy values. The import of this article can also be seen in a related and more popular literature—the burgeoning research on spirituality and religion in psychology. That is, Bergin 1980 was not just about values in psychotherapy; it was about *religious* values in psychotherapy. This article was one of the very first to explicitly address and explore the interface between religious doctrine and psychological "doctrine" concerning mental health (as recognized by the 1998 award from the American Psychiatric Association and the 1990 Williams James Award from the American Psychological Association Division 36, Psychology and Religion).

Although religious affiliation had been used for years as an independent or a dependent variable, few psychologists had taken religious *values* into account (for an exception, see Collins, 1977). Almost no psychologist had taken seriously the contrast between these values and the secular values implicit in psychotherapy. In this sense, the heuristic influence of Bergin 1980 is better understood for the role it played in the coming torrent of research involving religion and mental health (Keating & Fretz, 1990; Richards & Bergin, 1997; Shafranske, 1996; Watson et al., 1989; Zinnbauer & Pargament, 2000). In this arena, a number of investigators have explicitly honored Bergin and his most pivotal position statement—Bergin 1980. Most notably, Eric Swedin (1999) viewed Bergin historically as one of the main "characters" in the "integrating of modern psychologies and religion" (p. 13).

Bergin's prestigious 1989 award from the American Psychological Association—Distinguished Professional Contributions to Knowledge—also evidences the crucial importance of the research begun by Bergin 1980. An excerpt from the award citation makes clear Bergin's pivotal role in the religion and values research: "Allen Bergin has established himself as a leading expert in psychotherapy research, and has challenged psychological orthodoxy to emphasize the importance of values and religion in therapy" ("Allen E. Bergin: Citation," 1990, p. 474). With this recognition, it is apparent that Bergin 1980 was integral not only to the reinvigoration of values research in psychotherapy but also to the entire spectrum of investigations involving mental health and religion. Surely again, Bergin 1980 meets our criteria for facilitating, if not spurring, programs of research. In this sense, it surpasses all our criteria of significance.

THE NARRATIVE OF BERGIN 1980

How, then, do we go about understanding the meaning of this significance? Here we conducted a qualitative analysis of sorts. We used qualitative methods somewhat informally to examine pertinent documents (e.g., letters) and to query the author about his experiences in writing Bergin 1980 (Kvale, 1996). We met Professor Bergin at his home for a 2-hour interview, which we then transcribed and analyzed into what we would term "the narrative of Bergin 1980." That is, we specifically asked Bergin to address the temporality of Bergin 1980—the relevant context that immediately preceded his writing of the article, his experiences in actually writing the article, and his experiences related to the article following its publication. We regret that space limitations prevent us from lengthy quotations, but the transcription is available from the authors. Needless to say, we are grateful to Bergin for his time and support of this project.

Before

It is interesting to note that Bergin felt strong emotions about the ideas of his 1980 article many years before the article was formally conceived. He reported experiencing a "kind of brooding feeling" that a large part of his professional desires and aspirations were "unfulfilled, frustrated, and wanting expression." Although he believed that much of his training (Massachusetts Institute of Technology, Stanford University, University of Wisconsin) prevented this expression, he views several presentations and publications before Bergin 1980 (Bergin, 1977, 1978, 1979) as approximate expressions. In this sense, Bergin 1980 was "not a sudden thing," because it had been brewing and brooding for a long while. However, these approximate expressions were frustrating because they lacked a "complete voice."

One likely turning point in his struggle for full expression was Bergin's move from Columbia University to Brigham Young University (BYU). BYU is the flagship university of The Church of Jesus Christ of Latter-day Saints, Bergin's own religious affiliation. Although Bergin was very accomplished at Columbia—establishing himself as a full professor and one of the premier psychotherapy researchers of his day (e.g., Bergin & Garfield, 1971; Bergin & Strupp, 1972; Swedin, 1999)—the atmosphere surrounding values, especially religious values, was dramatically different at the two universities. On the one hand, Columbia was the prototypical secular university; religious rhetoric, for example, was considered inappropriate in psychology courses. BYU, on the other hand, actively encouraged the comparison of the sacred and the secular—with sacred (religious) values actively discussed alongside secular values. In this sense, the move to BYU provided a local venue for Bergin to give free and full expression to his professional desires and aspirations.

The discipline at the national and international levels was another matter entirely. Psychologists generally maintained a staunch secular position on the issue of values, although they rarely viewed this as a "position." Most considered secularism as a kind of value-free neutrality, which they assumed complemented the objectivism and scientism of the discipline (Slife, in press). Although this position was, from Bergin's perspective, a "misconception" as well as an obstacle to his nascent project, he also saw many encouraging signs in the years leading up to his 1980 contribution. For instance, he took encouragement from the founding of the American Psychological Association Division of Psychology and Religion (Division 36) in 1976 and the publishing of Collins's (1977) book on religion and psychology. These signs also emboldened Bergin. He found himself framing clearer and clearer statements of his own ideas, along with an increasing resolution to present them to his discipline.

Three elements seem to have played a major role in this increasingly bold and resolved stance: clarity of vision, sense of injustice, and willingness to take risks. Regarding the issue of clarity, the mid- to late 1970s was a time in which Bergin believed he finally saw that the "emperor had no clothes." That is, he finally realized how the vaunted neutrality and objectivism of psychology was really an illusion or a sham. From Bergin's perspective, the seeming neutrality and secularism of psychology was actually a set of value-laden opinions about how psychology and psychotherapy should be conducted. Secularists, in this sense, were able to express their value-laden opinions through academic jargon (e.g., at Columbia), as though it were scholarship rather than an ideological agenda. Why was he, a religious person, prevented from expressing his views in standard academic forums?

This perceived prevention led Bergin to get his "Irish up," as he puts it. He sensed an injustice in academic psychology that had important consequences for its applied realms. For instance, the devout religious beliefs of clients were consistently being discounted in therapy (Richards & Bergin, 1997). Although most psychotherapists assumed that they valued these client values, regardless of their own beliefs, empirical research demonstrated otherwise (Richards & Bergin, 1997, 2000). Consequently, Bergin felt he had to address this injustice. Secularism had become its own unacknowledged brand of religion, with secularists attempting to "convert" religious people (Tjeltveit, 1999).

With his "Irish up," Bergin found a new willingness to take risks as well as new approaches to address these issues. He "experimented" with this courage and these approaches in many university colloquia and national conferences. He remembers distinctly saying to himself at one point, "I think my academic career is over." That is, he somehow realized that the only way he could even begin to give complete expression to his views was to face and overcome the possibility of professional death. As long as he was concerned about his professional reputation, he knew that he would never give full voice to what he felt was the injustice of his discipline.

At one point in 1977, however, Bergin realized he had gone too far. He describes this presentation as "bombastic" and a "bridge burner," and his startled audience apparently told him so. Sensitive to this reaction, Bergin immediately took stock. He resolved to take an evolutionary rather than a revolutionary perspective and look to the long term for change in his discipline. This long-term perspective allowed him to feel less pressure, stow some of his indignation, and concentrate on "building rather than burning bridges." Interestingly, his 1980 article was a direct result of this perspective. Bergin knew he had finally found the right tone for this article (and his entire project) when his erstwhile mentor, Carl Rogers, remarked on reading Bergin 1980, "Allen, I'm so happy that you are finally speaking from your own gut" (A. E. Bergin, personal communication, March 19, 2001).

During

Bergin reported that the writing of his 1980 contribution was relatively easy. Indeed, the manuscript seemed to "write itself," undergoing far fewer drafts than his usual papers. This ease, however, was no surprise. The ideas of the manuscript had been fermenting for many years, and he had a strong sense of his audience. Although he was keenly aware of the potential disciplinary opposition to this sort of paper, he somehow knew that there were "lots of other people out there like me" who were "in the closet." In this sense, he perceived the importance of the paper before it was written.

In terms of writing organization, Bergin believed (in retrospect) that he unconsciously adopted the writing style and content structure of his other most highly cited article—Bergin (1966; reprinted in 13 anthologies). He had long viewed the writing of his 1966 article as his most accessible and readable, although he had not specifically attempted to write in this manner since. The structure of the 1966 article has each main and secondary point outlined and bulleted, so that readers can readily gain the primary concepts of the paper in 2 minutes and the secondary concepts in 5 minutes. Indeed, Bergin 1980 is so well organized in this regard that readers only need to read the "fine print" (supporting material) if they have a problem with a main point. Even here—in the supporting material—the prose is cogent enough to satisfy all but the most opposed of readers.

What enabled Bergin to write so accessibly and convincingly? Bergin considered his writing ability to be "God given," although he admitted it was greatly enriched by the "uncompromising critique of others." His own critique of the work of others, particularly his graduate students, also facilitated his writing skills. Bergin felt especially "blessed" by students because his "Irish was often up" on their behalf. "I love students," he explained, "I felt they were often mistreated by the obfuscations and pedantry of very bright people who were massaging their egos with all those big words." Bergin struggled with the torturous prose of many journal authors himself, having served on the editorial boards of 14 professional journals, so he especially empathized with students. He also believed his religious convictions helped him avoid a "big ego" and put the emphasis in his writing where it should be—clarity of expression.

After

Following publication, Bergin reported that the response of readers to his 1980 contribution "blew" him away. Although he had some confidence that the article would be important, he clearly underestimated the degree of both positive and negative reactions from his professional colleagues. The first sign, of course, was the veritable flood of reprint requests and letters, numbering more than 1,000. He was surprised at the high quality and emotionality of the letters that accompanied these requests (as discussed earlier), many writers confessing their most privately held beliefs and convictions to him. Several published responses followed the reprint requests, along with numerous invitations to speak and discuss his proposals and conclusions.

At the same time, Bergin was a little surprised at the level of opposition that resulted from the article's publication. Ellis's (1980) response is perhaps indicative of this opposition: "Religiosity is in many respects equivalent to irrational thinking and emotional disturbance" (p. 636). In our interview with Bergin, however, he was struck more by his experience in presenting his ideas in Amsterdam, The Netherlands. There, the level of opposition and even indignation at his presentation was unexpected. After all, from Bergin's perspective he had "toned it down" and was in his "building bridges" mode. Unfortunately, even the modulated version of his ideas was met with utter (perceived) disdain, reminding Bergin of the disciplinary obstacles in his path. Subsequent debates with Ellis—a charismatic lecturer and debater—also drove a similar point home.

Bergin came to see that the 1980 article set a research agenda for many scholars, including himself. Still, he admitted to some disappointment in what seemed like an inordinate delay in the initiation of this research. Although Bergin stated several clear hypotheses for subsequent research in his 1980 article, these hypotheses did not seem to be investigated until a few years later. In retrospect, this disappointment may have been due to his impatience about getting things under way. In fact, the research "wheels" were probably rolling all the time, in terms of funding, organizational support, and experimental designs. Most important, later in the decade, Sir John Templeton, Christian philanthropist, founded the Templeton Foundation for research on the religion/science relation, and David Larson organized the National Institute for Health Care Research in 1991 to investigate religion in relation to mental and physical health.

In the end, the article was reprinted six separate times, with many follow-up articles written by Bergin (Bergin, 1980a, 1980b, 1991). Bergin admitted to some disappointment with the reception of a recent follow-up—the 1991 *American Psychologist* article. Despite its being published in perhaps the most visible and well-read journal of the discipline, its reception was "nothing" compared with the 1980 article. Bergin believed that its relatively bland reception indicates how far the discipline of psychology has come in accepting his 1980 ideas. No longer are they quite as scandalous or even as positive as they once were. The provocative context in which the original article was conceived is no longer present. Bergin truly felt that a new atmosphere, tolerant of research on spirituality and religion, is evident in the discipline.

THE LESSONS OF THE NARRATIVE

What does this narrative have to offer us about the meaning of significance? Like many stories, it offers several lessons or morals that are not so much universal principles as they are rules or guidelines. Universal principles—if they even exist in this case—apply universally, regardless of the context. Lessons and morals, on the other hand, are more context or story dependent, although they are rarely context or story bound (Slife & Reber, 2001). That is, the application of a lesson probably requires modification to the particular context of its listener or reader, but a lesson is rarely applicable only to the original narrative context. What, then, is the moral to the story of Bergin 1980? What do Bergin's experiences teach about what to consider in attempting to write a significant theoretical article?

1. *Have a passion for the ideas.* A genuine passion appears to help immensely. Too often, researchers write about intellectualized and specialized ideas in which they experience little personal or emotional investment. Bergin, however, had a strong sense of injustice about the privileged status of secular values, made personal by his compassion for students and religious clients. At Columbia, for instance, his students were imbued with secular values, often without their being labeled or distinguished as personal biases, and the secular therapists of New York City frequently discounted their religious clients' values. At BYU, on the other hand, many of Bergin's students were frustrated by the lack of spiritual perspectives in standard disciplinary readings. Recall that Bergin's "Irish" was up on many occasions, and he felt the need to right the seeming wrongs of the discipline. This passion provided

him with the energy needed to develop and publish his ideas as well as the motivation to be as clear as possible.

2. *Direct and refine the passion.* Unfortunately, as Bergin learned, an unbridled passion can also obstruct his message. Passion must be harnessed in a hearable, respectful style. Bergin's Irish was only productive when he was building bridges to his audience rather than burning them. The opposition can be perceived as ignorant fools who lack your brilliance, or as respected colleagues who can teach you as you teach them. The former can result in a rhetorical style that is shrill and accusatory, whereas the latter can lead to a mutual dialogue, with lessons learned by all. Anyone who reads Bergin 1980—clearly a controversial stand on a controversial subject—will attest to its respect for the reader as well as its tough, yet conciliatory tone.

3. *Develop an encouraging environment.* A time and a place are needed to formulate and develop ideas. Few truly significant theoretical contributions could be written without academic freedom, in many senses. Controversial or revolutionary ideas rarely spring to the fore, whole cloth. They require time for their development (e.g., "brooding" and "fermenting") and a place in which the author can feel encouraged to develop them. However, this encouragement appears to require more than simply academic freedom in the technical sense, which Columbia surely provided Bergin. The development of truly controversial and revolutionary ideas may also require the presence of explicit encouragement.

4. *Evaluate the environment's practical constraints.* The context of any institution carries with it informal parameters or limits about what is appropriate or inappropriate. Bergin, for example, did not feel it appropriate at Columbia to discuss explicitly Christian values in psychology classes, because psychology was considered a secular discipline. Columbia, in this sense, was a world-class bastion of secularism—participating in the same "injustice" and curtailment of (practical) religious freedom as the discipline of psychology. Interestingly, BYU has sometimes had its more technical academic freedom questioned (American Association of University Professors, 2001), whereas the technical academic freedom of Columbia has never been doubted, as far as we know. Still, Bergin experienced greater academic freedom, in the practical sense, at BYU. His experiences at Columbia were integral to Bergin 1980 because they helped him see the reduction of practical freedom in secularism (i.e., the emperor's new clothes). The BYU experience, in this respect, served as a dramatic practical contrast.

5. *Develop a clear sense of vision.* With a bridled passion and encouraging work environment, an aspiring scholar is now ready to ask, What do I truly have to say? Too often, it seems, scholars do not ask this question and opt instead to "play the publication game." Many readers may see this statement as unfair and certainly an overgeneralization. Still, it is difficult to read psychology's journals without coming to this conclusion in some measure (cf. Sternberg, 1992; Tulving & Madigan, 1970). Bergin, on the other hand,

was "blessed," as he put it, with a strong sense of disciplinary vision. Although he needed time and an encouraging place to clarify and elaborate this vision, its seeds were planted long before he could remember. Could it be that all true scholars have such "seeds," if they were to seriously seek and nurture them?

6. *Risk disciplinary disapproval.* Here, we believe one of the "morals" to the Bergin 1980 story is that these necessary conditions (points 1–5) are still insufficient and incomplete. Another crucial element is courage—the willingness to risk disciplinary disapproval in the development of a theoretical vision. As this story highlights, theoretical significance is often correlated with disciplinary controversy. Sternberg's (1992) assessment of highly cited articles seems to concur: "behind almost all stunning successes in journal writing are risks and that these authors took a stand for what they believed and how they believed they should write about it" (p. 388). If controversial ideas were not enough, the author of such ideas must also fumble around— often through trial and error, often for many years—to find the right tone, vocabulary, venue, and rhetoric for the presentation of these ideas. New visions and new ideas, by their nature, require new frameworks, vocabulary, and so on. Therefore, the courage needed to write significant articles involves not only the controversial nature of the ideas but also the sometimes humbling experiences one has in formulating and refining them.

7. *Have a clear sense of audience.* Given that writing is the medium of ideas, we cannot overlook how interconnected the content of an article is with its process. That is, the writing style and organization of a significant article is not inconsequential; it is integral to the message being presented as well as the follow-up expected from readers. Here, we believe, Bergin 1980 is a model, particularly in this era of too-much-information-in-too-little-time. As the narrative of Bergin 1980 shows, Bergin's composition began with a strong sense of his audience and a strong sense of caring for that audience.

8. *Write clearly.* Clarity of expression also appears to be vital to clarity of communication. Although this would seem to go without saying, any careful reading of psychology's journals shows how often this bears repeating. Recall that Bergin wanted to save his students from multisyllabic vocabularies and strings of convoluted sentences. Unfortunately, journal editors are often perceived as encouraging such "specialized" writing and vocabularies. We believe that it is far easier for researchers to write to a more specialized than generalized audience. Moreover, complicated prose is frequently a cover for fuzzy thinking.

9. *Allow the idea organization to mature.* As important as clarity of audience and focus of expression are, the importance of article organization may even surpass these. The difficulty is that good organization almost always requires maturity of thinking. That is, the ideas frequently need to be, as Bergin put it, "brooding," "fermenting," and "crystallizing" for a long time before their organizational structure emerges. This is not to say that trial

presentations and articles—intermediate to this emergence—should not be published. Indeed, without some sort of public distribution, vital feedback from colleagues would be curtailed. Rather, we are asserting that maturity of thinking is probably necessary for the organization of a truly significant article. Even a brief scan of Bergin 1980 illustrates our point, particularly if it is juxtaposed to the run-of-the-mill theoretical article.

10. *Make the organization easily accessible.* Good organization also broadens an already overly pressed audience. Few professionals these days can truly peruse the entire "fine print" of an article, but many professionals can take in a few well-crafted main points. Consequently, if authors want an idea or point to stand out, they must make it stand out in the text, separating and clearly demarcating main and secondary points from their supporting materials. Authors should never assume that readers will make this separation and demarcation for themselves. Similarly, authors should never assume that readers will know how to follow up the article's ideas. Bergin, for example, explicated nine hypotheses that can be investigated as a result of his ideas. The authors of significant articles must be explicit about how readers can "join in" to the ideas presented.

CONCLUSION

We hope, in conclusion, that these 10 points make explicit how the reader can join in to the ideas presented here—the narrative of Bergin 1980. These points cannot provide a recipe (or a set of principles) for writing a particular article of significance. There are too many other factors, such as professional culture and timing, that enter into the evaluation of significance. Still, these points can, we would hold, provide lessons for orienting one's scholarly life. Although many of them might be anticipated (e.g., clarity of writing), many seem to have been forgotten in today's psychology, such as bridled enthusiasm, professional courage, and practical constraints. Perhaps most importantly, there simply is no substitute for scholars to ask of themselves—sincerely and honestly—What is my passion? What do I truly have to say?

REFERENCES

Allen E. Bergin: Citation. (1990). *American Psychologist, 45,* 474–476.

American Association of University Professors. (2001). *Censured administrations.* Retrieved in April 2001 from http://www.aaup.org/censure.htm#list.

Bergin, A. E. (1966). Some implications of psychotherapy research for therapeutic practice. *Journal of Abnormal Psychology, 71,* 235–246.

Bergin, A. E. (1977, August). *Conceptual basis for a religious approach to psychotherapy.* Paper presented at the 85th Annual Convention of the American Psychological Association, San Francisco, CA.

Bergin, A. E. (1978). In behalf of a revealed approach to counseling. *AMCAP Journal, 4*(1), 3–9.

Bergin, A. E. (1979). Bringing the restoration to the academic world: Clinical psychology as a test case. *BYU Studies, 19,* 449–473.

Bergin, A. E. (1980a). Psychotherapy and religious values. *Journal of Consulting and Clinical Psychology, 48,* 95–105.

Bergin, A. E. (1980b). Religious and humanistic values: A reply to Ellis and Walls. *Journal of Consulting and Clinical Psychology, 48,* 642–645.

Bergin, A. E. (1985a, August). *Dialogue with Albert Ellis and others.* Symposium on Religion and Mental Health conducted at the 93rd Annual Convention of the American Psychological Association, Los Angeles, CA.

Bergin, A. E. (1985b). Proposed values for guiding and evaluating counseling and psychotherapy. *Counseling and Values, 29,* 99–117.

Bergin, A. E. (1991). Values and religious issues in psychotherapy and mental health. *American Psychologist, 46,* 394–403.

Bergin, A. E. (1996, August). *Dialogue with Albert Ellis and others.* Symposium on Rational Emotive Behavior Therapy and Religion conducted at the 104th Annual Convention of the American Psychological Association, Toronto, Ontario, Canada.

Bergin, A. E., & Garfield, S. L. (Eds.). (1971). *Handbook of psychotherapy and behavior change.* New York: Wiley.

Bergin, A. E., & Strupp, H. H. (1972). *Changing frontiers in the science of psychotherapy.* Chicago: Aldine.

British Broadcasting Company. (2001). *Doctor Who: Remembrance of the Daleks* [DVD & video]. London: BBC Shop.

Chaddock, T. P., & McMinn, M. R. (1999). Values affecting collaboration among psychologists and evangelical clergy. *Journal of Psychology and Theology, 27,* 319–328.

Collins, G. R. (1977). *The rebuilding of psychology: An integration of psychology and Christianity.* Wheaton, IL: Tyndale House.

Cronbach, L. J. (1955). Processes affecting scores on "understanding of other" and "assumed similarity." *Psychological Bulletin, 52,* 177–193.

Danziger, K. (1990). *Constructing the subject: Historical origins of psychological research.* New York: Cambridge University Press.

Douglas, R. J. (1992). How to write a highly cited article without even trying. *Psychological Bulletin, 112,* 405–408.

Ellis, A. (1980). Comments. Psychotherapy and atheistic values: A response to A. E. Bergin's "Psychotherapy and religious values." *Journal of Consulting and Clinical Psychology, 48,* 635–639.

Ellis, A. (1985, August). *Dialogue with Allen Bergin and others*. Symposium on Religion and Mental Health conducted at the 93rd Annual Convention of the American Psychological Association, Los Angeles, CA.

Ellis, A. (1996, August). *Dialogue with Allen Bergin and others*. Symposium on Rational Emotive Behavior Therapy and Religion conducted at the 104th Annual Convention of the American Psychological Association, Toronto, Ontario, Canada.

Keating, A. M., & Fretz, B. R. (1990). Christians' anticipations about counselors in response to counselor descriptions. *Journal of Counseling Psychology, 37,* 293–296.

Kuhn, T. S. (1970). *The structure of scientific revolutions* (2nd ed.). Chicago: University of Chicago Press.

Kvale, S. (1996). *Interviews: An introduction to qualitative research interviewing*. Thousand Oaks, CA: Sage.

Larson, D. B., Swyers, J. P., & McCullough, M. E. (Eds.). (1998). *Scientific research an spirituality and health: A consensus report*. Rockville, MD: National Institute for Healthcare Research.

Miller, R. B. (Ed.). (1992). *The restoration of dialogue: Readings in the philosophy of clinical psychology*. Washington, DC: American Psychological Association.

Richards, P. S., & Bergin, A. E. (1997). *A spiritual strategy for counseling and psychotherapy*. Washington, DC: American Psychological Association.

Richards, P. S., & Bergin, A. E. (2000). *Handbook of psychotherapy and religious diversity*. Washington, DC: American Psychological Association.

Rosenthal, D. (1955). Changes in some moral values following psychotherapy. *Journal of Consulting Psychology, 19,* 431–436.

Shafranske, E. P. (Ed.). (1996). *Religion and the clinical practice of psychology*. Washington, DC: American Psychological Association.

Shafranske, E. P., & Malony, H. N. (1990). Clinical psychologists' religious and spiritual orientations and their practice of psychotherapy. *Psychotherapy, 27,* 72–78.

Slife, B. D. (1998). Raising the consciousness of researchers: Hidden assumptions in the behavioral sciences. *Adapted Physical Activity Quarterly, 15,* 208–221.

Slife, B. D. (in press). Theoretical challenges to therapy practice and research: The constraint of naturalism. In M. Lambert (Ed.) *Handbook of psychotherapy and behavior change* (5th ed.). New York: Wiley.

Slife, B. D., & Reber, J. (2001). Eclecticism in psychotherapy: Is it really the best substitute for traditional theories? In B. D. Slife, R. Williams, & S. Barlow (Eds.) *Critical issues in psychotherapy: Translating new ideas into practice* (pp. 213–234). Thousand Oaks, CA: Sage.

Slife, B. D., & Rubinstein, J. (1992). *Taking sides: Clashing views on controversial psychological issues* (7th ed.). Guilford, CT: Dushkin.

Slife, B. D., Smith, A. M., & Burchfield, C. (in press). Psychotherapists as cryptomissionaries: An exemplar on the crossroads of history, theory, and philosophy.

In D. B. Hill & M. J. Kral (Eds.), *About psychology: Essays at the crossroads of history, theory, and philosophy*. Albany: SUNY Press.

Slife, B. D., & Williams, R. N. (1995). *What's behind the research: Discovering hidden assumption in the behavioral sciences*. Thousand Oaks, CA: Sage.

Smith, A. M., & Slife, B. D. (in press). *Managing values in psychotherapy*. Thousand Oaks, CA: Sage.

Sternberg, R. J. (1992). *Psychological Bulletin's* top 10 "hit parade." *Psychological Bulletin, 112,* 387–388.

Sternberg, R. J. (1996). The anatomy of impact: What makes an article influential? *Psychological Science, 7,* 69–75.

Swedin, E. G. (1999). Integrating the modern psychologies and religion: Allen E. Bergin and the Latter-day Saints of the late twentieth century. *Journal of the History of the Behavioral Sciences, 35,* 157–176.

Tjeltveit, A. C. (1999). *Ethics and values in psychotherapy*. London: Routledge.

Tulving, E., & Madigan, S. A. (1970). Memory and verbal learning. In P. H. Mussen & M. R. Rosenzweig (Eds.), *Annual review of psychology* (Vol. 21, pp. 437–484). Palo Alto, CA: Annual Reviews.

Walls, G. (1980). Values and psychotherapy: A comment on "Psychotherapy and Religious Values." *Journal of Consulting and Clinical Psychology, 48,* 640–641.

Watson, P. J., Morris, R. J., & Hood, R. W., Jr. (1989). Sin and self-functioning: Part 4. Depression, assertiveness, and religious commitments. *Journal of Psychology and Theology, 17,* 44–58.

Worthington, E. L., Jr. (1988). Understanding the values of religious clients: A model and its application to counseling. *Journal of Counseling Psychology, 35,* 166–174.

Zinnbauer, B. J., & Pargament, K. I. (2000). Working with the sacred: Four approaches to religious and spiritual issues in counseling. *Journal of Counseling and Development, 78,* 162–171.

11

IMPACT AS SUBSTANCE
AND AS FASHION

Daniel N. Robinson

The chapters written for this volume, instructive and important in their own right, are based on the realistic and defensible assumption that impact is impact. Experiments and theoretical contributions that have moved others to change course and perspective, to abandon well-rehearsed and seemingly successful methods, surely answer to the sense of impact. But as the editor and authors of this volume well know, there remains something at once suspect and potentially misleading in the uncritical adoption of the common sense notion of impact. Accordingly, this chapter considers just those factors that have been neglected historically, thereby permitting less-than-worthy endeavors to have the wrong sort of impact, even as ultimately fruitful contributions were overlooked or undervalued. Here, then, is another look at "impact."

"IMPACT" EXAMINED

My assailant pushed me into a dark corner off the main boulevard and away from the street lights. He put a gun to my chest and said, "Hand over your watch and your wallet, or I'll kill you." I must say, these words had a very great impact on me!

Impact, as with *force* or *velocity*, arouses neither sentiment nor judgment until its context and consequences are specified. That an uncommonly great force was exerted to free the cat caught under the fallen tree is cause for praise. The same force, delivered as a fatal blow to the victim of a crime, leads to a very different estimation. Adolf Hitler's *Mein Kampf* had great impact on his readers. Would that it had not been so.

In the history of science, strong personalities and original ideas have often had an impact well beyond their intrinsic worth. There have also been instances of buried treasure, in which the real and significant value of a contribution was not discovered until many years after it was made. There are, then, many examples of manifest treasure, buried treasure, fool's gold, and the evanescent power of fashion, all capable of conferring on people and their ideas the quality of impact.

As the record is so worrisomely mixed in this regard, it would be of great value were there a set of stable methods, epistemological standards, and logical canons with which any competent person could judge the real rather than the apparent value of new ideas. Thus, might there be some protection against the vagaries of enthusiasm, the often dreadful consequences of "village credulity." Candidate methods, however, tend to illustrate rather than check enthusiasm and credulity. All too many otherwise highly educated (trained?) people are confident that something called *scientific method* is the corrective, as if the history of science itself were not littered with silly notions, dangerous errors, and costly distractions to which entire legions of the best and the brightest had attached themselves.

There is, of course, no set of stable methods, epistemological standards, and logical canons either unique to the scientific enterprise or universally applicable across its many missions. The significant sense in which theory is underdetermined by data renders hopeless any prospect of finding full sanctuary in the comforting environs of "the lab." Indeed, if there is a place in which every type of enthusiasm and credulity finds nurturance among those not otherwise intoxicated, it may well be the laboratory, or at least some laboratories. Where else is there such fidelity to the stock notions of an age, to such formulaic modes of inquiry, to such dubious attempts to mimic or model reality? Two examples expose the genre: Where else would one regard chimpanzees housed for life in a small cage as fit specimens for understanding their nature and capacities? Where else would one claim great gains in "ecological validity" by permitting "subjects" to make their usual earthly rounds while summoned periodically by an attached buzzer or bell to report what they are now thinking or feeling? Readers can only imagine the essential quality of their day knowing that at any moment, and often throughout that day, their cell phones will ring and they will be tested on the phenomenology of the moment! As for the former example, readers surely cannot imagine the range of effects produced by a lifetime spent in a box.

To this might be added another if obvious consideration. The good researcher and the good astrologer are both practitioners within a venerable tradition. Both are scrupulous in recording data, maintaining records, and following accepted methods. Accordingly, where there is a penchant toward simplistic thinking, rash reasoning, and self-deception, no great immunity is achieved merely by careful observation, accurate record keeping, and orderly methods. One must, therefore, not claim too much for the laboratory. It is sufficient to acknowledge that the strictures of experimentation afford a measure of protection against innocent credulity and fanatical enthusiasms. It is, however, not unlike the protection that people of common sense and an Erasmian appreciation of life's ironies have always enjoyed. In some respects, it is but an attempt to reduce this to a formula. It would be saying too much to attempt to quantify the degree of protection in either case, or to proclaim it to be sufficient unto the task.

Needless to say, were there a virtually flawless mode of defense, the phenomenon of impact would soon become the norm, for there would soon be no field of scientific rubbish to clear. But there is no flawless mode. There is no mode or method not itself subject to the sorts of challenges that might come to have great impact on the nature of inquiry and on a fuller understanding of what such inquiry might yield.

If impact as it pertains to psychology is the subject, and if it is what some are pleased to call scientific psychology that should be the test case, who better to begin with than Wilhelm Wundt? All would agree that in establishing not only a laboratory at Leipzig but also a journal devoted to the publication of experimental findings, Wundt had great impact on the discipline; so too did he as the teacher of those who would establish comparable programs of research at major universities; so too as the author of numerous books and articles that defined fruitful areas of inquiry.

Wundt's impact is a matter of record. On the surface, one would then place him as something of an early term in a causal sequence whose effects would include research of a certain kind, facilities of a "Wundtian" sort, perspectives faithful to those he had defended in his many publications. But examined more deeply, the actual record is rather more complex, the causal model rather less convincing. In a manner of speaking, if Wundt had two richly developed and defended agendas for psychology, only one of them was permitted to have great impact. A few words about the curious reality of impact are in order.

THE REAL WORLD

To the extent that Wundt retains paternity rights in the matter of modern "scientific" psychology, there is much to be learned by tracing out this curious fact: Virtually no attention whatever is paid to the most sustained, voluminous, and systematic works of his that stand as the culmination of a life of scholarship and critical inquiry. Only a fraction of his multivolume *Volkerpsychologie* (1911–1920) is available in English, and even that fraction is rarely cited in books and articles otherwise encomiastic in their treatments of Wundt's place in the history of psychology. For all the time, talent, and deep and original thinking that went into *Volkerpsychologie*, its impact has been negligible. As it happens, it is also a work laced with incisive and original thinking of the sort that can still excite the prepared mind. The moral of the tale so far is that impact and significance do not run in parallel paths in the history of science or within the larger culture of thought. Moreover, less like toothache than moral counsel, impact is not felt until one decides to feel it.

While the world of psychology registered its indifference to this massive chapter in Wundt's extraordinarily productive life, it was nonetheless doting on every page delivered to an eager audience by Sigmund Freud. So great has been his impact that, were a scale to be constructed, all others would be assigned scores expressed as millifreuds with perhaps only B. F. Skinner approaching the parity level of 1,000. It would not be beside the point, of course, to note that Franz Joseph Gall's phrenology flourished as long as has psychoanalytic theory, that its findings and sayings filled a score of journals, and that educated citizens in all the right and interesting centers of culture were serious about palpating each other's heads. Thus does another moral intrude itself: Impact per se establishes nothing regarding the validity or adequacy of works that have or lack the impact initially, later or ever.

About 40 years after the final volume of the *Volkerpsychologie*, there appeared the first volumes of Sigmund Koch's landmark *Psychology: A Study of a Science* (1963). No comparable collection preceded it. Between the covers of the volumes are chapters by the leading lights of the discipline, prodded and guided by Koch to make known their core assumptions, the grounds of their methodological commitments, the implications they judged to be warranted by the specialty fields they worked with such diligence and success. To be included in any of the volumes, authors must have by then already had a considerable impact on the discipline. Alas, and again at a distance of 40 years, one is amazed to discover how little of all those high-impact efforts has even the slightest influence on current projects and perspectives. The moral of the tale may now be extended to include, in the manner of a Greek chorus, the reminder that triumph is composed of ephemeral stuff.

Little more than oblique contact with the history of science is needed to document all this and to recognize it less as truth than as truism. It is surely unnecessary to rehearse, typically in ways rather more dramatic than the actual records warrant, the trials and tribulations of revolutionary thinkers, often dead for years or decades before their keen and initially unpopular or ignored insights are numbered among the stock ideas of an age. The inertial constants of the body scientific are such as to keep the project on a more or less steady course, at least until someone notices that it is a course either bending back on itself or going nowhere in particular. None of this should be taken as affording unstinting supporting to Kuhnian notions of "normal science" and "revolution." Rather, as it is difficult to be especially clever at anything, it should not be surprising that it is more difficult by orders of magnitude to be clever about the workings of the heavens or of the entities found in and under them.

This much granted, it will be argued that impact—whatever its course and its half life—stands as a powerful motive, a cause for praise, and a measure of something that matches up with the prevailing values and standards of those most qualified to judge such achievement. As such, it warrants study. Indeed. However, nearly every word in this very passage calls for closer scrutiny: motive, cause, praise, measure, prevailing, values, standards, qualified, judge, and achievement. To wit:

1. Ideal exceptions duly noted, the sources of motivation are not invariably internal and authentic, let alone noble. A system of patronage, of financial inducements now typically in the form of grants and contracts, tied in with a system of professional advancement and tenure, can install quite powerful motives for engaging in any number of activities, some of them otherwise trite and tiresome. Seeking to have an impact, in the circumstance, may amount to no more than seeking to retain one's position and widen one's access to its sundry perquisites.

2. Impact, next considered as a legitimate "cause" for praise, calls for further attention to the causal modality itself, as well as to the sources of the praise. An example: The majority of phrenologists were likely to praise those judged to be the really gifted phrenologists, the institution of praise at once validating the entire enterprise while identifying those who could be presented by others as being at least in principle in the running for comparable accolades.

3. Prevailing values, too, are subject both to subtle and to rather gross forms of manipulation. Within those halls of ivy now housing departments of psychology, there is a somewhat strident, some would say shrill, response to any challenge directed toward the alleged superiority of experimental modes of inquiry; to any who would resist that species of cant according to which problems that do not admit of experimental address are either nonproblems or are too "unscientific" to be settled. However, as the shrill part of the register is also occupied by those likely to have most of the funding, their protestations fall fully within the range of sounds to which academic administrations are most sensitive. A cynic might describe the bureaucrat's audiogram as peaking in the frequency range occupied by cash registers. The main point, of course, is that the "prevailing values" within the profession may have little to do with intrinsic value. Further, what makes them prevail may be more akin to what allows a standing army to prevail.

4. If it is the standards that must be met or exceeded by contributions that would have an impact, one must then be clear as to the genre from

which the standards are drawn. There are standards of precision, of care, of ingenuity, of integrity—nearly all the nouns that refer to values are subject to comparison with a given standard. For a quarter of a century, the impact of Skinnerian behaviorism on research and theory within academic psychology was without parallel. What standards were at work during that period that are no longer capable of sustaining such allegiance? Standards, as it happens, had nothing to do either with behaviorism's occupancy of or its departure from center stage. Instead, what actually changed was the particular flavor or brand answering to the description, "just my cup of tea." This is not to say that there were no good conceptual or empirical grounds on which to shift attention away from operant behavior and toward, say, cognitive processes. Rather, such grounds had been available long before the episodic hegemony of behaviorism. It was not discovery, then, that ushered in a new orthodoxy, nor was it the adoption of new "standards."

5. Who is "qualified to judge" in such a way as to increase the impact of a contribution? Just what is it that is judged? The predictions put in place by Einstein's theory of relativity could not be tested for years but were so charged with implications as to have an impact on thought and theory long before the collection of supporting evidence. Judgment of the power of the theory was based on little more than sufficient scientific and mathematical preparation to follow the lines of argument and test them against the resulting data. However one would understand either the "behaviorist revolution" launched by Watson and brought to fruition by Hull, Spence, and Skinner, or the "cognitive revolution" that then replaced it, neither can be plausibly explained chiefly on the basis of empirical predictions, greater theoretical reach and coherence, or greater implications for practice. As noted, there was a cognitive psychology in place long before the rise of behaviorism. Something within the general culture of the discipline changed, as did the patronage of those holding the formidable powers of the purse.

At the risk of being controversial, it is tempting to conclude that, where allegiances shift so completely in the absence of compelling empirical or conceptual inducements, there is really no basis on which to accord the status of "qualified judge." Put another way, this time as a question, what range of findings or conceptual formulations made clear to competently trained psychologists that Skinner's descriptive science of behavior was no longer viable? What conceivable range of future findings or conceptual formulations would make it clear to current students that "cognitive neuroscience" is not a viable framework within which to advance the science and practice of psychology? At the level of observation and measurement, what might lead those of judicious temperament to reject the claim that the mission of cognitive neuroscience is the discovery of "mechanisms" by which to explain the processes of language, memory, and thought? The right answer may be none.

6. The achievement, then, that leads to increased impact is less one of discovery than of rhetoric: One group, recording its methods and arguments

in the official journals, finally convinces ever increasing numbers of those who read the same journals, that it is worth following the (allegedly) new leads. Watson's polemics are the extreme version of the process. Skinner's quasi-popular writings were of the same sort. Popular magazines have covers boldly asking whether infidelity is in our genes, and bolding proclaiming that God is in the brain. The actual research on which this fluff depends could not begin to support such conclusions, but impact now is the gift not of achievement but of publicity.

WHAT'S WRONG WITH THE REAL WORLD?

One need not defend trends and tendencies of this sort by noting that they are widespread across all fields of science and scholarship and have been at work in all ages. On this account, the sources of impact in psychology are essentially those operating as much in physics as in political science, as much early in the 21st century as in the Athens of Aristotle. It is simply the way things work in the real world. It is no cause for pouting or for lamentations for, over the long haul, things average out, the chaff falling to the ground as azure fields of grain spring up everywhere.

It may well be that, under the selection pressures of free-market scholarship, whereby all ideas and findings and methods vie for impact, the best of the lot finally come to have it. Metaphorically speaking, the "long haul" here can be suddenly cut short by the unexpected but highly desirable mutant strain, that rare genius who puts matters on new footing. At any rate, not only does the real world operate in such a manner, but alternative schemes, like the "scientifically planned economies" of what was once the Soviet Union, merely verify the productive power of self-interest. As with Mandeville's bees, let each scientist act on the basis of highly individuated impulses and the hive will flourish, even when that is not the aim of any bee at all.

What is wrong with this picture? To begin, it is a false picture, partly for reasons set forth in the previous section. Funding practices do not create or sustain a free market of ideas but function more in the manner of those very planned economies in which a centralized bureaucracy determines what is in the national interest. The vaunted distinction between "pure" and "applied" research (which the history of science itself shows to be misleading when not meaningless) creates the illusion of liberated thought. Reality, however, indicates otherwise as every "purist's" application for patronage is inevitably justified in terms of earthly needs and hopes. Exceptions may be found in those areas of physics reaching the very large and the very small, but even the cosmos and the muon can be identified as serving the "national interest." After all, the cosmos is where we live, isn't it?

The history of patronage is a subject at once vast and subtle. The motives of the patron are often elusive, sometimes fickle, now and then even sinister. For every Medici, Julius II, Fugger, or Hapsburg who possesses the rare combination of financial, political, and aesthetic powers of discernment, there are scores of well-meaning know-nothings who supply the means by which mediocrity leaves its rubbish, ultimately to be cleared by a later age. Science has but a few built-in defenses against this sort of thing. George Berkeley had a commanding knowledge of optics and mathematics, was a philosopher of originality and intellectual power, and was confident that tar water was the right treatment for gall stones. A wise patron would have supported Berkeley's work in optics, even his intended college in Bermuda. The tar water, which nearly killed Berkeley himself, was a different matter, but there is no reason to think that even the more discerning patron is able to make all the right distinctions. It would take a brave Study Section to give Isaac Newton a bad score, even if the proposal centered on Newton's own strong beliefs in alchemy and astrology. The halo effect works often in mindless and pervasive ways, so much so that some would base political decisions on the words of folk singers, or choose a washing machine favored by a wrestler. All this is really at work in "the real world." Thus, does one begin to see the form of self-deception that treats the real world as if it really were a free marketplace of ideas.

In actuality, the contemporary scientific bureaucracy is not devoted to an open and free marketplace of ideas but to what, in the new-speak of the age, are called "prioritized missions" promising "to impact" one or another problem, one or another national interest. The language alone must raise suspicions, if only because serious persons tend not to speak this way. However, once one's own "mission" happily falls high on the list of the prioritized ones (this outcome scarcely coincidental!), and once one satisfies those "peers" sitting in judgment that the proposed work will "impact," one's daily labor undergoes a sudden transformation: The overworked teacher discovers a miraculous lightening of the teaching "load," the latter now picked up by a paid assistant. Books and journals once ignored by the librarian now appear in multiple copies. Previously unavailable space is swept and cleared for research. Money descends on the lucky contestant for travel and equipment, for conferences and computers, for typists and clerks.

There is a price to be paid by those thus paid, and the price is the command to produce. The award of a grant sets a timer in motion marking off in months and then weeks and then hours the date of the renewal application. Between now and that moment, the project must generate palpable yield, this in the form of "regular publication in peer-review journals." Needless to say (and this is readily verifiable), most of the pages of these journals feature work that has been thus funded. It stands to reason that those with space, equipment, assistants, and related impedimenta will be more "productive" than those still writing proposals, let alone those who merely sit and think. Thus, if to have some impact one must reach the many, and if the vehicle of one's thoughts and discoveries is the peer-review journal, it follows that "impact" must be at least partly the gift of patronage. By the same rationale, the further conclusion is that the odds of having an impact get better as that patronage continues, for it is by this means that one publication builds on another, then another, till one has, as it were, covered a "field" (as in *my field*) with them.

Then, too, one's subsidized students are now out in that semireal world, fully prepared to do what they have been doing; namely, more of the same. Room here for reducing cognitive dissonance is vast. Thus, if the research were actually prosaic, why would it be so richly supported? If there is little intrinsic value in the project, why are the results eagerly accepted by the better journals? If we were not on to something really significant, why would so many able students commit themselves to our work? Those who read *All the President's Men* by Carl Bernstein and Bob Woodward or saw the filmed version will recall that moment in the shadows of an indoor parking lot when the desperate investigative reporter admits to "Deep Throat" that progress has come to a full stop and that, absent further clues and guides, the whole investigation will be abandoned. And what clue is forthcoming? "Follow the money."

Perhaps it is not the idealist after all but the putative realist these days who has an innocent perspective on the nature and sources of impact in psychology and similar areas of study and scholarship. One must, however, be clear on what is not suggested here: The thesis is not a challenge to the surface reasonableness of the process or to the integrity of scientist or patron. Each, it is plausible to assume, has sound motives for choosing or sponsoring a program of research. The choice of problems, not surprisingly, is guided by what the most established and respected investigators have been productively exploring. Their efforts are recorded in the authoritative and highly selective journals. Surely it only makes sense to commit inevitably limited resources to what is judged, however imperfectly, to be most promising, and these journals are reasonably seen as good guides. Surely the horses that have run well in the past are the ones to bet on now. So, again, it is not surprising that in the funding process the rich will either stay rich or get richer. Surely proposals regarded as most worthy by those who themselves are experienced and productive deserve to be supported.

All this is, as it were, the surface grammar of the process but not its deep structure. The more fundamental level turns up factors that have had and now especially have a corrupting effect. Consider that actual Department of Psychology—this a major department that need not be identified here— featuring an honor roll prominently displayed in the corridor used by students, staff, and faculty daily. The honor roll lists all members of the faculty who have published three articles that year in peer review experimental journals. No hermeneutic analysis is required here. The meaning is clear to all: Experimental psychology qualifies for honors; all the rest is tolerated. Just in case nontenured members of such a department were to consider, in a prudent and reasonably self-interested fashion, where to invest their intellectual energies, is there any doubt as to the path they should follow? The honor roll in this instance is but one of a number of devices designed to render impact "official." It is, of course, garden-variety censorship, no less patent for the withholding of epithets or even more vulgar forms of control.

SETTING THE BAR

Whether or not a contribution will have great impact, as now should be clear, may have very little to do with its intrinsic value, which might take years or even centuries to be widely perceived. The relationship between a contribution and its impact, then, is not unlike that between rhetoric and the attending audience. The effect of the content will depend, of course, on the content itself, but also on the perceived standing of the speaker, the powers and purposes of those who hear it, the inevitable "noise" in the system, the selective and evanescent nature of memory, and competing signals coming from other and comparably authoritative sources.

One of the burning questions raised in Plato's Protagoras is whether virtue is teachable. This is a burning question but, rightly understood, not an "empirical" question as such. The audience of busy psychologists may hear it and decide it is not reducible to an experimental format, thus not fundable, thus not worth their attention. Rather, "It's philosophy, and that's in the building at the other end of campus." In time, all such questions are consigned to some other building. In time, there are few in the Psychology Department who can keep up even with confused undergraduates having their first encounter with Plato. In time, the intellectual bar has been so lowered that little more than narrow, specific, context-free miniproblems can be absorbed. What has occurred is the debasement of critical thought.

IMPACT RECONSIDERED

There is a temptation, not without warrant, to distinguish the right forms of impact from mere enthusiasm by expecting the former to be far more persistent. But, as noted, any number of dead-ends and fanciful oddities has possessed both the better minds and the average ones for years, decades, centuries. The "witch theory" was not a rank superstition adopted by simpletons but a well-developed set of propositions sturdy enough to support highly sophisticated adjudicative procedures in the most advanced countries of the time; and the time here was the better part of three centuries.

If there is to be a defensible guide in attempts to differentiate impact and enthusiasm, it will be one largely indifferent to the number of adherents and to the temporal span over which allegiances hold firm. The ideas that have authentic impact are those that generate a veritable cascade of comparably influential ideas. For example, once a stable form of experimental science was in place, presaged as early as the Oxford movement led by such original thinkers as Roger Bacon, whole realms of inquiry were on a horizon not yet fully visible. Only when these anticipations became more or less standardized and grounded firmly in what, in the very nature of things, was a metaphysical foundation, would there arise experimentalism able to summon worthy disciples. This was the achievement chiefly of the 17th century, the age that numbered in its leading ranks Francis Bacon, Isaac Newton, Robert Boyle, Robert Hooke, Christian Huygens, Galileo, and René Descartes. What was invented now was the method of invention itself. A new and unforeseen range of intellectual and investigative possibilities suddenly was obvious. In a word, a different way of seeing things was inaugurated, a different sense what it means to know something.

Less important than the flood of technical and theoretical outpourings of the age was this new vantage point. Long after the technical claims were either refined or revised or abandoned, and long after the early generalizations were absorbed into more general theories—or shown to be far more limited than even a Newton might have suspected—the perspective retained its original promise. All too many experiments are trite and pointless, but the experimental outlook on the world of the knowable remains a great achievement of the imagination and one that has had an impact on nearly every realm of inquiry and practice.

The point worth making here is that impact, in contrast to enthusiasm, operates chiefly at the level of metaphysics; the level at which fundamental questions are raised as to what really exists, and just what resources are available by which we might presume to know what really exists. It is in the service of these core ontological and epistemological questions that technology earns its stripes. The ontological realm was expanded beyond all earlier expectation by the inventions of microscope and telescope. The epistemological realm was transformed first by Aristotle's logical treatises and then, centuries later, by probability theory, number theory, and Fregean analytic philosophy. It would be idle in light of these contributions to count the number of persons competent to accept or reject them, or the number of years they have been influencing various specialists. Again, neither the number of disciples nor that temporal life of the contribution compares in importance with this defining element of authentic impact.

But suppose no one were to accept such discoveries or see their implications? Then, for seasons of unpredictable length, what otherwise would have been the progress and refinement of the understanding would have instead been a period of stasis and relative torpor. And this would be no less so even if, at the level of behavior, large aggregates continued to engage with great enthusiasm in all the old familiar ways.

Phrenology was cited earlier as evidence of an influential and widely adopted bit of quackery to make clear that popular enthusiasm is often the counterfeit of authentic impact. Phrenology, however, was but the failed implication of what in fact was a highly "impactful" perspective—a perspective at once daring and productive, and able to generate just that cascading effect previously noted. The perspective, laboring now under the heading "cognitive neuroscience," was one that would come to grips with the vexing issues raised within philosophy of mind and would recast these as problems in functional neuroanatomy. Gall as the father of phrenology is a target of highbrow humor. Gall as an informed advocate of a brain science able to address issues of social, moral, and legal consequence is a figure warranting admiration. There is, then, yet another moral of the tale: The same original thinker, often standing behind the same core assumptions, may be the source of both authentic impact and mere popular enthusiasm. A later age reserves the right to remember the Newton of the calculus while remaining respectfully amnesic in the matter of Newton the astrologer.

AUTHENTIC IMPACT IN PSYCHOLOGY

By the standard defended in the previous section, very few ideas propounded specifically within the discipline of psychology can lay claim to authentic impact. Figures such as Franz Gall, John Stuart Mill, Hermann Helmholtz, Herbert Spencer, Charles Darwin, and Francis Galton had considerable impact on whole schools of psychology, but these thinkers stand as external influences. Within psychology proper, perhaps only Freud and Skinner have had comparable impact. Like the others, although both Freud and Skinner were well-trained experimentalists (and although Skinner himself was a relentless gatherer of data), their actual impact has been chiefly at the metaphysical level. The theory of unconscious motivation, as developed by Freud, enlarged the ontological domain of psychology in ways that transformed the prosaic into the deeply meaningful. Skinner, almost in the form of counterpoint, located significant sources of human striving not within the person but in the world surrounding the person. As Freud featured what had been overlooked in the psyche, Skinner pointed to subtle, ubiquitous influences seemingly requiring no psyche at all.

Lest recognition here signal assent, I should note that, in my own estimation, both the Skinnerian and the Freudian perspectives are not only defective and limited but based on any number of conceptual confusions. The same, of course, was true of Gall's system and Galen's much earlier. This is largely beside the point, however. Skinner and Freud required a reexamination and reinterpretation of ordinary experience. They offered as a working hypothesis the possibility that the received understanding of the essential nature of human nature was simply mistaken and that the correct story was very different.

It is doubtful in the extreme that an impact of such magnitude will be generated within the discipline, as it is now understood, taught, defined. Another decade of functional magnetic resonance imaging will reveal ever more precisely just where Gall was right and where he was wrong, but it will have been Gall (and Pierre Paul Broca, Carl Wernicke, David Ferrier, Henry Maudsley, Thomas Henry Huxley, Charles Sherrington, Wilder Penfield, John Eccles, Karl Lashley—the list is long) who made all this possible, setting the stage of others to compute the third and fourth places after the decimal. It is doubtful in the extreme that any of those now working on these decimals will look away long enough to inaugurate a voyage in a different and comparably promising direction.

If one these days is to follow the money, it will lead not to the sources of impact but to the sources of enthusiasm: teamwork, joint projects, institutes, compound nouns, hyphenated advanced degrees, peer review plaudits, increased space, a deanship! There is nothing cynical in this appraisal. It is a matter of record that little in the prevailing institutional climate nurtures or is designed to nurture bold departures from mainstream thinking. Thought as such is not fundable and, in any case, cannot be graded in ways that might suggest inequalities of the offensive variety. But authentic impact is achieved only at someone's expense, if only the one whose authoritative theory is soon to be overturned. The conditions favoring impact are just those that favor ideas in collision, controlled passions pulling in every direction, the muses in chaotic and capricious modes of inspiration. None of this finds safe haven in today's tame, safe, lock step, "correct," and essentially entrepreneurial enclaves. It is in these places that each "worker" has the metes and bounds of his or her "field" clearly marked and posted. Criticism aimed toward that field is vandalism. The offender is asking for trouble. Those who doubt this—if they are experimentally inclined—can perform a modest test: Engage a colleague in conversation in which you firmly reject the claims of religion, or the soundness of the U.S. Constitution, or the rule of law itself, or the value of friendship, or punishments for treasonous acts. Next, engage the same colleague in conversation in which you express the view that your colleague's field of research is finally rather pointless, redeemed only by the fact that it is easy to perform and unlikely to produce anything controversial. Experienced academics need not perform the experiment, for the results are obvious a priori.

REMEDIES

Scholars know better than to attempt to pave shortcuts to what can be reached only through the disorderly dance of history. Apart from the chronic scarcity of native genius, the principal obstacles to authentic impact are institutional and cultural, here the culture being that of the discipline itself.

Consider how the activities of untenured members of a psychology faculty would be affected by the following provisions:

1. In applying for tenure, candidates are to submit only one written work, either published or unpublished, regarded by the candidate as his or her most original contribution to a recognized area of theory or practice.
2. Promotion in rank is reserved to those whose scientific or scholarly contributions are recognized as influencing the perspective of others engaged in the same or neighboring areas of inquiry.
3. For purposes of tenure and promotion, research grants per se are not considered as contributions to science or scholarship.

The point of citing these three provisions is not to recommend their adoption but to draw attention to the sheer power—the impact—that institutional cultures have on impact itself. In this connection, it may be instructive to suggest three additional provisions, these having to do with finance and bureaucracy:

4. Federal funding is reserved to those institutions that have prepared space and general facilities sufficient to host professional-level research. Accordingly, there is no federal funding of indirect costs.
5. Federal funds for research cannot be used to support any purely administrative office or personnel not directly engaged in the funded project.
6. Federal funding of research is available to full-time members of the faculty provided that during the period of funding they neither seek nor receive reductions in their teaching loads.

Again, these are not recommendations but reminders—reminders that financial arrangements can be contrived that render authentic impact more or less likely. Current practices summon too many of the wrong sort to undertake research for the wrong reasons while cluttering up the arena in which the right sort might otherwise find a bit of breathing room.

Finally, as structure ordains function, the prevailing academic structure is a powerful obstacle to originality, a veritable engine of intellectual complacency. Fish never discover water, for they are immersed in it. It constitutes all their possible worlds. Departments are fish bowls. There are big fish and smaller ones; fast ones and others who rest amid the algae. But all that is discoverable within such a murky concoction are slight changes in temperature; various patterns of unfocused light; cross-currents moving flotsam first one way, then another; and new stores of the same old food. Nonetheless, peril awaits those who leave the tank having found the "mainstream" to be a puddle.

Learning to live together in an actual mainstream is difficult; in a modest puddle it can be downright dangerous. Sensitivities arc acute. In place of collegiality—which, under nurturing conditions, includes the bloodlessly intellectual version of gladiatorial combat—one finds rather prissy modes of etiquette bearing the same relationship to respect that wallpaper bears to art. Prissy though it is, it is mandatory under penalty of rehabilitation. One might find oneself on the faculty of a religiously affiliated institution, nonetheless numbering agnostics and atheists among the staff. Classes may be organized to find something redeeming in pornography or polygamy. In yet other courses students learn that God is dead, that heroin should be legally available, and that gender is irrelevant to marriage. All this and more: Mao Tse Tung as liberator; George Washington as felon; Al Capone as Robin Hood. All this and still more. But never—and the word is never—shall one member of a department declare, on the basis of sober and deep reflection, that the research and writing of a colleague is trite. Authentic impact cannot help but be critical, for to have this sort of impact is to jar otherwise sleepy sensibilities and challenge the orthodoxy. Find a department with an honor roll for articles in peer review journals, and there you can be sure no impact will be fashioned or, for that matter, felt.

Departmental structure, then, must be understood as a weight on thought, a low ceiling on critical assessments. Getting rid of it, however, can actually be achieved by a stroke of the pen. To wit:

7. As of Fall 2003, the current Departments of Psychology, Philosophy, Sociology, Economics, History, and Political Science will be merged into the School of Humanistic Studies. In any 2-year period, it is expected that members of each of these former departments will offer at least one course in one of the other disciplines.
8. Room and space assignments in the new School of Humanistic Studies will be determined alphabetically.
9. All university laboratories are located in buildings in which there are neither faculty offices nor classrooms.
10. The position of Dean of the School of Humanistic Studies is by faculty election, for a term not to exceed 4 years.

Of the 10 provisions cited above, readers will decide which are intended as playful and which as deadly serious, which are readily implemented and which seemingly impracticable, which would aid in the nurturance of creative thought and which would not. The 10 provisions are intended to convey a world in waiting, different from the one now in place on nearly every American campus, in nearly every Psychology Department. If having an impact is what each of them longs for, at least one of them will have to break away from the pack. The 10 provisions listed above are free to any and all.

REFERENCES

Koch, S. (1963). *Psychology: A study of a science*. New York: McGraw Hill.

Wundt, W. (1911–1920). *Volkerpsychologie* [Cultural psychology] (Vols. 1–10). Leipzig, Germany: Alfred Kröner.

12

IMPACT IN PSYCHOLOGY: FINAL REFLECTIONS

FRANK C. RICHARDSON

Unlike most of the contributors to this volume, I had the opportunity to read the entire book before writing my chapter. I expected the book to be interesting and stimulating to people like myself and its authors, all of whom are distinctly philosophically minded psychologists, most of whom have long been associated with the Division of Theoretical and Philosophical Psychology (Division 24) of the American Psychological Association. Certainly these chapters will be interesting and stimulating to the likes of us. However, having read the book, it seems to me that it should and may very well gain a wider audience. I cannot imagine teaching Sigmund Freud again without utilizing Stanley B. Messer and Nancy McWilliams's appreciative and critical discussion of Freud's impact on psychology and culture (this volume, chapter 4). Their clinical illustrations alone make it a worthwhile read. Most or all of the book would make for valuable reading in graduate courses I teach on personality psychology, the history of psychology, or the philosophy of social science. Also, I imagine that many advanced undergraduates would find this book fascinating. Here is some of the rich historical and critical material that sadly is bleached out of most psychology textbooks, depriving students of information they need to appreciate both the real greatness and the "all too human" flaws of great thinkers and texts in their field—insights they require to be equipped for the struggle for excellence in their own pursuits.

Many academics and students in various areas of psychology are passionately dedicated to their studies, but they also have doubts about their fields. They worry about whether the theories and findings of much modern psychology have the intellectual value or social significance they would like them to have. Perhaps they wonder why so much published work in their fields seems to reflect more "fashion" than "substance," to use Daniel N. Robinson's felicitous terminology in chapter 11 of this volume. Many of them have the sense, even though they are drawn to many topics in their field, that in the contemporary social sciences, in Robinson's words, "the intellectual bar has been so lowered that little more than narrow, specific, context-free miniproblems" can be discussed. I have found that even dedicated students and researchers in psychology usually chuckle and cast a rueful look when quoted the philosopher Charles Taylor's (1985) remark that too much social science fails to come up with more than "wordy elaborations of the obvious" (p. 1).

Robert J. Sternberg's preface indicates that this book is dedicated to helping students and scholars cultivate the aspiration to accomplish more than just publish research that is read by only a very small number of people and quickly forgotten. In other words, it is dedicated to shedding light on ways whereby we might more often produce work that is both excellent and has impact on our field and the wider society. This is a worthy ideal, to say the least. It seems to me that the examples, analyses, and lessons to be drawn provided by these chapters largely speak for themselves and do not need to be reiterated or summarized. I have confidence that they will beneficially delight, sometimes shock, and enlighten most serious readers concerning the nature of worthy impact, even though none of them nor anyone else can explain such impact fully. Neither these chapters nor their conclusions mesh together perfectly. They reflect the diverse biases and commitments of their authors. But that is as it should be. Undergraduate and graduate students in psychology are too often presented with conventional, assured, "canned" versions of research methods and clinical procedure. However, rather than assure success, produce impactful writings, or engender a truly rewarding career, they tend to breed both triviality and arrogance. They are a recipe for failing to do the many things suggested by this book's authors toward the end of their essays—things like read widely, question assumptions, reflect on the cultural challenges and dilemmas of one's time and place, write at least in part for thoughtful citizens or laypersons rather than only for self-appointed experts in one's field, think outside the box, dare to be original, and so forth.

DISCIPLINARY DILEMMAS

At the end of this book, however, it may be useful to offer a few reflections about how psychology got to the place where such advice is so badly needed. It is hard to diagnose such disciplinary dilemmas, but not so hard as coming up with solutions to them! Still, diagnosis of a problem is often the first step toward solving it. Moreover, theoretical and philosophical psychologists such as this book's authors have been struggling with the problem of diagnosis for several decades and have come up with a number of ideas that seem illuminating and potentially beneficial. This is not to suggest that they have unearthed anything like a surefire method for producing works of quality and impact. Indeed, it is probably absurd to think that there are ever more than a few highly original works in a generation. Moreover, those who produce them modestly attribute them, in part, to the good fortune of having been at the right place and the right time where some fresh insight could finally crystallize. Like the great Newton, world famous in his own lifetime, who is said to have attributed his stunning accomplishments to having "stood on the shoulders of giants." Or the great American philosopher Alfred North Whitehead, who remarked that all of Western philosophy was "a series of footnotes to Plato." Perhaps most of us should be content to be footnotes to footnotes. That would purchase us the virtue of humility, rid the world of much damaging narcissism, allow us to participate in and richly enjoy exciting and ennobling ideas, and position us to have the great pleasure of teaching them to others, to the next generation. In my department, by contrast, every student who is granted a PhD is assured that he or she has met the standard of having produced an "original contribution to knowledge." How sweetly complimentary, how admirably democratic, and how patently absurd.

Daniel N. Robinson (this volume, chapter 11) forces us to be brutally realistic about the question of "impact." He points out that if we mean by impact something more weighty or worthy than mere "fashion" or "enthusiasm," then sheer number of publications or the length of time a certain approach is in vogue (phrenology would win that contest) cannot serve as the standard of "authentic impact." Popularity does not necessarily earmark excellence, even over the long run. Instead, drawing on examples from physics, Robinson argues that authentic impact "operates chiefly at the level of metaphysics" and touches on "core ontological and epistemological questions" as to "what really exists and as to what resources are available by which we might presume to know what really exists." So far as the human or social sciences are concerned, I would say that "metaphysics" is always involved and important in Robinson's sense. I would add that authentically impactful writings in our field characteristically offer new explanations, descriptions, or narrative accounts of individual or social phenomena that shed fresh light on them and help us deal with or come to terms with them within our cultural and moral horizons. Also, I would contend that the understanding they bring— even when they claim otherwise—is anything but strictly value neutral. They are, in part, inescapably evaluative accounts of meaningful and value-imbued phenomena, accounts that change the meaning such events or experiences have for us and alter the trajectory of our lives in significant ways.

Robinson suggests that within psychology, "perhaps only Freud and Skinner have had an impact" of this fundamental sort, and he has major reservations about both of their approaches, feeling that they contain serious conceptual confusions and significantly distort human experience. Nor is Robinson sanguine about the immediate future. He finds that "the prevailing academic structure is a powerful obstacle to originality, a veritable engine of intellectual complacency," a place where money and careerism have way too much influence, and that "little in the prevailing institutional climate nurtures or is designed to nurture bold departures from mainstream thinking." I agree with most of Robinson's analysis and share some of his pessimism. But I have in mind a kind of complementary or supplementary viewpoint on the dilemmas of psychology and the social sciences that suggests to me some reason for hope for better developments in the foreseeable future. Perhaps that hope is in vain, but it seems to me that we ought to try to conjure up as much rational hope as possible, along with a cold-eyed look at our shortcomings.

First of all, it seems to me that it is a mistake to think of psychology on the model of physics, mathematics, or engineering, that is, as a relatively straightforward, objective theoretical or applied science. There are branches of psychology that are virtual natural sciences. There are others that deal appropriately with relatively circumscribed, technical problems and applications—although even these only exist as part of a wider social and moral context that we ignore at our peril. But much of clinical, social, or personality psychology at least overlap with the humanities. They are interpretations of individual, social, and cultural dynamics. Their subject matter is essentially, in part, the sorts of meanings and values that imbue and animate our personal and social existence, and their interpretations are always framed partly in terms of such meanings and values, however much they may try to obscure that fact through the use of neutral-sounding terms such as *functional* or *effective*. I take this to mean that we need to realize the enormous extent to which all our theories and research findings are deeply embedded in history and culture, indeed part of the historical flux. We need to think of psychology partly as a flesh and blood human institution, social undertaking, or cultural movement rather than as a relatively neat, tidy academic or professional enterprise that can be smoothly managed like a supermarket or post office branch. We should think of it as one of what the 19th-century German historian Johann Gustav Droysen called the "moral forces that rule history," for better or worse.

TOWARD A CULTURAL PSYCHOLOGY

Many psychological theorists are beginning to think of our field and their work in these terms. In this effort, they draw on diverse perspectives, including ordinary language philosophy, psychoanalytic theories, postmodern thought, the critical theory of the Frankfurt school and Jürgen Habermas, hermeneutic philosophy, Lacanian theory, and others (Cushman, 1990, 1995; Gergen, 1994; Malone & Friedlander, 2000; Polkinghorne, 1988; Prilleltensky, 1997; Richardson, Fowers, & Guignon, 1999; Slife & Williams, 1995; Smith, Harré, & Langenhove, 1995; and others). Jerome Bruner (1990, p. 1) captured much of this idea with his proposal for a "cultural psychology." The basic subject matter of such a cultural psychology is what Bruner called "acts of meaning." He described how, during what has come to be known as psychology's Cognitive Revolution of the late 1950s and 1960s, he and some of his colleagues "intended to bring 'mind' back into the human sciences after a long cold winter of objectivism." Unfortunately, in his view, the "new cognitive science" that has emerged has gained "its technical successes at the price of dehumanizing the very concept of mind it had sought to reestablish," with the result that it has "estranged much of psychology from other human sciences and the humanities" (p. 1).

Bruner (1990, pp. 2–5) advocated a "renewed cognitive revolution—a more interpretive approach to cognition concerned with 'meaning-making.'" This approach would focus on the "symbolic activities that human beings employ in constructing and in making sense not only of the world but of themselves." Regrettably, in Bruner's view, much cognitive psychology today tends to reduce the "construction of meaning" to the "processing of information." There is a place, of course, for the properly scientific investigation of human cognitive capacities. But the kind of "meaning and the processes that create everyday [human action]" are "surprisingly remote from what is conventionally called 'information processing.'" The notion of information used by many cognitive psychologists is quite narrow and limited. As a rule, they adopt an approach according to which "computability [is] a necessary criterion of a good theoretical model." Such an approach, however, precludes important but, in their view, "ill-formed questions as 'How is the world organized in the mind of a Muslim fundamentalist?' or 'How does the concept of Self differ in Homeric Greece and in the postindustrial world?'" In Bruner's view, human beings

> do not terminate at their own skins; they are expressions of culture. To treat the world as an indifferent flow of information to be processed by individuals each on his or her own terms is to lose sight of how individuals are formed and how they function. . . . Given that psychology is so immersed in culture, it must be organized around those meaning-making and meaning-using processes that connect [humans] to culture. This does *not* commit us to more subjectivity in psychology; it is just the reverse. By virtue of participation in culture, meaning is rendered *public* and *shared*. Our culturally adapted way of life depends upon shared meanings and shared concepts and depends as well upon shared modes of discourse for negotiating differences in meaning and interpretation. (pp. 12–13)

WINNOWING AND TRANSFORMATION

To use a homely analogy, one might think of the enterprise of psychology on the model of the American Democrat party, another "moral force" that has influenced the history of our times. I am a fairly loyal, lifelong Democrat who has usually, not always, voted for Democrats. I judge that the party got significantly off the track of wisdom during the period of the "McGovern years" that started several decades ago, righted itself significantly with the "New Democrats" of the Clinton era, albeit at the price of a certain amount of integrity and confusion about what it stood for any longer, and now faces an enormous challenge in adapting its fundamentally liberal principles to sharp new concerns of many in contemporary American society (which I share) about the erosion of community and the effects of a shallow consumerism on the quality of our lives. (The specifics don't matter. Please don't be distracted by them.) The point is that I can find many things that I value and disvalue in my political party's stands and assertions over the years and that my view of these matters changes with continuing experience and reflection. Many of my opinions about exactly what is worthy or shoddy about past achievements are uncertain and will vary according to new conclusions about the social and political good I arrive at in the present, partly in response to new and unforeseen challenges. For example, while still a Democrat, I now see certain programs of the modern welfare state as tending to do for people certain things that they, their families, or their communities ought to and properly only do for themselves.

Perhaps something similar is true for those of us who participate in the enterprise of modern psychology. For all of its dross and trivia and bizarre oversimplifications of human life and living, 20th-century psychology has been a medium for and a contributor to many of the exemplary cultural and moral trends of our time. It has raised our consciousness about the existence and anguish of many human maladies and deficits, sensitized us to numerous ways the human psyche can tie itself in knots in response to various deprivations and abuses, and afforded a number of tools and techniques for relieving pain and enhancing human autonomy and dignity. In fact, there is evidence that profoundly limited theories and approaches can serve worthy ends, at least for a time. Freud's highly constricted and rather dehumanizing view of the superego as strictly an agent of internal punishment for violating extant social norms has served, nevertheless, as a vehicle for reconsidering and relaxing irrational moralisms that do no one any good. Skinner's narrowly behavioristic conception of operant conditioning has shed new light on and fostered practical new approaches to such diverse human activities as toilet training, classroom discipline, debilitating phobias, and even marital dysfunction. Heinz Kohut's influential self psychology celebrates an ideal of "healthy narcissism" (of all things) that regrettably downplays the importance of lasting social ties and responsibilities. But its account of the crucial healing role of "empathy" in psychotherapy and human relationships generally beneficially illuminates important human dynamics. It seems that for a time these oversimplified and reductionistic models are used by many researchers and practitioners against the tacit background of a much subtler appreciation of human intentionality, creativity, and the cultural and moral context of human action. They are not absolutized. Their limitations are at least implicitly recognized. As a result, they may do more good than harm.

For example, in his widely read little book, *Soul Searching: Why Psychotherapy Must Promote Moral Responsibility*, William Doherty (1995) argued that most 20th-century therapy theory and discourse reflect a kind of one-sided individualism that rejects and often scoffs at conventional morality. They enshrine ideals of personal autonomy and self-realization that may help liberate us from a narrow ethic of blind self-sacrifice and inauthenticity, Doherty felt, but they afford nothing adequate to put in their place. To borrow a line from Erich Fromm a half a century ago (1941/1969), we moderns have cultivated a profound sense of what we want to be "free from" but have only the vaguest notion of what we want to be "free to" or "free for" in terms of substantive possibilities for a cultural or moral existence. From this modern "ambiguity of freedom," Fromm deduced the inevitability of many of the ethical confusions and emotional maladies of individuals living in our kind of modern society, including "depersonalization," "alienation," and "emptiness."

In Doherty's (1995) view, during the "Golden Years" of psychotherapy in the 1960s into the 1980s, psychotherapists "saw the oppressiveness of cultural norms dressed up as moral principles" and saw "themselves as agents of emancipation" (p. 11). By doing so, he felt, they contributed to our recent slide into a "culture of narcissism." Therapists inadvertently perpetuated the problem in the cure. They contributed to a kind of irresponsible "nonjudgmentalism," excessive self-preoccupation, loss of any sense of wider purpose, and decay of community by which many people feel we have subsequently become swamped. However, according to Doherty, we still were able to do much good during that period because many of the "moral rules of conventional society . . . could be counted on to provide the scaffolding upon which the client could build a more authentic life" (p. 11). Unfortunately, by "the 1990s . . . whatever has served as the moral center of mainstream culture seems not to be holding" (p. 11). Today, corruption, crime, violence, father absence, and disintegrating families, accompanied by "justifications based on personal entitlement, doing one's own thing, or victimization" (p. 11), are leading many ordinary people and social critics to feel that we need a renewed emphasis on character, moral integrity, community responsibility, and, where appropriate, a respect for tradition. Doherty's book outlines ways that psychotherapy, without abandoning much of its traditional wisdom and skills, can respectfully broach the moral dimension and help the many clients who need it to grow in ethical and social responsibility as well as pursue "self-actualization." Older ideas and approaches may be more or less extensively revised or transformed in the process. New theory is called for since the old models had a kind of one-sided individualism built into their very premises about human dynamics. Exactly what the world will look like when that theory is elaborated, or what our assessment of traditional techniques and of our very conceptions of the goals of therapy and its role in society will turn out to resemble, we cannot say in advance. All we can say with near certainty is that it is unlikely that we can rest on our laurels (we never can for long) or that the past will be radically forsaken (it rarely is). Theory and research that have impact in the next few decades will probably be those that help execute such a transvaluation of values.

In their recent book, *The Psychology of Human Possibility and Constraint*, Jack Martin and Jeff Sugarman (1999) made a similar claim for academic psychology. These authors searched for a genuine third alternative to the polarized options in much of today's psychology of scientism and postmodernism. The first viewpoint greatly reifies and substantializes the human "self" whereas the other decenters the subject completely and reduces it, at best, to a mere performer of culturally fabricated scripts. Martin and Sugarman boldly addressed basic questions concerning the nature of reality and the nature of the human person. They challenged the Cartesian, dualistic legacy of our field that forces us to choose between unacceptable, opposed viewpoints. For example, they contended that we confront a cognitive psychology that tends to isolate the mind and its development from the sociocultural world and a social constructionism or textualism in which the phenomena of psychology disappear into the cultural text. The challenge, the authors argued, is to discern how neither dualism nor this antidualist reaction really overcomes our Cartesian legacy. They outlined a fresh metaphysical account of individual psychological phenomena and their place in the world, namely a "dynamic interactionism" that acknowledges the "mostly sociocultural origins and practices of human psychology" but "still leaves room for bona fide psychological phenomena of agency, intentionality, self, and creativity" (p. 3) Both societies and selves are seen as "emergent and mutable" and existing in "dynamic relation," never taking final or fixed form but nonetheless tangible and real as purposive, responsible agency. The authors provided a number of telling examples of how most theory in psychology may aim at capturing human reality of this sort but ends up either preserving agency and intentionality by cordoning it off from wider social forces or reducing it to a mere effect of the forces and meanings of our sociocultural embeddedness.

I believe that many in psychology today are looking for a credible alternative to scientism and postmodernism, and I am drawn to the general thrust of Martin and Sugarman's (1999) proposal. To what extent their approach succeeds in detail is not my concern at the moment. Rather, I would draw your attention to their suggestion that within the framework of a new metaphysics of the self in the world such as they proposed, "much extant inquiry in social science and psychology" may be able to be stripped of "vestiges of objectivism and positivism" and reinterpreted as "fallibilist" and "necessarily socioculturally and temporally constrained demonstrations of what is possible and influential in human practices, actions, and experiences" (Martin & Sugerman, 1999, pp. 55–56). In other words, some theory and models from the abundance of findings in the 20th century are likely to be able to be retrieved and reformulated from this new perspective. To what extent that is true, or in what way, no one can say in advance. But theory and research that have impact in the years ahead may be those that undertake the arduous task of such retrieval and reformulation.

I suppose the main implication of this line of thought is that, if true, the producers of genuinely excellent social science theory and research in the next few decades are going to have to follow the sort of advice proffered in this book and become much broader and subtler in their approach to social inquiry. Social scientists will have to become competent in analyzing the ideological and moral value underpinnings of both social phenomena and psychological theory itself. They will need to appreciate that their research and theory is underpinned by a metaphysics of one sort or another, and gain the ability to reflect on and contribute to the reformulation of such philosophical premises. And they will have to continue, as so many are today, to rethink what are proper methods—quantitative, qualitative, interpretive, all of the above in one or another creative blend—in social and psychological inquiry. Surely one hallmark of a new and better social science will be that we have learned to adapt our methods to our subject matter rather than truncate or trivialize our subject matter to capture it with our preferred methods, as we so often have done in the era just past. Part-time cultural critics. Part-time metaphysicians. Part-time epistemologists. Hardly what most of us signed on for in graduate school! But that may be just what is required for authentic impact in the future.

REFERENCES

Bruner, J. (1990). *Acts of meaning*. Cambridge, MA: Harvard University Press.

Cushman, P. (1990). Why the self is empty. *American Psychologist, 45*, 599–611.

Cushman, P. (1995). *Constructing the self, constructing America*. Menlo Park, CA: Addison-Wesley.

Doherty, W. (1995). *Soul searching: Why psychotherapy must promote moral responsibility*. New York: Basic Books.

Fromm, E. (1969). *Escape from freedom*. New York: Avon. (Original work published 1941)

Gergen, K. (1994). Realities and relationships: Soundings in social constructionism. Cambridge, MA: Harvard University Press.

Malone, K., & Friedlander, S. (2000). *The subject of Lacan: A Lacanian reader for psychologists*. Albany: State University of New York Press.

Martin, J., & Sugarman, J. (1999). *The psychology of human possibility and constraint*. Albany: SUNY Press.

Polkinghorne, D. (1988). *Narrative knowing and the human sciences*. Albany, NY: State University of New York Press.

Prilleltensky, I. (1997). Values, assumptions, and practices: Assessing the moral implications of psychological discourse and action. *American Psychologist, 5*, 517–535.

Richardson, F., Fowers, B., & Guignon, C. (1999). *Re-envisioning psychology: Moral dimensions of theory and practice*. San Francisco: Jossey-Bass.

Slife, B., & Williams, R. (1995). *What's behind the research? Discovering hidden assumptions in the behavioral sciences*. Thousand Oaks, CA: Sage.

Smith, J., Harré, R., & Langenhove, L. (1995). *Rethinking methods in psychology*. London: Sage.

Taylor, C. (1985). *Human agency and language: Philosophical papers* (Vol. 1). Cambridge, England: Cambridge University Press.

AFTERWORD: HOW MUCH IMPACT SHOULD IMPACT HAVE?

ROBERT J. STERNBERG

The goal of this book is to argue for the importance of *impact* in psychological theory and research, as well as to evaluate the factors that underlie impact. In a book devoted to the importance of impact, a chapter such as Daniel N. Robinson's chapter (chapter 11), which takes a critical look at impact, provides an important balance. Robinson reminds us that impact is not always for the good, that sometimes it is misjudged, and that concentrating on it may lead us away from concentrating on other important aspects of the valuing of psychological theory and research. He values the study of impact but raises questions about the way it is often studied and assessed. I end this book by considering some of Robinson's and other people's arguments questioning the importance of impact and by stating why, despite the merits of their arguments, I still believe the study of impact to be important. I do so in a question-and-answer format, addressing questions raised by Robinson and others who may wonder whether the concept of impact itself perhaps merits less impact than this book purports to give it. In writing this Afterword, I am in no way "targeting" Robinson or anyone else. Quite the contrary, I am grateful to Robinson for raising fundamental issues that need to be addressed. Recognizing the importance of the critics such as Robinson, I here am attempting to address the important issues that Robinson and others have raised over the years and that merit some response.

OBJECTION 1: AN IDEA CAN HAVE GREAT IMPACT AND YET BE FALSE

This argument is, of course, correct. Karl Marx's ideas have had great impact, but many of them have not well withstood the test of time. Robinson

223

points to Sigmund Freud and B. F. Skinner as thinkers who had great impact yet whose ideas were lacking in many respects as well.

It is indeed necessary to distinguish impact from truth. The fact that such a distinction exists, however, does not make impact less important. Rather, it perhaps points out that both elements need to be considered in evaluating work. For example, were I to seek to publish an article showing that IQ test scores often provide modest to moderate prediction of achievement test scores, I would be seeking to publish an article that told the truth but that was likely to have little impact, because the point it had to make has been made so many times before, and because the message of my article is merely an empirical relation rather than a psychological explanation. So, just as things can be false but have impact, so can things be true but have little impact. We need to consider both veridicality and impact in evaluating psychological work.

We need further to realize that very few of our psychological theories—perhaps none of them—actually will prove to be wholly correct over the long term. The best we can hope for, perhaps, is that our theories will have heuristic value, helping the field move from one set of ideas to a better, or at least different, set of ideas. Even many psychological findings that seem robust when they are first published turn out to replicate only under certain circumstances. The goal of any one article or set of articles is usually not to present the whole truth but to help science move along the road to truth.

Thus, it may well be that Freud and Skinner had many incorrect ideas. So did Jean Piaget, Lev Vygotsky, and many others. The contribution of a great psychological researcher is perhaps not to find the ultimate truth but to move science along in a process that is, ultimately, self-correcting. The fact that we now know that many of these ideas were incorrect is a testament to the fact that, at some level, science does what it should, namely, correct its own ideas. And for all the wrong ideas Freud, Skinner, or anyone else may have had, those ideas did help us understand important aspects of human behavior. We should not throw out the baby with the bath. Great minds in science are not great because they find ultimate truth but because they help science progress toward such truth, even though it may never quite arrive at its destination. Freud and Skinner are great not because they were right in all or even most respects but because their ways of thinking had such a profound influence on other scientists, including those who disagreed or continue to disagree with them.

OBJECTION 2: IMPACT IS NOT NECESSARILY FOR THE GOOD

This argument, of course, is correct. In the political realm, Adolf Hitler had great impact, but it was negative. The impact of Franz Gall and phrenology perhaps was not so great either, at least in some ways, although any damage done cannot be compared with that done by Hitler and his ideas. Prefrontal lobotomies were among the most notorious examples of impact gone awry, and they did cause considerable damage. What conclusions, then, are we to draw?

In discussing impact, it is important to make certain distinctions—between the short and the long term, between ideas from which we can learn little or nothing and ideas from which we can learn a lot even if it is by way of correction, and between impact and morality. First, for whatever influence phrenology or prefrontal lobotomies may have had when they first were proposed, that influence is long gone. In the scientific realm, there are not many phrenologists left in the world or surgeons performing prefrontal lobotomies. Such individuals may exist, but outside the boundaries of science as we know it today. No doubt, scientists of the future will point to some of the work we are doing today; thank goodness that such work is a matter for history! In the long term, science self-corrects, and work that may have a great deal of short-term influence later often proves to have little long-term impact.

Second, part of the reason to study the history of science, or the history of anything, is to learn from the mistakes of the past so that we do not repeat those mistakes. There is a great deal to be learned from Hitler, the phrenologists, the prefrontal lobotomists, and many others whose mistakes we do not wish to repeat. One can regret many of the things they have done. But what is done is done. We need to study what they did to learn from it so that we do not do more of the same. Sometimes, there is more to be learned from the mistakes of the past than from the correct decisions of the past.

Truth is not always a saving grace. There are countless scientific articles whose findings, as far as they go, are true but also trivial. Perhaps the only lesson to be learned from this work is a lesson that applies not to individual works but to the class of work as a whole—namely, the need to eschew the true but trivial.

Third, impact is not about morality. The morality of ideas needs to be studied separately from, although perhaps in relation to, the impact of the work. It is risky to conflate the two. At various times in history, religious and even scientific groups have sought to suppress ideas that have had great impact on history but that were viewed at the time as somehow immoral or heretical—such as that the Earth revolves around the Sun. Morality is important; impact is important; but they are simply not the same. The fact that an idea can be perceived as moral but as having little impact, or as having great impact but not as being moral, only shows the need to look at both morality and impact rather than to look at one to the exclusion of the other.

OBJECTION 3: THE SYSTEM OFTEN IS WEIGHED AGAINST WORK THAT SHOULD HAVE IMPACT

Robinson (chapter 11) and others, including myself, have pointed out that there are many aspects of the current scientific system that can be self-defeating. Inordinate emphasis on sheer numbers of publications, or sheer numbers of dollars of grant money acquired, or sheer number of courses taught, can have deleterious consequences. What is impressive is that science has progressed as far as it has despite such obstacles.

My colleagues and I have argued (e.g., Sternberg, 2002; Sternberg & Lubart, 1995) that creative individuals typically defy the crowd: They often reject ideas that are popular with others and propose instead alternative ideas of their own. The reaction they receive is often one of deprecation and even scorn. But they persist despite this reaction and frequently succeed in changing other people's minds. Indeed, according to our theory, changing other people's minds is a practical part of the creative process. Thus, the fact that there is opposition, and sometimes organized opposition, against one's ideas does not mean that, in the long run, those ideas cannot or will not have a major impact. Rather, it means that creative people have to strive hard to get others to accept their own ideas; sometimes, acceptance may come only after a long struggle, and sometimes not even within one's lifetime. As Robinson points out, "It is surely unnecessary to rehearse, typically in ways rather more dramatic than the actual records warrant, the trials and tribulations of revolutionary thinkers" (chapter 11). The fact that we do have such documentation, and that it is their lives rather than the lives of more ordinary thinkers, that are so well documented, suggests that the revolutionary thinkers often succeeded after all in their goal of shaping history.

I believe that all scientists have to choose what is really important to them. Some will go for grant money, others for large numbers of publications, others for plum administrative positions, and still others for an easy life. Many will go for some combination of these and other goals. Those striving for impact often pay a price in terms of other things they may have wished for in their life. They may not get the most grant money, or the most publications, or the easiest life. But they have made their choice, and there is no reason why science or society should necessarily cooperate with them in their goal. Often they get little cooperation. Indeed, I have sometimes thought that creative individuals not only encounter obstacles in their work but may even at times create obstacles. Perhaps many creative individuals are people who need to be pushing against something in order to succeed.

OBJECTION 4: SOMETIMES THE IMPACT OF WORK SEEMS TOTALLY OUT OF PROPORTION TO ITS QUALITY

Robinson (chapter 11) correctly points out how sometimes great work seems to have less impact than it deserves, whereas not-so-great or even poor work sometimes has impact far beyond what it deserves. At times, it feels as though we have a problem of the blind leading the blind. Probably all of us wonder at the impact of some contemporary work that seems to us shoddy at best, and we also wonder at the lack of impact of work that we may consider to be of much higher quality. But what is to be concluded?

First, no system of judging anything is wholly adequate. There will always be artists, musicians, writers, political leaders, scientists, and other people whose impact is far beyond what, according to some standards, it should have been, whereas there will be others whose impact is far less. Probably on average, the system works more or less the way it should, but it would be foolhardy to deny that there are exceptions. And these exceptions can be so galling that we lose sight of the fact that, at least in science, the system typically works, over the long run, more or less the way it should. Gadflies may pay a price.

Second, there probably always has been, and always will be, a short-term advantage bequeathed upon those who follow the fads and fashions of the times. In the long run, however, the accolades may go more to those who challenged these fads and fashions but also proposed better alternatives of their own.

Third, to the extent that the system is flawed, we need to propose ways to improve it. Robinson, for example, has done this in his chapter. Whether one accepts his particular suggestions or not, he has taken the right kind of step. It will be incumbent upon him, or anyone else who wants to change the system, to persuade others to do so, and the path to doing so typically is a long and tortuous one strewn with many obstacles along the way.

Although I have often been critical of the system as it exists, I probably am more sanguine than Robinson. I think that most departments—or, at least, good departments—try to see beyond numbers of publications, or sheer amount of grant funding, or other gross quantitative measures of productivity. Many of them, I think, try to assess impact, flawed though their measures of impact may be. They may seek out letters from distinguished referees, consult sources such as the *Social Science Citation Index,* critically read a candidate's work, and so forth. No matter how much they do, they may make mistakes, and frequent ones. The system is flawed, as are the people who implement it. But there are no easy solutions.

For example, Robinson suggests that candidates submit just a single work to be evaluated. Should candidates be judged by just their single best-written work, as Robinson suggests? This system, too, has problems. For example, it might overvalue "one-idea" scholars—scholars who do have one very impressive idea but then who never have another impressive one. Or it might overvalue those who lack any kind of reasonable standard of productivity, for example, people who just publish a single work in their entire professional career.

As another example, should research grants not count at all in promotions and tenure? A case can be made that it should be the outcomes of the research, rather than the grants themselves, that matter. But a case also can be made that there is something to be said for being able to convince one's peers that one has an active and potentially meaningful research program. There are certainly people who get grants and do nothing with them. But if they do nothing, they may find it quite a bit more difficult to get funded in the future than they did in the past.

I raise these questions with regard to Robinson's proposals not to attack them but rather to point out that any system, including Robinson's, is likely to have weak as well as strong aspects. There almost certainly is no perfect system, and in substituting a new system for an old one, we may solve some old problems and create some new problems in the process. The question is likely to be whether we would prefer to live with the new problems or the old ones.

There is no single gold standard to what makes a difference in a scientific career. Each scientist must decide for himself or herself what goals to pursue. But I continue to believe that impact is a particularly meaningful goal to set for oneself, and I hope that, through the essays in this book, I will have encouraged other readers to think the same way.

REFERENCES

Sternberg, R. J. (Ed.). (2002). *Psychologists defying the crowd: Stories of those who battled the establishment and won*. Washington, DC: American Psychological Association.

Sternberg, R. J., & Lubart, T. I. (1995). *Defying the crowd: Cultivating creativity in a culture of conformity*. New York: Free Press.

AUTHOR INDEX

Numbers in italics refer to listings in the references.

Farr, A. L., 172, *175*
Fechner, G. T., 47, *68*
Feinstein, H. M., 32, *39*
Feist, G. J., 8, 13, *16*
Fenigstein, A., 12, *16*
Feshbach, S., 144, *157*
Festinger, L., 118, *122, 123,* 133, *135*
Fisher, R. I., 148, *158*
Fisher, S., 82, *87,* 147, *158*
Flavell, J. H., 101, *106*
Fowers, B., 217, *222*
Fraisse, P., 101, *106*
Fretz, B. R., 184, *194*
Freud, S., 72, 73, 76, *87,* 102, *106*
Friedlander, S., 217, *222*
Fromm, E, 219, *221*
Fullinwider, S. P., 32, *40*

Gage, N. L., 143, *158*
Galanter, E., 28, *41*
Galton, F., 5–8, 10, 11, 14, 15, *16,* 103, *106*
Gardner, H., 4, *18,* 103, *106*
Garfield, E., 172, *175*
Garfield, S. L., 185, *193*
Gay, P., 73, *87*
Gergen, K., 217, *221*
Gerrig, R. J., 144, *159*
Gerst, M., 174, *175*
Glauberman, N., 96, 97, *106*
Goffman, E., 126–129, 132, *135*
Goleman, D., 103, 104, *106*
Gorman, M. E., 8, *16*
Gould, S. J., 90, *106*
Gouldner, A., 135, *135*
Greenberg, R., 82, *87*
Guignon, C., 217, *222*
Guntrip, H., 152, *158*

Hale, N. G., 73, *88*
Halgin, R. P., 144, *158*
Harré, R., 217, *222*
Hartmann, E., 83, 86, *88*
Harvey, J., *122*
Hay, R. A., 168, *175*
Hearnshaw, L. S., 60, *68*
Heidbreder, E., 22, *40*
Helmholtz, H., 47, *68*
Henley, T. B., 22, 23, *40*
Henri, V., 91–93, *105*
Henry, M., 77, *88*
Herman, J. L., 78, *88*
Herrnstein, R. J., 7, *16*

Herzog, M., 27, *40*
Heyduk, R. G., 12, *16*
Hill, C. E., 86, *88*
Hill, C. O., 59, *68*
Hilts, V. L., 10, *16*
Hogan, R., 130, *135*
Holt, E. B., 28, *40*
Hood, R. W., Jr., 184, *195*
Hornstein, G. A., 64, *69*
Hull, D., 34, *40*
Hung, S. S., 6, *18*
Huston, T. L., *122*

Jacoby, R., 96, 97, *106*
James, H., III, 31, 32, *40*
James, W., 20, 23–26, 28–30, 32, 35, 38, *40*
Jensen, A. R., 102, *106*
Johnson, M. G., 22, 23, *40*
Jourard, S. M., 143, *158*
Judd, C. M., 168, *175*

Kadanoff, L. P., 111, *122*
Kamin, L., 98, *106*
Keating, A. M., 184, *194*
Kelley, H. H., 118, *122, 123*
Keltner, D., 130, *135*
Kenny, D. A., 163, 168, *175*
Kimble, G. A., 33, *40*
Koch, S., 37, *40,* 212
Koestler, A., 110, *122*
Kohut, H., 152, *158*
Kosslyn, S. M., 22, *41*
Kraus, O., 59, *69*
Kroeber, A. L., 8, 11, *16*
Kuhn, T. S., 179, *194*
Kvale, S., 185, *194*

Ladd, G. T., 23, 24, *40*
Laing, R. D., 142, *158*
Langenhove, L., 217, *222*
Larson, D. B., 184, *194*
Leahey, T. H., 49, 61, 63, *69*
Leary, D. E., 22, 28, 31, 32, 34, 35, 37, 38, *40*
Lehman, H. C., 11, *16*
Levinger, G., *122*
Leviton, L. C., 166, *175*
Lewin, K., 113, 116–118, *122, 123*
Librardi, M., 60, *67*
Lippitt, R., 117, *123*
Locke, J., 22, *41*
Lomas, P., 143, *158*

Searle, J. R., 65, 69
Sears, P., 118, *123*
Seashore, C. E., 23, *41*
Selye, H., 121, *123*
Shadish, W. R., 163, 166, 168, 169, 172, *175*
Shafranske, E. P., 184, *194*
Shaw, C. R., 130, *136*
Sherif, M., 117, *123*
Siegler, R. S., 90, 101, *106*
Simon, T., 93–96, 100, *105*
Simons, P., 52, 62, 69
Simonton, D. K., 4–6, 8, 11–14, *17, 175*
Slife, B., 178, 183, 184, 189, *194, 195*, 217, 222
Sloane, P., 86, 88
Smith, A. M., 184, *194, 195*
Smith, B., 50, 65, 69
Smith, J., 217, *222*
Smith, L. D., 64, 69
Smith, L. M., 148, *159*
Smith, M. B., 28, *41*
Smither, R., 130, *135*
Snow, C. P., 120, 121, *123*
Social Sciences Citation Index, 129, *136*
Social Sciences Citation Index Five-Year Cumulation, 10, *17*
Sokal, M. M., 20, 23, *41*
Solms, M., 86, 88
Solomon, R. L., 22, 23, *39*
Spiegelberg, H., 51, 69
Stanley, J. C., 161–163, *175*
Sternberg, R. J., 102, *107*, 144, *159*, 173, *176*, 178, 181, 190, 191, *195*, 226, 228
Stolorow, R., 152, *159*
Strupp, H. H., 185, *193*
Strykowski, B. F., 6, *18*
Stumpf, C., 59, 69
Suchman, E. A., 169, *176*
Sugarman, J., 220, 221, *222*
Sullivan, H. S., 30, *41*
Sulloway, F. J., 73, 88
Swedin, E. G., 184, 185, *195*
Swyers, J. P., 184, *194*

Taylor, C., 214, *222*
Taylor, E., 23, 37, *42*
Teigen, K. H., 8, *17*
Terman, L. M., 6, 97, *17, 107*
Thibaut, J. W., 118, *122, 123*

Thinès, G., 44, 69
Thompson, M. G., 149, 152, *159*
Thorndike, E. L., 25, *42*
Titchener, E. B., 48, 62, 69
Tjeltveit, A. C., 186, *195*
Tolman, E. C., 28, *42*
Trochim, W. M. K., 168, *176*
Tulving, E., 190, *195*

Van Kaam, A., 143, 150, *159*
Varela, F. J., 65, 69
Vasari, G., 7, *18*
Velarde-Mayol, V., 50, 51, 65, 69
Vico, 45, *70*
Viney, W., 49, *70*
Vonnegut, M., 144, *159*
Vygotsky, L. S., 99, *107*

Walberg, H. J., 6, *18*
Walls, G., 183, *195*
Walters, J., 4, *18*
Wann, T. W., 60, *70*
Watson, J. B., 20, *42*, 63, 69
Watson, P. J., 184, *195*
Watson, R. I., 3, 4, *15*
Watson, R. I., Sr., *18*
Waugh, N. C., 28, *42*
Weber, E. H., 47, *70*
Weiner, B., 144, *157*
Weiss, C. H., 169, *176*
Wertz, F. J., 60, *70*, 152, *159*
Westen, D., 102, *107*
Whitbourne, S. K., 144, *158*
White, R., 117, *123*
Whitehead, A. N., 19, 34, *42*
Williams, R., 178, *195*, 217, 222
Wirth, L., 130, *136*
Wolf, T. H., 100, 101, *107*
Wollheim, R., 61, *70*
Worthington, E. L., Jr., 184, *195*
Wortman, A. G., 143, *159*
Wundt, W., 47–49, *70*, 114, *123*, 200, *212*

Zander, A., 114, 117, *122*
Zazzo, R., 91, *107*
Zimbardo, P. G., 144, *1591*
Zinnbauer, B. J., 184, *195*
Zorbaugh, H. W., 130, *136*
Zusne, L., 3, 4, *18*
Zuza, F., 90, *107*

SUBJECT INDEX

Free association, 79
Free Society for the Psychological Study of Children, 94
French Academy of Medicine, 92
Freud, Sigmund, 3, 11, 13, 15, 19, 71–87, 102–104, 153, 177, 200, 208, 213, 218, 224. *See also The Interpretation of Dreams*
  and Franz Brentano, 60–61
  case study and free association methods of, 79
  impact of, 77–78
  influences on, 72–73
  and Pierre Janet, 77–78
  personal myth created by, 73–74
  prolific output of, 76–77
  self-confidence of, 75
  willingness of, to change his ideas, 78–79
  writing style of, 75–76
Fromm, Erich, 145, 219

Galen, 208
Galileo Galilei, 14, 15, 73, 207
Gall, Franz Joseph, 200, 208, 209, 224
Galton, Francis, 3–15, 103, 208. *See also Hereditary Genius*
  career output of, 11–12
  continuing importance of, 3–4
  influences on, 4–5
  lessons to be learned from, 14–15
Gandhi, Mahatma, 75
Gardner, Howard, 103, 104
Garfield, Sol, 182
Gates, Bill, 174
Generality, 166
Generativity, 167–168
Genetic psychology, 53
Genius, 6–8
Gestalt psychology, 27, 59, 61
The Ghetto (Louis Wirth), 130
Given acts, 128
Given off acts, 128
Goddard, Henry, 96, 103
Goffman, Erving, 125–135. *See also The Presentation of Self in Everyday Life*
The Gold Coast and the Slum (Henry Zorbaugh), 130
Goleman, Daniel, 104
Goodman, Nelson, 19n1
Greeks, ancient, 8–9
Group dynamics, 114, 116–119

Habermas, Jürgen, 217
Habit, 23–25
Hall, G. Stanley, 4, 23n3
Halo effect, 204
Hannibal, 73
Hegel, Georg, 51
Heidbreder, Edna, 22
Heidegger, Martin, 60, 66
Helmholtz, Hermann von, 3, 11, 19, 47, 208
Henri, Victor, 91–93, 98
Hereditary Genius: An Inquiry Into Its Laws and Consequences (Francis Galton), 5–15
  adaptive fitness described in, 6–7
  conceptual content of, 12–14
  eugenics discussed in, 8–9
  familial inheritance discussed in, 7–8
  and Galton's career, 11–12
  individual differences, probability distribution of, 5–6
  lessons to be learned from, 14–15
  professional influence of, 9–11
"Hereditary Talent and Character" (Francis Dalton), 4, 15
Histoire des Sciences et des Savants depuis Deux Siècles (Alphonse Candolle), 10
Historical acts, contextualism of, 133–134
Historiometrics, 8
A History of Experimental Psychology (Edward G. Boring), 62–63
Hitler, Adolf, 117, 135, 198, 224
Höffding, Harald, 59
Holmes, Richard, 110
Holt, E. B., 28n6
Hooke, Robert, 207
Hughes, Everett, C., 130
Husserl, Edmund, 56, 59, 60
Huxley, Thomas Henry, 209
Huygens, Christian, 207
Hypnosis, 90

I, 29, 30
Imagination, 5
Impact, 197–211
  aspects of, 201–203
  authentic, in psychology, 208–211
  common-sense notion of, 197–198
  complexity of, in psychology, 199–200
  and context of "real world," 203–206
  and disciplinary dilemmas in psychology, 214–216
  enthusiasm vs., 206–208

McWilliams, Nancy, 213
Me, 29, 30
Mead, George Herbert, 30, 133
Mead, Margaret, 119, 126
The Meaning of Things: Domestic Symbols and the Self (Mihaly Csikszentmihalyi & Eugene Rochberg-Halton), 29
Mein Kampf (Adolf Hitler), 198
Meinong, Alexius von, 59, 60
Mendeleev, Dmitriy, 49
Menninger, Karl, 184
Mental Fatigue (Alfred Binet & Victor Henri), 91–93
Mental phenomena, 56–58
Messer, Stanley B., 213
Metric Intelligence Scale, 94–98, 101
Mezan, Peter, 146–147
Michelangelo, 7
Mill, John Stuart, 208
Modern Ideas on Children (Alfred Binet), 91, 98–100
Monte, C. F., 144–145
Mosteller, Fred, 164
Motivation, 7
Mulcaster, Richard, 8
Müller, Johannes, 11
Multiple discovery/invention, 5

Narrative of an Explorer in Tropical South Africa (Francis Dalton), 12
Nash, John, 120
National Academy of Sciences, 9
Natural ability, 5–7
Natural Inheritance (Francis Galton), 12
Natural intelligence, 7
Natural selection, 8
Nature vs. nurture, 7–8
Nero, 135
Newcomb, Theodore, 133
Newton, Isaac, 4, 14, 73, 204, 207, 208, 215
Nietzsche, Friedrich, 77
Nixon, Richard, 110
Nobel Prize, 9
Normal curve, 6, 7

Obsessions, 78n2
Olsen, Ken, 174
On the Several Senses of Being in Aristotle (Franz Brentano), 60, 66
Ontological security, 139–141
Operant conditioning, 25
Origin of Species (Charles Darwin), 4, 11

Otis, Arthur, 103
Outlines of Psychology (Rudolph Lotze), 47

Paradigms, 169
Park, Robert, 126
Passion (in writing), 189–190
Pasteur, Louis, 174
Pavlov, Ivan, 3, 13
Penfield, Wilder, 209
Pepper, Stephen, 19n1, 133
Performance teams, 128
Phenomenology, 56, 60, 139
Philosophical (introspective) psychology, 45, 46
Phrenology, 90, 207–208, 224
Physical phenomena, 56–58
Physiological (experimental) psychology, 45–50
Piaget, Jean, 13, 90, 101–102, 104, 145, 224
Plato, 3, 19n1, 206
Policy Studies Organization, 163
The Politics of Experience (R. D. Laing), 145–146
The Presentation of Self in Everyday Life (Erving Goffman), 125–135
  central message of, 126–127
  conceptual categories in, 127–129
  contextualism in, 133–134
  impact of, 129–134
  writing style in, 131–132
  and zeitgeist, 132–133
Principles of Physiological Psychology (Wilhelm Wundt), 47–49, 62, 114
The Principles of Psychology (William James), 20–31, 35n9
Psychoanalysis, 74, 79, 152–153
Psychognosy, 53
Psychology: Briefer Course (William James), 20n2
Psychology From an Empirical Standpoint (Franz Brentano), 43–67
  and act psychology, 58–60
  and American psychology, 62–64
  Book One of, 52–56
  Book Two of, 56–58
  and experimental method, 46–47
  and Sigmund Freud, 60–61
  historical context of, 44–49
  impact of, 43–44, 58–65
  and impact of psychology texts in general, 65–67
  and introspective method, 46

on mental phenomena in general, 56–58

origins of, 49–52

and phenomenology, 60

on psychology as science, 52–56

revival of interest in, 64–65

and Wundt's *Physiological Psychology*, 47–48, 62

The Psychology of Affiliation (Stanley Schachter), 118

The Psychology of Human Possibility and Constraint (Jack Martin & Jeff Sugarman), 220–221

Psychology of science, 9

"Psychotherapy and Religious Values" (Allen E. Bergin), 177–178, 180–192

abstract of, 180

citations of, 181–182

lessons to be learned from, 189–192

origins of, 185–187

reception of, 182–185, 188–189

writing of, 187–188

PsycSCAN, 145, 152, 153

Pure ego, 29, 30

Putnam, Hilary, 19n1

Quality, impact and, 226–228

Quasi-experiments, 162, 163

Quételet, Adolphe, 5, 11

Racial hierarchy, 8

Rationalism, 73

Realigning reactions, 129

Reception, quality of, 179–180

"The Reflex Arc Concept in Psychology" (John Dewey), 27–28

Religion, 32

Rickert, Heinrich, 45

Robinson, Daniel N., 214–216, 223–228

Rochberg-Halton, Eugene, 29

Rogers, Carl, 60, 145, 147, 152, 153, 184, 187

Rorty, Richard, 19n1

Rosenthal, Robert, 164

Royal Military College, 6

Royal Society of London, 8

Sacks, Oliver, 19n1

Salovey, Peter, 103, 104

Sandler, Howard, 164

Sarbin, Theodore, 133

Sartre, Jean-Paul, 126

Schachter, Stanley, 118

Scheibe, Karl, 129

Schizophrenia, 138–142

Scientific inquiry, 44, 52–56, 72–73, 91–93

Selection, 36–37

Selective attention, 26

Self, 28–31, 128, 217

Self-reflection, 55

Selye, Hans, 121

Sense of Touch and the Common Sensibility (Ernst Heinrich Weber), 47

Shakespeare, William, 8

Shaw, Clifford, 130

Sherif, Muzafer, 117

Sherrington, Charles, 209

Simmel, Georg, 126

Simon, Theodore, 90–91, 94–98, 100

Simplicity (of writing), 164–165

Skinner, B. F., 13, 25, 35n9, 60, 102, 104, 145, 153, 200, 202, 208, 218, 224

Snow, C. P., 120, 121

Social context, 169

Social criticism, 153

Social Darwinism, 9

Social Sciences Citation Index, 10, 129–130

Social self, 29–30

Soul Searching: Why Psychotherapy Must Promote Moral Responsibility (William Doherty), 219–220

Southwest German school, 45

Spencer, Herbert, 72, 99, 208

Staging talk, 128–129

Stake, Robert, 164

Stalin, Joseph, 135

Stanford–Binet Intelligence Scale, 6, 97, 101

Stanford–Binet–IV, 89

Stanley, Julian, 162–174. *See also Experimental and Quasi-Experimental Designs for Research*

Stein, Gertrude, 19n1

Sternberg, Robert J., 214

Stevens, Wallace, 19n1

Strategic secrets, 128

Strumpf, Carl, 59

Studies in Hysteria (Sigmund Freud), 72n1

Stufflebeam, Daniel, 164

Stumpf, Carl, 111

Subjectivity, sense of, 30

Sugarman, Jeff, 220–221

Sullivan, Harry Stack, 30

Swedenborg, Emanuel, 32

Symbolization, 81

ABOUT THE EDITOR

Robert J. Sternberg is most well-known for his theory of successful intelligence, investment theory of creativity (developed with Todd Lubart), theory of mental self-government, balance theory of wisdom, and triangular theory of love and theory of love as a story. The focus of his research is intelligence and cognitive development. Dr. Sternberg is the author of over 800 journal articles, book chapters, and books and has received about $15 million in government grants and contracts for his research. He is 2003 President of the American Psychological Association (APA) and editor of *Contemporary Psychology*. He received his PhD from Stanford University in 1975 and his BA summa cum laude, Phi Beta Kappa, from Yale University in 1972. He has won many awards, including the Early Career Award from APA, Outstanding Book Awards from the American Educational Research Association, the Distinguished Lifetime Contribution to Psychology Award from the Connecticut Psychological Association, the Cattell Award of the Society for Multivariate Experimental Psychology, and the Award for Excellence of the Mensa Education and Research Foundation. He has held a Guggenheim Fellowship as well as Yale University Senior and Junior Faculty Fellowships. He has been president of the Divisions of General Psychology, Educational Psychology, Psychology and the Arts, and Theoretical and Philosophical Psychology of the APA and has served as editor of *Psychological Bulletin*.